QUALITATIVE RESEARCH TOPICS IN LANGUAGE TEACHER EDUCATION

Many students and novice researchers may have a general idea of a topic they would like to research, but have a difficult time settling on a more specific topic and associated research questions. Addressing this problem, this book features contributions from over 30 diverse and experienced research supervisors, mentors, and principal investigators in the field of language teacher education. The chapters are autobiographic in nature, with each contributing author reflecting on relevant, current, and innovative research topics through the lens of their own professional life and research work. Offering explicit research topics and strategies for each area of expertise, this book will serve as a useful reference for the seasoned qualitative or narrative research practitioner, and a helpful guide for the new researcher narrowing down their own research topics.

Gary Barkhuizen is professor of applied linguistics at the University of Auckland, New Zealand. His teaching and research interests are in the areas of language teacher education, teacher and learner identity, study abroad, and narrative inquiry. He is editor of *Reflections on Language Teacher Identity Research* (Routledge, 2017) and co-author of *Narrative Inquiry in Language Teaching and Learning Research* (Routledge, 2014).

QUALITATIVE RESEARCH TOPICS IN LANGUAGE TEACHER EDUCATION

Edited by Gary Barkhuizen

NEW YORK AND LONDON

First published 2019
by Routledge
52 Vanderbilt Avenue, New York, NY 10017

and by Routledge
2 Park Square, Milton Park, Abingdon, Oxon OX14 4RN

Routledge is an imprint of the Taylor & Francis Group, an informa business

© 2019 Taylor & Francis

The right of Gary Barkhuizen to be identified as the author of the editorial material, and of the authors for their individual chapters, has been asserted in accordance with sections 77 and 78 of the Copyright, Designs and Patents Act 1988.

All rights reserved. No part of this book may be reprinted or reproduced or utilised in any form or by any electronic, mechanical, or other means, now known or hereafter invented, including photocopying and recording, or in any information storage or retrieval system, without permission in writing from the publishers.

Trademark notice: Product or corporate names may be trademarks or registered trademarks, and are used only for identification and explanation without intent to infringe.

Library of Congress Cataloging-in-Publication Data
A catalog record for this title has been requested

ISBN: 978-1-138-61812-1 (hbk)
ISBN: 978-1-138-61814-5 (pbk)
ISBN: 978-0-429-46134-7 (ebk)

Typeset in Bembo
by Taylor & Francis Books

CONTENTS

1 Introduction: Qualitative Research Topics in Language
   Teacher Education 1
   Gary Barkhuizen

2 Working with Doctoral Dissertation Writers 15
   Christine Pearson Casanave

3 Going Beyond Familiarity and Doing the Opposite in
   Language Teacher Education 21
   Tan Bee Tin

4 Learning to Teach Languages 27
   Donald Freeman

5 Researching Language Ideologies 33
   Carolyn McKinney

6 Language Teachers' Professional Learning in China 39
   Wen Qiufang

7 The Impact of Language Teacher Professional Development 44
   Simon Borg

8 Language Teacher Psychology Research 50
   Sarah Mercer

9 Emotions in Language Teacher Education and Practice 56
   Elizabeth R. Miller and Christina Gkonou

10	Researching Emotion in LTE *Matthew T. Prior*	63
11	Beliefs and Emotions in Language Teaching and Learning *Ana Maria F. Barcelos*	70
12	Language Teacher Identities in Teacher Education *Bonny Norton and Peter De Costa*	76
13	Understanding Language Teacher Identities: Conceptualizations, practices and change *Maria Ruohotie-Lyhty*	81
14	Researching LTE through a Vygostkian Sociocultural Theoretical Perspective *Paula R. Golombek*	86
15	Context in Sociocultural Theory *Anne Feryok*	92
16	Academic Writing: Linking Writers, Readers and Text Content *Rosemary Wette*	98
17	English L2 Writing in International Higher Education *Jim McKinley*	104
18	Academic Writing: The Human Side *Pat Strauss*	110
19	Critical Questions in English for Academic Purposes *Gregory Hadley*	115
20	Race in Critical Research *Ryuko Kubota*	120
21	Gender and LTE *Harold Castañeda-Peña*	126
22	Researching English as an International Language *Heath Rose*	131
23	Multilingualism in (Foreign) Language Teaching and Learning *Anne Pitkänen-Huhta*	137
24	English Language Teaching in Multilingual Contexts *Christa van der Walt*	143

25	Social Representations of Multilingualism *Alice Chik and Sílvia Melo-Pfeifer*	149
26	Language Teacher Education in Study Abroad Contexts *John L. Plews*	155
27	Study Abroad for Language Teachers *John Macalister*	161
28	Generating Action Research Topics *Anne Burns*	167
29	Researching Teacher Research *Daniel Xerri*	174
30	Teacher Researchers *Kenan Dikilitaş*	180
31	Exploring Issues in Language and Content Instruction *Sandra Zappa-Hollman and Patricia A. Duff*	186
32	LTE in Primary and Secondary Schools *Takaaki Hiratsuka*	192
33	Researching Task-based Teaching and Assessment *Martin East*	198
34	Language Teaching Approaches *Jessie S. Barrot*	204
35	Strategy Instruction *Carol Griffiths*	210
Index		*216*

1

INTRODUCTION

Qualitative Research Topics in Language Teacher Education

Gary Barkhuizen
UNIVERSITY OF AUCKLAND, NEW ZEALAND

As an experienced supervisor/advisor of graduate student qualitative research I am constantly reminded of the difficulty students have deciding on a *topic*. As novice researchers, they may have an idea about a broad, general *research area* (e.g., teacher identity, gender in the classroom, study abroad), but they struggle to nail down a specific topic and its associated *research questions*, and often when they do, the study may be unfeasible for a variety of reasons. It is not only my graduate students, however, who struggle to decide on a topic. Teacher researchers and the early career academic researchers I have mentored also sometimes have difficulty identifying a topic they feel academically and personally comfortable with. Even more experienced researchers don't always find it easy to select topics for new projects, particularly in contexts where institutions and funding bodies require continuous research activity and the regular roll out of new innovative projects.

Perhaps part of this difficulty with topic selection has to do with the planning and processes associated with qualitative research, as Christine Pearson Casanave says in Chapter 2, "it could take a year to develop a feasible and sustainable topic. Research questions change, grow, and develop; inquiry processes drag out as researchers get familiar with participants and follow change over time." The inductive mechanisms of qualitative research mean that topics and research questions, as well as interpretations of the data, change and become refined over time. Nevertheless, although this is the case with much qualitative research, researchers still need to have selected a research *topic* (more narrow than a broad research area and less narrow than specific research questions) before their study can begin, knowing that over time it will reconstruct into a more "feasible and sustainable topic." In other words, there needs to be a (starting) point at which researchers feel that they have identified a topic for their study.

This book is primarily about research *topics* in second, foreign and multilingual language teacher education (LTE). Specifically, it aims to raise awareness about current and future research topics in the field, and secondarily to suggest ways to go about *choosing* a topic. The focus is on research topics suitable for investigation using qualitative and narrative research methodologies. The book is not a research *methods* book, although various qualitative methodological approaches and specific methods of research design, data collection and data analysis are suggested in relation to the many topics put forward. The remainder of this introduction chapter provides a brief rationale for the book, summarizes the main strategies for choosing a research topic suggested by the authors, outlines the structure of the book, and then for easy reference concludes with a list of the five topics suggested in each chapter.

Qualitative Research Topics in Language Teacher Education

The title of this book has three main parts: qualitative research, topics, and language teacher education (LTE). *Topics* has already been covered in the paragraphs above. In this book, they fall into a wide range of LTE-related research areas, including the following:

- doctoral dissertation writing
- language teacher learning and professional development
- language teacher psychology
- emotions in language teaching, learning, and teacher education
- language teacher identities
- sociocultural theoretical perspectives on LTE
- L2 and academic writing
- English for academic purposes
- race and gender
- English as an international language
- multilingualism in language learning, teaching, and LTE
- LTE and teacher study abroad
- teacher research and action research
- teaching and assessment approaches
- strategy instruction

The chapter titles at the end of this chapter and the accompanying list of five research topics per chapter provide further information about these research areas. Each of the listed topics are described in much more detail within the chapters.

As explained by the authors in the book, the topics they suggest are suitable for investigation using *qualitative research* methods. I find Denzin and Lincoln's (2011, p. 8) broad definition adequate for the purposes of framing this work:

Qualitative researchers stress the socially constructed nature of reality, the intimate relationship between the researcher and what is studied, and the situational constraints that shape inquiry. Such researchers emphasize the value-laden nature of inquiry. They seek answers to questions that stress *how* social experience is created and given meaning.

Richards (2009), reviewing qualitative research in language teaching, expands on this definition. He says that qualitative research is (p. 149):

- locally situated: it studies human participants in natural settings and conditions, eschewing artificially constructed situations
- participant-oriented: it is sensitive to, and seeks to understand, participants' perspectives on their world
- holistic: it is context sensitive and does not study isolated aspects independently of the situation in which they occur
- inductive: it depends on a process of interpretation that involves immersion in the data and draws on different perspectives.

I would add that these four should be thought of as *more-or-less* features of qualitative research, that is, with each falling along a continuum. For instance, with the final feature, inductive, potential exists for qualitative research analysis to include deductive methods. A thematic content analysis, for example, may start with a set of theoretically derived codes (or themes) determined even before the analysis of the data begins.

The qualitative research *methodologies* suggested in relation to the topics and research questions in the book cover the full spectrum found in language teacher education and applied linguistics research, including (critical) discourse analysis, conversation analysis, content and thematic analysis, narrative inquiry, and (critical) ethnography. A broad range of methods, some quite innovative, associated with these approaches are also evident: interviews, observations, digital storytelling, visual narratives, open-ended surveys, critical incident techniques, teacher journals, video recordings of classroom interaction, social media postings and commentaries, document analysis, language portraits, linguistic (school, classroom) landscapes.

The third part of the title is *language teacher education*. In this book it is used in its broadest sense, to refer to language teachers' professional learning, development and practice in pre-service and in-service phases of their careers.

Strategies for Choosing a Research Topic

Strategies for going about selecting a topic are surprisingly superficially addressed in research methodology textbooks, if at all, and so for this book I asked contributors to draw on their own experiences and to suggest strategies they have seen effectively implemented, either by themselves or the student and teacher researchers they have worked with. They have suggested many, including some of the more obvious but essential ones, such as reading relevant literature, talking to colleagues, and focusing on personal interest, but they have also recommended some quite innovative approaches to topic selection. I conducted a content analysis of the 'Strategies for choosing a research topic' section in all the chapters and categorized them as below. For each strategy, I provide a heading followed by sub-categories, which inevitably interconnect with other categories. The strategies are not in any particular order, and all are elaborated on within the chapters.

Read Theoretical and Empirical Literature

- be attentive to current debates and developments
- read content pages and abstracts of recent, relevant journals
- become familiar with classical literature in the field

Follow Interests and Passions

- reflect on own experience
- be constantly engaged in critical self-reflection
- ground topic in context you know and care about
- connect topic to own life history, including language learning history

Engage with Professional and Academic Community

- reflect on formal courses taken or take new ones
- join professional associations and read their research agendas and missions
- network and talk to members
- if a student, connect to supervisor's research interests and projects
- attend conferences, and be a critical listener
- observe teacher educators in classes and seminars/workshops
- participate in online forums, discussion groups, and webinars

Engage with Teachers

- observe teachers in classrooms
- observe activity in your own workplace
- consider what issues teachers and learners face in their contexts, from their perspectives
- ask teachers whether potential research addresses their needs

Be Curious

- become aware of own geo-political context
- pay attention to debates and discussion in the media
- reflect on own professional problems and issues and reasons for them
- pursue questions you really don't have answers to and are really curious about

Explore Your Own Workplace

- talk to colleagues
- survey colleagues
- consider collaborating in research teams
- draw on own particular professional knowledge and teaching practice in the workplace

Be Practical

- ensure you have access to appropriate participants
- stick close to what you know
- ensure you have access to appropriate facilities and institutions
- consider whether you have the necessary research skills needed to conduct the research
- consider whether there are sufficient resources (i.e., human, financial, time, bibliographic) needed to conduct the research

Be Prepared for the Unexpected

- be on the lookout for topics that may find you in your work
- be on the lookout for topics that emerge when busily researching something else
- take notice of discomfort, ambiguities and puzzlement in your work, from which topics might emerge

Go Beyond the Familiar

- look at big issues beyond your own professional community
- push yourself beyond your level of research expertise
- read across disciplinary boundaries
- explore other related disciplines and consider transdisciplinary topics
- tackle topics already studied by others and use different methodologies and participants, in varying geo-political contexts
- examine and challenge old issues and debates (e.g., teaching methods, practices, policies) in light of new and emerging theories.

To end this section I quote Matthew Prior from Chapter 10, who summarizes nicely some of the deliberations we probably all engage in to some extent as we go about *constructing* a topic for our next research project:

> Because there are many ways to frame a topic – all shaped by experience, personal preferences, assumptions, beliefs, methodological choices, and professional alignments – I must consider what my particular "story" of this topic might look like: Is it something I can or really want (or need) to tell? Am I the right person to tell it? Is this something other people will want to hear or read? After carefully weighing such matters, I find that I am better prepared to demonstrate how my study relates to other research stories on the topic and how it might contribute new insights or findings.

Organization of the Book

Contributors to this book are experienced qualitative research supervisors/ advisers, mentors, and principal investigators in the field of language teacher education, including language teaching and learning, literacy education, the preparation of pre-service teachers, and the professional development of in-service language teachers; and by language teachers I mean those teaching in contexts that are variously described as second language, foreign language, multilingual, and bilingual.

The chapters are autobiographical in nature, with contributors reflecting on relevant, current and innovative research topics within their own area of work. To varying degrees they embed their discussions within accounts of their professional life and research work. The book aims to accomplish the following:

1. On a practical level, it offers explicit research topics within the contributors' areas of expertise, and even more specifically, actual research/guiding questions that reflect these topics.
2. Also, practically, it offers suggestions for strategies to use to decide on these research topics and questions.
3. Overall, the chapters offer broad coverage of current thinking about research in LTE.

Following this introductory chapter, there are 34 chapters, each organized into the following separately headed sections:

- a brief biographical statement by the author, positioning their area of research within LTE and briefly introducing the chapter
- suggestions for strategies to use when selecting a research topic within a qualitative/narrative research paradigm

- *five* proposed research topics
- *ten* specific research questions or guiding questions that reflect the five topics
- a maximum of ten key references

This is not a book I expect to be read from beginning to end. As such there is no particular order to the sequencing of the chapters, except that they are loosely grouped by common research area; for example, you will find a grouping on emotions in language teaching, learning, and teacher education, followed by another on language teacher identities, and then one on sociocultural theoretical perspectives on LTE. I anticipate that readers will go to chapters that relate to topics that might already interest them, and then read 'outwards' from there to explore new areas. Following is a list of the chapters together with the five topics suggested by their authors.

Research Topics

Chapter 2: Working with Doctoral Dissertation Writers (Christine Pearson Casanave)

1. Graduate LTE students' and faculty's past and present experiences with L1 and L2 academic reading and writing activities
2. Influences of graduate LTE programs on the literacy activities that graduates design for their own students
3. Literacy-related identity changes: (a) in graduate students over the duration of their graduate programs; (b) in faculty over the duration of a career
4. Tales of successful and unsuccessful academic literacy experiences in LTE programs
5. Reasons why some LTE writers do not assimilate into the academic literacy activities of a disciplinary community

Chapter 3: Going Beyond Familiarity and Doing the Opposite in Language Teacher Education (Tan Bee Tin)

1. Research on creativity in language use, language learning and teaching
2. Research on interest and language learning/teaching
3. Research on language learning and teaching in diverse contexts
4. Research on teachers: Teacher talk
5. Research on students: Students' language learning experiences in diverse contexts

Chapter 4: Learning to Teach Languages (Donald Freeman)

1. Teacher knowledge and knowledge-for-teaching languages
2. How people learn to teach (languages)

3. Teacher knowledge and ELT 'policyscapes'
4. Equitable classroom practices and pedagogies
5. Understanding how professional development 'works'

Chapter 5: Researching Language Ideologies (Carolyn McKinney)

1. Teachers' language ideologies (in multilingual contexts)
2. Children's/students' language ideologies
3. Language ideologies informing school policies, including language policy
4. Language ideologies underpinning language curricula and assessment
5. Impact of language ideologies on language pedagogy and language practices across the curriculum

Chapter 6: Language Teachers' Professional Learning in China (Wen Qiufang)

1. Novice English teachers' professional development in an inter-university community
2. Particular aspects of professional learning
3. Emotional challenges and responses in an inter-university community of professional learning
4. Mechanisms for developing an inter-university community of professional learning
5. Sustaining the effects of an inter-university community of professional learning

Chapter 7: The Impact of Language Teacher Professional Development (Simon Borg)

1. Instructional practices
2. Teacher language proficiency
3. Teacher knowledge
4. Teachers' beliefs
5. Confidence

Chapter 8: Language Teacher Psychology Research (Sarah Mercer)

1. Teacher–learner relationship
2. Teacher mindsets
3. Teacher wellbeing
4. Positive language teacher education
5. Teacher emotions

Chapter 9: Emotions in Language Teacher Education and Practice (Elizabeth R. Miller and Christina Gkonou)

1. Emotion labor
2. Agency
3. Identity
4. Teaching as caring
5. Critical incidents

Chapter 10: Researching Emotion in LTE (Matthew T. Prior)

1. Anxiety
2. Positive emotions
3. Emotional labor
4. Emotion regulation
5. Emotion discourse

Chapter 11: Beliefs and Emotions in Language Teaching and Learning (Ana Maria F. Barcelos)

1. Identifying teacher and learner emotions
2. Teacher emotions and their relationship to action in the classroom and to student learning
3. Relationship between emotions, beliefs and identity
4. Emotions and teacher development/learning
5. Emotions and beliefs as a component in language teacher education courses

Chapter 12: Language Teacher Identities in Teacher Education (Bonny Norton and Peter De Costa)

1. Postcoloniality and LTI
2. Social class and LTI
3. Race and LTI
4. LTI in a digital world
5. LTI methodological issues

Chapter 13: Understanding Language Teacher Identities: Conceptualizations, Practices and Change (Maria Ruohotie-Lyhty)

1. Conceptualizations of language as part of language teacher identities
2. Language teachers' identities and practices
3. Teacher identities in the midst of change
4. Language teacher identity development across the career span
5. Supporting language teacher identity development

Chapter 14: Researching LTE through a Vygostkian Sociocultural Theoretical Perspective (Paula R. Golombek)

1. Greater attention to LTE pedagogy
2. Relationship of influence
3. The *social turn*
4. Emotion–cognition as dialectic in teaching/learning and teachers/learners
5. Ecologies of teachers' inner lives

Chapter 15: Context in Sociocultural Theory (Anne Feryok)

1. Formation of new beliefs and practices in context
2. Linking teaching to learning in context
3. Agency in context
4. Commitment in context
5. Perezhivanie in context

Chapter 16: Academic Writing: Linking Writers, Readers and Text Content (Rosemary Wette)

1. Disciplinary differences
2. Writing using sources
3. Synthesizing and integrating multiple sources
4. Stance and engagement
5. Models as textual mentors

Chapter 17: English L2 Writing in International Higher Education (Jim McKinley)

1. Standards and norms in English L2 writing
2. Social constructivism in English L2 writing education
3. Critical thinking and/or pragmatics in English L2 writing
4. Use of metalanguage in supporting English L2 writing
5. Assessment and/or washback in English L2 writing education

Chapter 18: Academic Writing: The Human Side (Pat Strauss)

1. What we don't know (but need to) about the academic writing challenges facing L2 student cohorts
2. The first years of study – how do L2 students adjust to the demands of academic writing?
3. The positioning of L2 (thesis) writers
4. Discipline faculty and academic writing
5. The role of academic writing teachers

Chapter 19: Critical Questions in English for Academic Purposes (Gregory Hadley)

1. International students
2. EAP pedagogy
3. EAP teacher identity
4. EAP management
5. EAP in context

Chapter 20: Race in Critical Research (Ryuko Kubota)

1. Race and learner beliefs or subjectivities
2. Race and teacher beliefs or subjectivities
3. Race and classroom interaction
4. Race and learning materials
5. Race and education policies

Chapter 21: Gender and LTE (Harold Castañeda-Peña)

1. Gendered identities in LTE
2. Gendered discourses (educational and non-educational) in LTE
3. Gendered representations (in language learning materials and media)
4. Gendered classroom interaction in LTE
5. Gendered teacher education

Chapter 22: Researching English as an International Language (Heath Rose)

1. Evaluation of the curriculum for global Englishes content
2. Approaches for teaching English as an international language
3. Attitudes of learners towards variation in English
4. Challenges associated with English medium instruction
5. Multilingualism in EMI and ELT classrooms

Chapter 23: Multilingualism in (Foreign) Language Teaching and Learning (Anne Pitkänen-Huhta)

1. Multilingual learners in foreign language classrooms
2. Teaching practices in a multilingual group
3. Teaching/learning materials for multilingual groups
4. Discourses of multilingualism/monolingualism in policy documents
5. Teacher's conceptualizations of language vs. their teaching practices

Chapter 24: English Language Teaching in Multilingual Contexts (Christa van der Walt)

1. Multilingual language teachers' linguistic knowledge over time
2. Translanguaging classroom practices
3. Family language policies
4. English language teachers as gatekeepers
5. Urban and non-standard varieties in education

Chapter 25: Social Representations of Multilingualism (Alice Chik and Sílvia Melo-Pfeifer)

1. Representations of individual multilingual repertoires
2. Students' language representations of their language education at school
3. Language representations in initial teacher training
4. Heritage language education and its representation
5. Refugees' multilingual repertoires: Deficit and divided

Chapter 26: Language Teacher Education in Study Abroad Contexts (John L. Plews)

1. LTE source and destination
2. The whole teacher
3. The social is professional
4. Specialized programming
5. Post-sojourn transfer

Chapter 27: Study Abroad for Language Teachers (John Macalister)

1. The rationale for study abroad
2. Bringing the local into the classroom abroad
3. Creating the conditions for change
4. Dealing with constraints and resistance
5. Measuring impact

Chapter 28: Generating Action Research Topics (Anne Burns)

1. Your own classroom issues
2. Teachers becoming researchers
3. Action research and teacher identity
4. Support needs of teacher researchers
5. Sustaining action research

Chapter 29: Researching Teacher Research (Daniel Xerri)

1. Teachers' conceptions of research
2. Research and teacher identity
3. Supporting teacher research
4. Teachers' research literacy
5. Benefits and challenges

Chapter 30: Teacher Researchers (Kenan Dikilitaş)

1. Impact on student learning and teacher practices
2. Autonomy development in doing research and teaching
3. Identity reconstruction and development
4. Self-efficacy building and motivation in research and teaching
5. Teachers' research writing experiences: Narratives of teachers as researchers

Chapter 31: Exploring Issues in Language and Content Instruction (Sandra Zappa-Hollman and Patricia A. Duff)

1. Developing effective, sustainable, interdisciplinary collaborations
2. Developing curriculum that integrates language and content instruction
3. Using technology to optimize learning, communication, and assessment
4. Deepening connections between research, theory, and practice
5. Developing expertise in (new) linguistic orientations and pedagogical approaches

Chapter 32: LTE in Primary and Secondary Schools (Takaaki Hiratsuka)

1. Early English language education
2. Teaching English through English
3. Reflective teaching
4. Teacher research
5. Team teaching

Chapter 33: Researching Task-based Teaching and Assessment (Martin East)

1. Pre-service teachers' emerging beliefs about TBLT
2. In-service teachers' developing beliefs about TBLT
3. Comparing pre-service and in-service teachers' beliefs about TBLT
4. Comparing teacher and student beliefs about TBLA (survey)
5. Comparing teacher and student beliefs about TBLA (interviews/focus groups)

Chapter 34: Language Teaching Approaches (Jessie S. Barrot)

1. Isolated and integrated form-focused instruction (FFI)
2. Technical–practical knowledge among teachers
3. Constructive alignment
4. Task-based language teaching
5. Technology-enhanced language teaching

Chapter 35: Strategy Instruction (Carol Griffiths)

1. The relationship between language learning strategies and successful learning
2. The relationship between context and language learning strategy use
3. The relationship between individual differences and language learning strategy use
4. The relationship between learning target and language learning strategy use
5. The relationship between complex/dynamic systems theory and language learning strategies

References

Denzin, N.K., & Lincoln, Y.S. (2011). Introduction: The discipline and practice of qualitative research. In N.K. Denzin & Y.S. Lincoln (Eds.), *The Sage handbook of qualitative research* (4th edition) (pp. 1–19). Thousand Oaks, CA: Sage.

Richards, K. (2009). Trends in qualitative research in language teaching since 2000. *Language Teaching*, 42(2), 147–180.

2

WORKING WITH DOCTORAL DISSERTATION WRITERS

Christine Pearson Casanave

TEMPLE UNIVERSITY, JAPAN CAMPUS, JAPAN; MIDDLEBURY INSTITUTE OF INTERNATIONAL STUDIES AT MONTEREY, USA

Although I wrote academic papers in Spanish at the master's level, my PhD work was all in English. Then, for many years post-PhD, I lived in Japan, where I taught EFL to undergraduates at a Japanese university. While there, I added graduate level teaching in two different TESOL language teacher education (LTE) programs at American university branch campuses. My work since leaving Japan continues at one of these, mainly online. I specialize in academic writing and qualitative inquiry, so much of my current work involves helping students write qualitative doctoral dissertations on a variety of Japan-related EFL topics. These students are all mid-career teachers of EFL, needing only to finish their dissertations to complete their doctoral program. As working English teachers, they naturally build their dissertation projects around issues in their own EFL teaching, just as my own topics for writing and publication stem from my interests in academic writing and qualitative inquiry generally and dissertation writing specifically.

Strategies for Choosing a Topic

Helping L1 and L2 doctoral students develop topics for qualitative dissertation projects is one of the most challenging aspects of my work at a Japan branch of an American university, as well as for me in my own work. Some advice says 'make a list,' and 'choose a topic.' It doesn't work this way. Even the how-to-write/ supervise-a-PhD-dissertation books and articles (Bitchener, 2018; Kamler & Thomson, 2008; Paltridge & Woodrow, 2012) pay insufficient attention to topic development, especially for messy qualitative projects (Li & Flowerdew, 2008). Such resources tend not to emphasize that it could take a year to develop a feasible and sustainable topic. Research questions change, grow, and develop; inquiry processes drag out as researchers get familiar with participants and follow change over time. It helps if LTE doctoral project topics develop from issues close at hand.

To be specific, the topics for my own academic writing and for my students' qualitative dissertation projects grow out of the complexities of our teaching and out of puzzles that we have noticed but not been able to understand or resolve. Often these curiosities have something to do with invisible processes and phenomena: change, intention, motivation, beliefs, cognitive processes, understanding, identity, and sometimes subtle cultural issues. However, in my doctoral advising I find that students often wish to describe their 'new' teaching method, give a test or analyze writings to see if anything has improved after instruction, and then interview students about changes. But descriptive studies of pedagogy don't lend themselves well to research that addresses invisible puzzles. Moreover, measures of writing improvement tend to describe rather superficial aspects of writing, ones that can be counted easily. It is difficult to characterize and document deeper, more abstract features of writing and of writers' experiences.

The point is, a topic in writing research needs to go beyond mere description and instead concern puzzles that require careful inquiry. For instance, I have been interested since my own PhD days in how people start a graduate program with one identity and leave some years later with what seems like a different identity (Fujioka, 2008). I started my own PhD program as an ESL teacher and ended it as something else – not quite a fully-fledged researcher, but no longer an ESL teacher. The changes were intimately tied to literacy activities – the years of reading and writing I had done in the PhD program. In more recent work I have watched how my L1 and L2 students' dissertation project work has changed them (Casanave, 2010, 2019). At the very least, students develop an aura of confidence and expertise that were not there when they started. Hence the question that has guided my own writing and my graduate advising: How do high level academic literacy practices change people?

Stemming from these personal and professional experiences, I provide this advice to myself and to my doctoral students: (a) Choose a dissertation topic close to home and close to the heart; (b) Pursue questions you really don't have answers to.

Topics and Suggested Qualitative Methods

Graduate LTE Students' and Faculty's Past and Present Experiences with L1 and L2 Academic Reading and Writing Activities

It is important for LTE researchers to begin with a clear idea of what both students and faculty know about academic reading and writing in their disciplines, and with what L1 and L2 experiences they bring to their program. Textbook knowledge cannot replace first-hand and experiential knowledge of students and faculty. Such knowledge allows instructors to start where students are, and to fill in gaps in their own knowledge and experience.

Learning about L1 and L2 academic writers' past experiences can involve retrospective narrative-style interviews about how writers learned discipline-specific reading and writing. Although some work exists on this topic, differences across disciplines and cultures can benefit from further inquiry. Such a study would gather background narratives and multiple interviews as a way to ensure a thorough and consistent coverage of participants' reports. Documents would also be used, such as journal reflections and evaluator feedback done on writing, as would copies of participants' earlier and later L1 and L2 writing. Current literacy activities and understandings could be monitored through online postings and electronic journals.

Influences of Graduate LTE Programs on the Literacy Activities that Graduates Design for their own Students

It is often the case that once LTE students graduate from a program, faculty and researchers lose track of them. The resulting lack of follow-up means that we never really know if graduate students' experiences with academic literacy influence the next generation of students – their own students. Such follow up would provide valuable feedback to an LTE program and to researchers who study career-long professional development.

To study this topic, researchers would need evidence of what literacy activities are practiced in the LTE program, and then what graduates do in classes of their own students in relation to what they learned in their program. It would be important both to observe graduates' classes multiple times and to collect syllabuses, handouts, textbooks, and samples of writing from their own students. Discourse-based interviews with graduates and their students and content analysis of teaching materials could be used to document the design and interpretation of writing activities. Observations would provide evidence of how the activities are actually carried out.

Literacy-related Identity Changes: (a) In Graduate Students over the Duration of their Graduate Programs; (b) In Faculty over the Duration of a Career

Identity is a difficult topic to investigate, given the abstractness of the concept and the difficulty identifying concrete evidence for it. However, one of the assumptions of graduate education is that students' identities change in ways that help them socialize into a disciplinary community. An extension of this idea is that over the career of an LTE faculty member, identity evolves as expertise develops (Casanave, 2019). Tracing this development of expertise over time would contribute to this effort.

Because researchers cannot be present for the full development over time of an LTE student's or faculty member's professional identity, research needs to rely to a great extent on retrospective and reflective interviews and analysis of past and present academic writing, including writing for publication. Researchers would note changes over time in writers' views of themselves as central or peripheral members of a disciplinary community, in their writing goals, and in changing aspects of writing itself.

Tales of Successful and Unsuccessful Academic Literacy Experiences in LTE Programs

An academic literacy experience will be considered successful or unsuccessful depending on how more-powerful others (professors, other evaluators) respond to what students do, from early on in an LTE program or a faculty career (Li & Flowerdew, 2008). These experiences can sometimes be painful, as LTE students struggle to meet expectations in their academic writing that might not always be clear. Students' private struggles with their academic writing might also remain invisible unless students are able to share them in storied form with faculty or researchers. Faculty themselves may struggle with their writing, for example, in writing for publication, but hide these struggles, given that they are supposed to be experts by virtue of their status (Casanave, 2019).

In all cases, researchers need to build trust with participating writers or the 'real' stories might not be told. With trusting relationships, researchers can benefit from open and honest interviews and from shared documents that participants might ordinarily keep private (reflective journals, early drafts of academic work and critical feedback, failed attempts at publication, etc.). Multiple approaches are needed to collect valid storied data (Polkinghorne, 2007) about successes and failures in their academic writing lives.

Reasons Why Some LTE Writers Do not Assimilate into the Academic Literacy Activities of a Disciplinary Community

Studies of failure to assimilate into an academic literacy community can be difficult to conduct. In the first place, students and faculty who do not assimilate may leave the field, making it problematic to follow them and their work. However, studies of failure are critically important for language teacher educators and researchers. It is through such studies of what goes wrong that we learn how to make changes to a program and its academic literacy requirements. Such studies require that LTE researchers closely observe struggling students and faculty who do not seem to be assimilating well, and that they try to follow up with interviews and examination of storied textual evidence over time that might point to some difficulties.

Guiding Research Questions

1. What are graduate LTE students' experiences with literacy activities in their programs?

This question asks what students are reading and writing in their programs and what their attitudes and experiences are toward their academic reading and writing.

2. What literacy activities do faculty in LTE programs undertake themselves?

Faculty who teach in an LTE program ideally are themselves L2 learners of a language as well as writers (in their L1 or L2) of discipline-specific writing. Learning more about what faculty experiences are with academic literacy activities will shed light on the kinds of activities they design for students and on their expectations for students' academic writing.

3. How do faculty literacy activities influence those that students take up?

Faculty academic literacy activities, if shared with students, can serve as models for professional development and for insights into what faculty expect from students.

4. What literacy-related changes can be observed in doctoral students' and faculty's identities over time?

In the cases of changes in graduate students' and faculty's professional identities, evidence might be found in the writing and other professional activities writers engage in over time. Change can be documented in topics for publication and presentation, research paradigms, and venues for written work, all of which have identity-related implications. Multiple samples of past and present writing need to be collected and discussed with writers.

5. What reasons lie behind some students' and faculty's lack of assimilation into disciplinary literacy activities?

Studies of failure to assimilate are especially important if researchers of academic literacy in LTE are to understand how to promote success and limit failures. Research on this topic involves 'why' questions, and requires that researchers find ways to follow up with graduate students and faculty who have left a program or field. Insights can also be gained by interviews with colleagues or instructors of those who have withdrawn from a program.

6. How do the L2 writing experiences of writing teachers parallel the activities they design for their students?

Connections between teachers' own writing activities and those they design for their students can reveal the values and expectations teachers have for themselves and their students, and the compatibility, or not, between what they themselves do and what they teach students to do. Researchers would note cases where faculty assign tasks to students that they themselves have not done, and inquire as to reasons for mismatches.

7. How can an L2 writing teacher who has not written much or at all in an L2 teach L2 writing?

It is likely that many academic writing teachers throughout the world are placed in positions of teaching L2 writing when they themselves have had little or no experience writing in an L2. This dilemma is especially salient for L1 users of English, many of whom have not studied a foreign language deeply or done what they ask their students to do. Learning how teachers with little experience in L2 writing manage to teach writing can help us understand how to provide needed support and encouragement for them to continue learning.

8. What is the balance of book knowledge and first-hand experience that L2 writing teachers need about L2 writing?

Many teachers of L2 writing throughout the world have little or no book knowledge about writing (theories, methods, processes of development, etc.). We need to know more about how such teachers manage their classes and their instruction. On the other hand, it is possible that teachers of L2 writing have only, or predominantly, book knowledge about writing theories and practices. Learning how this book knowledge plays out in actual classrooms will help inform L2 writing pedagogy and practice in LTE programs.

References

Bitchener, J. (2018). *A guide to supervising non-native English writers of theses and dissertations: Focus on the writing process.* New York: Routledge.

Casanave, C.P. (2010). Taking risks?: A case study of three doctoral students writing qualitative dissertations at an American university in Japan. *Journal of Second Language Writing*, 19, 1–16.

Casanave, C.P. (2019). Performing expertise in doctoral dissertations: Thoughts on a fundamental dilemma facing doctoral students and their supervisors. *Journal of Second Language Writing,* 43, 57–62.

Fujioka, M. (2008). Dissertation writing and the (re)positioning of self in a 'community of practice.' In C. P. Casanave & X. Li (Eds.), *Learning the literacy practices of graduate school: Insiders' reflections on academic enculturation* (pp. 58–73). Ann Arbor: University of Michigan Press.

Kamler, B., & Thomson, P. (2008). The failure of dissertation advice books: Toward alternative pedagogies for doctoral writing. *Educational Researcher*, 37(8), 507–514.

Li, Y., & Flowerdew, J. (2008). Finding one's way into qualitative case studies in Ph.D. thesis research: An interactive journey of a mentee and her mentor. In C.P. Casanave & X. Li (Eds.), *Learning the literacy practices of graduate school: Insiders' reflections on academic enculturation* (pp. 105–120). Ann Arbor: University of Michigan Press.

Paltridge, B., & Woodrow, L. (2012). Thesis and dissertation writing: Moving beyond the text. In R. Tang (Ed.), *Academic writing in a second or foreign language: Issues and challenges facing ESL/EFL academic writers in higher education contexts* (pp. 88–104). London: Continuum.

Polkinghorne, D.E. (2007). Validity issues in narrative research. *Qualitative Inquiry*, 13(4), 471–486.

3

GOING BEYOND FAMILIARITY AND DOING THE OPPOSITE IN LANGUAGE TEACHER EDUCATION

Tan Bee Tin

UNIVERSITY OF AUCKLAND, NEW ZEALAND

I am a qualitative researcher with a desire to fulfil a personal quest for new, valuable knowledge for our field (second language teaching/learning). I choose not to follow a well-trodden path but to pave a new risky one by focusing on 'less-trodden' but valuable areas of research as evidenced in my research on *peripheral English language teaching contexts* (e.g., Tin, 2014), *creativity* (e.g., Tin, 2011), and *interest* in language learning (e.g., Tin, 2016). I travel to places where others have not normally gone to collect ethnographic data, to understand what happens not just in well-developed educational contexts in the West, but in those difficult contexts and classes in Asia (where my heart is, as I am Asian – my nationality being Burmese). Research for me is a part of my personal quest to understand what language teachers, learners and users are capable of achieving despite unfavorable external circumstances and constraints. Qualitative research tools used in my studies are ethnographic observations of what happens in real classrooms, and qualitative analysis of spoken data that emerges in various language learning tasks and teaching contexts.

The various topics described below arise from diverse activities I engage in: a teacher, a student, a researcher, a traveler, and a regular participant in creative writing workshops. Right from the very beginning of my career as a PhD candidate, I was intrigued by the *emergence of original ideas* during various group discussion tasks in higher education settings. This early interest surfaced again as I participated in various creative writing projects since 2000, leading to my current qualitative research investigating creativity with reference to language learning tasks. A closer look at the various topics of my research will show that there exists a common thread that ties them altogether: my core interest in what language learners, teachers and users are capable of achieving despite unfavorable external circumstances and constraints. I am interested in how topics of positive psychology such as interest and creativity apply to language teacher education in diverse contexts. It is important to generate research topics that reflect our core values and interests that will in return benefit the community and enrich our soul. In a nutshell:

> **R**esearch for me is
> **E**nriching
> **S**tudents' &
> **E**ducators' lives
> **A**dding value &
> **R**eaching out to
> **C**ommunities, and gradually …
> **H**ome-coming to one's self and soul.

Strategies for Choosing a Research Topic

Most of us do research for various pragmatic/utilitarian reasons: to get a tenured position, to get promoted, to get a postgraduate degree, etc. This utilitarian nature of research means that it is all the more important for us to have an opportunity to select research topics that we are passionate about and are intrinsically interested in. This will help us to maintain our interest and motivation, to overcome difficulties and frustration we encounter when conducting research. Choosing personally significant, new, valuable topics for research plays an important role not only in stimulating but also maintaining our interest in doing research. Several strategies can be used when looking for ideas for research within a qualitative framework.

Thinking outside the box: Going beyond the familiar to the unfamiliar. Going beyond the familiar classrooms, practices and discipline to unfamiliar contexts is a strategy I have used to generate new ideas for my research projects. Language teaching has been widely influenced by various disciplines. For example, the discipline of educational psychology has had a massive impact on generating new ideas for language teacher education (LTE) related research. Similarly, the concept of ecology, which has become popular in many qualitative LTE-related explorations, has its origin in the discipline of biology. Going beyond one's discipline requires exploratory, transformational and combinational thinking: trying to *explore* what has been going on in other fields, relating or *combining* other disciplines with one's familiar territory, and *transforming* our current knowledge in the discipline. Qualitative research, by nature, is suitable for such studies which involve discovering new terrains in a qualitative manner.

Taking advantage of unfamiliar, surprising experiences. Another strategy that can be used is taking advantage of unexpected experiences one encounters in the language teaching profession. Moving to a different pedagogic setting often leads to experiencing culture shock or surprising, unpleasant experiences. Such experiences can be exploited to generate ideas for qualitative research before they become so familiar that we no longer notice them as 'strange.' For example, my interest in 'interest' (e.g., Tin, 2016) started a long way back through a somewhat surprising unpleasant experience in a postgraduate paper I taught during the first year of my employment at the University of Auckland in 2004. A course that I thought was very interesting and that I thought I had 'taught so well' turned out to receive the lowest results in one particular item in the course evaluation form: 'The lecturer/the course stimulated students' interest in the course.' That unpleasantly surprising experience caught my attention, triggering my interest in the idea of 'interestingness' and led me to a ten-year long research journey: reading about theories related to interest, conducting my own empirical/exploratory studies on interest with reference to language teacher education programs, and then to language teaching programs in various Asian contexts.

Doing the opposite: Bringing the outlaws back. Another strategy that can be used is trying to be somewhat rebellious when selecting research topics. I believe in the importance of honoring traditional practices and values while keeping up with trends. Many topics that have gone out of fashion in language teaching such as traditional teaching practices (reading aloud, translation, teacher talk) can serve as fertile ideas for research (e.g., see Cook, 2010). Those issues can be revisited in the light of new emerging themes in language teaching. Similarly, well-established popular topics such as CLT (communicative language teaching) and TBLT (task-based language teaching) can be examined and challenged.

Current Research Topics

Research on Creativity in Language Use, Language Learning and Teaching

Recently, creativity has become an increasingly important topic in the discipline of language teacher education (e.g., Jones & Richards, 2016). Creativity – the ability and desire to produce new, valuable knowledge – is an important quality that drives humans not only to seek but also to create/construct new knowledge. My study (Tin, 2011) demonstrates how the need to produce new valuable knowledge plays an important role in language learning. In the process of using language to create new valuable knowledge, learners' language grows in complexity and develops. Understanding how creativity is reflected in our normal daily language use and classroom practices becomes a rich source of ideas for qualitative research. Ethnographic observation and discourse analysis are suitable methods for studying creativity in language classrooms. We can observe, record and compare people's behavior in various language learning tasks designed in accordance with principles of creativity to understand how creative language use can encourage language learning. More research is needed to understand how various language learning tasks can afford opportunities for creativity and language learning and what creative processes students undergo when engaged in such tasks.

Research on Interest and Language Learning/Teaching

Interest, which has been widely studied in mainstream education, is a neglected topic in LTE research. Interest is a positive emotion that emerges when a person interacts with an object of personal significance. Unlike other positive emotions such as enjoyment, interest is a knowledge-intensive emotion: only interest can generate knowledge-seeking behavior, a desire to seek knowledge. When students are interested in the learning activity, they are more likely to engage in higher order thinking, remember what they learn, and have a desire to explore further. Interest plays an important role in both learning in general and language learning (Tin, 2016). Most interest research in education has adopted a quantitative approach and there is an urgent need for qualitative research to understand how interest features in real language teaching/learning environments, and how it affects language learning and teaching. Suitable approaches to study interest are longitudinal studies, tracing the development of students' interest in various topics and how it relates to language learning. Ethnographic observations and getting participants to reflect on their level and nature of interest *while* participating in various language learning activities could also be used.

Research on Language Learning and Teaching in Diverse Contexts

Language teaching and learning takes place in multiple diverse contexts. Most theories of language learning/teaching have been criticized because they often originate from research conducted in ideal classrooms and contexts with favorable circumstances (e.g., Holliday, 2005). Exploring how language learning and teaching occurs in various underprivileged contexts is an important topic. Using an ecological approach (van Lier, 2000), describing the contexts in detail and understanding practices that have emerged to match the contextual constraints is an area for LTE research within a qualitative framework.

Research on Teachers: Teacher Talk

Driven by TBLT, most research has focused on tasks and interaction rather than talk, in particular teacher talk. A widespread assumption that exists in many language teacher training courses is that teacher talk should not be more than 20% of the total teacher–student interaction. Instead of outlawing teacher talk, studies could investigate the quality of teacher talk that can enhance language learning. In many classrooms around the world, teacher talk plays a major role and serves as a valuable, reliable source of input and inspiration for students' language learning (e.g., Tin, 2016).

Research on Students: Students' Language Learning Experiences in Diverse Contexts

To match the widespread studies of teachers' beliefs and experiences, we need more qualitative studies investigating students' learning experiences and views in diverse contexts. The language used in eliciting students' experiences plays an important role. Bilingual researchers fluent in students' L1 are suitable researchers to investigate students' views and experiences (especially when the English level of students is low and when interviews are used to elicit data). Interviews could be conducted using the students' L1 so as to facilitate the process of articulating students' views. Researchers should also be involved in reading the original data in the L1 rather than the translated data (e.g., Tin, 2014).

Research Questions

1. What does 'creativity' mean to language learners, teachers and researchers in various disciplines and contexts? How is creativity reflected in language teachers' practices and language learning tasks? And how does creativity facilitate language learning?
2. How do learners and students view the role of creativity in language learning/teaching?
3. How can we design language learning tasks to promote learners' creative language use? What happens when learners engage in various language learning tasks that are designed to promote creative language use?
4. What are the initial conditions and situational features that contribute to triggering student interest in learning a second/foreign language, transforming language into an object of personal significance and interest?
5. What maintains learners' interest in language learning in the long term and how does it affect their language learning? How do students develop interest in various language-related activities and topics?
6. How can language teaching be conducted in ways that cater to various types of interest?

7. How are language teaching and learning conducted in various diverse contexts? What is the culture of learning and teaching in those contexts?
8. What might be the sources and consequences of such practices? How can teaching practices be transformed to maximize teachers' and students' learning?

9. What are the features of teacher talk that promote students' interest and language learning? How do teachers utilize their talk in various circumstances to promote language learning?

10. How do students differ in their language learning experiences and how do those differences affect their language learning and performance?

References

Cook, G. (2010). *Translation in language teaching: An argument for reassessment.* Oxford: Oxford University Press.

Holliday, A. (2005). *The struggle to teach English as an international language.* New York: Oxford University Press.

Jones, R.H., & Richards, J.C. (Eds.). (2016). *Creativity and language teaching: Perspectives from research and practice.* London: Routledge.

Tin, T.B. (2011). Language creativity and co-emergence of form and meaning in creative writing tasks. *Applied Linguistics*, 32(2), 215–235.

Tin, T.B. (2014). Learning English in the periphery: A view from Myanmar (Burma). *Language Teaching Research*, 18(1), 95–117.

Tin, T.B. (2016). *Stimulating student interest in language learning: Theory, research and practice.* Basingstoke, UK: Palgrave Macmillan.

van Lier, L. (2000). From input to affordance: Social interactive learning from an ecological perspective. In J.P. Lantolf (Ed.), *Sociocultural theory and second language learning* (pp. 245–259). Oxford: Oxford University Press.

4

LEARNING TO TEACH LANGUAGES

Donald Freeman
UNIVERSITY OF MICHIGAN, USA

I fell into the work of language teaching, and that entry has shaped my fascination with language teaching knowledge and teacher learning, or more colloquially put, 'how teachers use what they know to do what they do.' I started out teaching French in a rural secondary school directly out of university, with no professional preparation. Although I hadn't planned on becoming a language teacher, I was hooked. I then did my Master of Arts in Teaching (MAT) in a program that was uncompromisingly focused on learning, following the aphorism, 'learning tells you how to teach.' This focus on learning and on experience has stayed with me throughout my career. I went on to teach English and to do teacher training (as we called it then) in Japan. My focus was shifting from my students' language learning to broader questions of how language teachers learn. I had the good fortune to join the faculty at the School of International Training (SIT), where for more than two decades we worked on issues of language teacher learning and teaching. Along the way, I did a doctorate, which catalyzed my research skills. The dissertation, along with my on-going work at SIT, led me to what I've called a 'design theory' for teacher education (Freeman, 2016). In 2007, I joined the education faculty at the University of Michigan, which has afforded more possibilities to research and to design teacher learning opportunities.

Choosing Research Topics

The first language I taught was 'foreign' to me. French was a language I had learned in and outside the classroom; it was not my home language, which I took for granted. This orientation led to my fascination with how, as teachers, we learn the language content that we teach, and how we use that knowledge in teaching. In this sense then, topics – or fascinations – have chosen me; it's more a matter of timing and serendipity than of intention. That said, however, I'd identify four drivers in selecting research topics.

Work on big topics that resonate beyond your particular professional community. In my case, the fascination with teachers' language and teaching knowledge fell within a group of critical sociopolitical issues. I came of professional age during the reign of what Johnston (1999) referred to as the 'post-modern paladins' – itinerant (usually white) 'native speaking' teachers from BANA countries (UK, Australia, New Zealand, Canada, and the USA). The notions of native-speakerism (Swan, et al., 2015) and linguicism (Skutnabb-Kangas, 2015) were dominating English language teaching globally. Researching teacher knowledge helped to challenge these widespread, unfounded notions that where you're born creates your subject-matter knowledge.

Build from what is known, but don't simply accept or defer to it. The whole notion of teacher learning was a new one when I was starting out as a researcher. In the 1980s, qualitative approaches that focused on documenting teachers' experiences and knowledge (see Freeman, 2016, Chapter 7) were upending the process–product research paradigm. In language teacher education, we drew on research in the general education community, finding that some of their ideas served us, while others – given the unique nature of language as classroom content – did not fit as well.

Ground your topic in a context you know and care about. Some researchers are fascinated by a setting and develop questions about it. I'm the reverse: I have a topic and I look for opportunities to place it in a familiar context that is important to me. The context then bounds and fills in the topic in particular ways. The known concreteness provides a counterpoint to the abstraction of the topic itself.

Develop the implications of your topic. I am fascinated by professional learning processes. An implication is that teachers themselves can access and document these processes and what they generate. Teachers are often positioned (through policies and professional development) as knowledge-receivers. Here again there is a socio-political dimension. Doing teacher-research – sometimes called 'working at the hyphen' – can position teachers as knowledge-generators, to be arbitrators of what counts as knowledge in their work.

Current Research Topics

Teacher Knowledge and Knowledge-for-teaching Languages

Teacher knowledge is a central concern in general teacher education research, where it encompasses a range of constructs such as 'practical knowledge,' 'pedagogical content knowledge,' 'decision-making,' 'metaphors' and 'beliefs,' and it overlaps with 'teacher thinking' or 'cognition.' The topic also includes 'content' knowledge, which is where *language* teacher knowledge starts to differ. Unlike disciplinary knowledge, in mathematics or the sciences for example, language as content knowledge combines discipline-related elements with the know-how of using it. This hybrid knowledge is now characterized as 'knowledge-for-teaching,' which highlights its purposes and starts to elaborate dimensions of how, where, and with whom it is used.

There are a range of ways to research this knowledge. Large-scale studies use defined constructs to collect data via surveys and analyze it using statistical modeling. More finely grained, qualitative work concentrates on documenting specific instances and uses of the knowledge through case studies and cross-case analyses. But the central methodological issue centers on how the researcher gains access to the participants' inner worlds of thinking, knowing, and sense-making. Any researcher in this domain needs to start by defining the terms and constructs, and relating them to the methodological choices they make about what constitutes evidence, and how they collect and analyze that data.

How People Learn to Teach (Languages)

As I noted above, the idea that teachers engage in a process of professional learning is relatively recent. There are different views on how that process happens. Cognitive positions (e.g., Borg, 2015) tend to study it in terms of individuals and the social and contextual elements that influence their learning. Sociocultural positions (e.g., Johnson, 2009) study learning as a socially distributed process that happens in, and so is shaped, by time. These two fabrics – of social mediation and interaction, called 'multi-voicedness,' and of past and present time, referred to as 'historicity' – are overlaid on one another.

As a topic, teacher learning tends to lend itself to idiographic research. The aim is to get inside these processes, to document them from the learners' perspectives. Like researching any process, studying those perspectives over time is key, which suggests a longitudinal approach.

Teacher Knowledge and ELT 'Policyscapes'

We know that educational policies do not usually align well with what teachers actually do. While policies themselves can be studied, to me the more crucial question is how they shape what happens in classrooms. Policies privilege certain definitions of what teachers need to know and do. These policies are enmeshed in what Mettler (2014, p. 1) has called national 'policyscapes,' "in which policies created in the past have themselves become institutions that shape governing operations, political behavior, the policy agenda, and the relationship between the state and society."

Studying how policyscapes play out generally requires a comprehensive theory that connects the macro and classroom levels. Cultural historical activity theory is often very productively used in this regard, as, for example, in Barahona's (2016) study of teacher preparation policies and practices in Chile.

Equitable Classroom Practices and Pedagogies

Understanding 'what works' in classrooms can be a fascinating, messy business. It depends on how successful outcomes are defined, and by whom. What works for the teacher may not work for all (or even some) students, and what used to work, may no longer. Because we know that – like all of us – teachers' ideas are anchored in their socialization and experience, and because classrooms are changing dynamically, how these inherited ideas (about who can do what, what works, etc.) play out becomes important. How can teacher preparation interrupt these inherited notions, or challenge them when they are problematic?

Understanding how Professional Development 'Works'

Most educational systems depend on professional development (PD) programming to improve what they do, reasoning that these programs will improve teaching that will then improve student outcomes. This causal view is the basis of most policy-making, and often shapes how professional development (PD) is delivered and evaluated. Missing in this formulation, however, are teachers: How do they as participants learn from and use PD opportunities (see Woodward, Graves & Freeman, 2018)? This topic is multifaceted, and includes versions of the previous four: defining the content of the PD (the first); what and how teachers learn from it (the second); how its goals and outcomes are embedded in policyscapes (the third); and defining what 'works' (the fourth). For these reasons, the topic can be studied at different levels – from the macro level of national systems that make and evaluate policies, to the meso level of the school building and local education authorities who implement these directives and expectations, to the micro level of what happens in particular PD sessions. Likewise, there are multiple perspectives – the PD designers and providers, those who deliver it, and those who participate. Given this layered complexity, the central challenge here is that, almost more than with the previous topics, the research methodology depends on, and creates, the perspective. Whether it is survey, case study, or mixed methods, the way in which the research is designed will shape what matters in and to the findings.

Research Questions

1. What is knowledge-for-teaching in language teaching?

If knowledge-for-teaching languages (Freeman, 2016) is to be a fully viable and useful construct, it needs further empirical work and definition. How is it comprised? How does it differ from what we call 'methodology'?

2. How does disciplinary knowledge figure in knowledge-for-teaching languages? What role does it play?

Content knowledge in language teaching has long been defined in disciplinary terms drawn principally from the literature of the language or from applied linguistics and second language acquisition. The advent of pedagogical content knowledge (or PCK) has focused on the question of how this knowledge actually works in classroom teaching. What role does it actually play?

3. What role does general English proficiency play in knowledge-for-teaching languages?

General proficiency is generally taken as a given qualification in language teaching, although we have scant research evidence of how it actually translates into classroom practice and student learning. And there is certain counter evidence that just because you can speak a language doesn't mean you can teach it.

4. How do teachers learn to teach a language that is their home language or mother tongue versus a second/additional language that they themselves are conscious of having learned?

We know that teachers' experiences of teaching their first versus their second languages are quite different, but what does this mean in the process of learning to teach?

5. Is the process of learning to teach languages over time better understood as a normative or an idiosyncratic one?

Both views are widespread and supported by interesting research in general teacher education. This is where learning to teach languages can be – or is – potentially different, however.

6. What role do national ELT policies [in a particular setting] play in classroom teaching? How do teachers make sense of what they are expected to do by [specific] policies?

There is a concept in sociology that the people who actually enact policies are, for all intents-and-purposes, creating them for the end user. How does this play out in ELT, where policies are widespread and often publicly debated?

7. How do teachers [in a particular setting] define 'what works' in their teaching? What are their criteria or bases for judgment? Where do these criteria come from? How are they developed?

This is a version of the 'why do you teach the way you do' question, posed from an etic perspective. The question is fundamental to making effective policies and to designing and implementing effective PD.

8. How effective are commonly held classroom ELT practices as judged by the student performance and outcome measures they generate?

Like any form of teaching, ELT is populated with myriad legacy classroom practices – from dictations and choral response to pair-work and gap-fill exercises. How effective are these common classroom practices in generating outcomes for student learning?

9. How do teachers [in a particular setting] adapt to new circumstances in their teaching?

This is a version of the 'changing/improving teaching' question, with two important caveats. First, it asks about 'adapting,' which assumes a process of modification. Second, it uses a placeholder, 'circumstance,' which needs to be particularly defined. This openness is purposeful. Circumstances can be actual – students, curriculum, technology, etc. – or they can by perceived by the teacher – students who are not motivated, a curriculum that is unworkable.

10. How is uptake facilitated in PD? How do teachers [in a particular setting] use what they experience in PD?

This is the central question of effectiveness in PD, but it is a deceptively complicated one. It starts by determining what 'use' means. From whose perspective is it defined?

References

Barahona, M. (2016). *English language teacher education in Chile: A cultural-historical activity theory perspective*. Abingdon, UK: Routledge.
Borg, S. (2015). *Teacher cognition and language education*. London: Bloomsbury.
Freeman, D. (2016). *Educating second language teachers*. Oxford: Oxford University Press.
Johnson, K. (2009). *Second language teacher education: A sociocultural perspective*. New York: Routledge.
Johnston, B. (1999). The expatriate teacher as postmodern paladin. *Research in the Teaching of English*, 34(2), 255–280.
Mettler, S. (2014). The politics of the policyscape: The challenges of contemporary governance for policy maintenance. Retrieved May 10, 2018 at SSRN: https://ssrn.com/abstract=2484837 or http://dx.doi.org/10.2139/ssrn.2484837.
Skutnabb-Kangas, T. (2015). Linguicism. In C. Chapelle (Ed.) *The encyclopedia of applied linguistics*. doi:10.1002/9781405198431.wbeal1460.
Swan, A., Aboshiha, P., & Holliday, A. (Eds.) (2015). *(En)countering native-speakerism: Global perspectives*. London: Palgrave.
Woodward, T., Graves, K., & Freeman, D. (2018). *Teacher development over time*. New York: Routledge.

5

RESEARCHING LANGUAGE IDEOLOGIES

Carolyn McKinney
UNIVERSITY OF CAPE TOWN, SOUTH AFRICA

As a teacher educator and language and literacy researcher, my research and teaching are shaped by my geographical and socio-political position. I grew up in apartheid South Africa, so it's not surprising that issues of social inequality and social justice have shaped my research focus. The relationships between apartheid, language, power, identity, multilingualism, and education are extremely complex. For example, at school I thought that a bilingual was a person who was equally fluent in English and Afrikaans! This was the enforced language policy for White South Africans, while Black South Africans were notoriously divided and separated geographically from White people and each other through the use of ethnolinguistic categories imposed by the state. In many post-colonial contexts language has been used to divide and rule, to oppress and exploit; but it has also been used for liberation.

In my research in a range of schools over the past ten years, my goal has been to understand why in South Africa, and many other post-colonial contexts, we continue to implement language policies that have clear discriminatory effects on African language speaking children, despite our constitutional principles of non-discrimination and redress of past inequalities. I have used the lens of linguistic ideologies – our beliefs about language – to understand how children from non-dominant groups are positioned as linguistically deficient and how monolingualism is erroneously taken as normative in our highly multilingual and unequal world (McKinney, 2017).

Choosing a Topic

As indicated above, for some researchers our geo-political location and context is an important starting point in thinking about what we choose to research; we may ask what the language and literacy challenges are in our own educational contexts and how these are different from/or similar to contexts that most often feature in published researched (e.g., in North America and Western Europe). Whether or not we are openly aware or conscious of this, I believe there is always a connection between ourselves as researchers and the topics and questions that we research.

For example, one PhD project I supervised (Botha, 2015) arose from the researcher's own challenges as a White English speaker attempting to learn an African language during apartheid. She became intrigued by how a small number of White people in the Eastern Cape who had also grown up through apartheid were fluent English/isiXhosa bilinguals. She went on to produce a fascinating project investigating the life histories of four elites learning a language of the oppressed and extended our understanding of relationships between language learning, power, race and identity.

In my own research choices, I have been guided by problems or phenomena that I have either experienced and observed in classrooms and schools, or identified from the research literature, and which I want to understand better and ultimately intervene in. For example, in my PhD study I chose to investigate first year university students' difficulties in dealing with the apartheid past as it was represented in the texts they had to study in an *English and Cultural Studies* course. Inspired by critical literacy and critical pedagogy, I had experienced student resistance to dealing with apartheid and issues of racism in my previous teaching. I wanted to understand this resistance and how I as a teacher could successfully intervene in it. At the same time as I had these experiences, my reading in the field of critical literacy/critical pedagogy showed that while some researchers had discussed the challenge of students resisting social justice focused teaching, this resistance was not well researched or understood. This helped me to identify a research gap.

Current Research Topics

While research on language ideologies is well established in linguistic anthropology (Woolard & Schieffelin, 1994), it is a fairly new field of enquiry in language and literacy education and in LTE. Language ideologies can be defined as "the sets of beliefs, values and cultural frames that continually circulate in society, informing the ways in which language is conceptualised and represented as well as how it is used. Such ideologies are constructed through discourse" (Makoe & McKinney, 2014, p. 659). As this definition suggests, like ideology more generally, language ideologies go beyond the ideas that one individual may have in one particular site, referring rather to a network of beliefs and values that exist across a number of people and sites, and deeply entwined with power relations. Recently, researchers have begun to show how language ideologies profoundly shape language-in-education policies, language curricula, prescriptions on how language and literacy should be taught, as well as what teachers do, or feel that they should do, in relation to language use in the classroom (Makoe & McKinney, 2014; Palmer, 2011).

Teachers' Language Ideologies (in Multilingual Contexts)

Teachers' beliefs about language including the kinds of language use they value, what they believe language is, as well as their views regarding their own and their learners' language use and language repertoires, very often shape both the pedagogical choices they make and the ways in which they position learners along the continuum of academic ability (Banda, 2018). In LTE, Palmer (2011, p. 106) points out that "teachers' unspoken and often unconscious assumptions about language can have a tremendous influence on the kinds of learning opportunities they make available to their linguistically diverse students." For example, if a teacher values a particular language or variety (including accent or phonological features) of a language over others, this will impact on what s/he perceives as good language use, and will likely influence how learners value their own and others' language use (e.g., Makoe & McKinney, 2014). Researching teachers' language ideologies would ideally involve both interview data where the teacher's beliefs are explored, as well as observational data where classroom observation would show ideologies as enacted, possible effects thereof, as well as the alignment or not of espoused and enacted beliefs. Linguistic ethnography (see Copland & Creese, 2015) is appropriate for this research as well as multimodal approaches such as language portraits (Busch, 2018) supported by interviews.

Children's/Students' Language Ideologies

It is not only teachers' language ideologies but those of the children or students in class that impact on how language is used and learned in and outside of classroom settings. In dual language settings, such as Spanish/English bilingual classrooms in the USA, children have been shown to subvert official language policy intentions in a number of ways, for example, with English dominant children expecting Spanish speaking children to use English during Spanish lesson times in two-way immersion classes (Volk & Angelova, 2007), or with bi/multilingual children using Spanish and English in officially English medium of instruction classes. Students' feelings towards a language are often shaped by language ideologies and can have important effects on their learning. Interviews including individual and group interviews and language portraits (Busch, 2018) can yield rich data if learners are old enough. Observational data is essential in exploring children's enacted language ideologies. Such observation needs to account for both formal (or on-the-record) language use, such as during whole class teaching (plenary), as well as informal (or off-the-record) communication while children are working together, in the playground and at break-times.

Language Ideologies Informing School Policies, including Language Policy

School language-in-education policies (and in some cases also admissions policies) can reveal the ways in which language is conceptualized and oriented to in the school space (Banda, 2018). This orientation will often show whether monolingualism or bi/multilingualism is considered the norm, and whether multilingualism is considered to be an asset or a problem. It will show how bi/multilingualism is understood in the programs on offer. It can also reveal language hierarchies as it is usually the language that is valued most, and thus with the highest status, that fulfils the role of medium of instruction in a school, even if this is only on paper. Studies of language policy and planning often make the distinction between policy as *text* (referring to the official policy document), policy as *discourse* (referring to talk or broader discourses about the policy), and policy as *practice* (referring to the enacted policy reflected in what is actually done in classrooms and the school community). The linguistic landscape and the physical use of space in an institution can be researched as a means to access language ideologies.

Language Ideologies Underpinning Language Curricula and Assessment

Although the curriculum often has a powerful effect on how language is taught and used, as well as how it is assessed, the language ideologies underpinning curricula have not to date been a focus of research. A powerful ideology of language that underpins many curricula, textbooks and forms of assessment is the notion that language competence is made up of four separate language skills: speaking, listening, reading, and writing. The assumption is that each of these skills can be assessed discretely. Language is also often conceptualized as a decontextualized and stable system as seen in the testing of learners' knowledge of grammar rules through multiple choice and sentence transformations where success in these assessments is seen as a marker of linguistic competence. Testing bi/multilingual learners as if they are monolingual, that is, allowing learners' to access the resources of only one named language at a time, shows how monolingual ideologies can shape assessments and curricula. Whether language teaching and learning is seen as the sole responsibility of a language teacher or of all teachers may be apparent from policy documents. This topic could be investigated through discourse analysis of curriculum and assessment documents, possibly supplemented with interviews of policy-makers. Critical discourse analysis would be an appropriate approach.

Impact of Language Ideologies on Language Pedagogy and Language Practices across the Curriculum

Choices about how to teach language as well as how best to use language to support learning across the curriculum cannot be separated from language ideologies. When it comes to language use in the classroom, this will be influenced by teacher and student language ideologies, school language policy, curricula, and wider societal beliefs about language (Banda, 2018). While linguistic diversity is the norm, classroom practice often prescribes linguistic homogeneity and the privileging of a single standardized variety of a language. In one of the few studies showing how language ideologies can impact the teaching of writing, Dyson and Smitherman (2009) show how a teacher's misunderstandings about and deficit positioning of African American Vernacular English (AAVE) prevent her from assisting a young African American writer constructively in her meaning-making processes. A linguistic ethnographic approach involving classroom observation, recording and micro-analysis of interactional data would be appropriate for this topic.

Research Questions

1. What language ideologies inform national and local language-in-education policy in one or more sites?
2. What is the relationship between language ideologies informing national language-in-education policy, a particular school's (or number of schools') policies, and enacted policy in practice?
3. What language ideologies inform language policy as text, as discourse, and as practice in a particular site?
4. How do teachers' language ideologies shape their pedagogical choices and their positioning of learners?
5. How do students take up language ideologies circulating in their own school context?
6. What is the relationship between teachers' and students' language ideologies in a particular school space?
7. What discourses about language are circulating or (re)produced in a particular classroom space and how do these discourses shape language and literacy pedagogy?
8. What does the linguistic landscape of a school/college/education institution or a number of institutions (including public signage and notices, environmental print in classrooms, official websites) reveal about language ideologies in that space?
9. How do language ideologies shape curriculum?
10. What language ideologies inform particular textbooks and learning support materials?

References

Banda, F. (2018). Translanguaging and English-African language mother tongues as linguistic dispensation in teaching and learning in a black township school in Cape Town. *Current Issues in Language Planning*, 19(2), 198–217.

Botha, L.J. (2015). *White men, Black language: Language learning, power, race and identity.* Bristol: Multilingual Matters.

Busch, B. (2018). The language portrait in multilingualism research: Theoretical and methodological considerations. *Paper 236 Working papers in urban language and literacy.* Accessed 24

August 2018. www.academia.edu/35988562/WP236_Busch_2018._The_language_portrait_in_multilingualism_research_Theoretical_and_methodological_considerations.

Copland, F., & Creese, A. (2015). *Linguistic ethnography: Collecting, analysing and presenting data*. London: Sage.

Dyson, A. & Smitherman, G. (2009). The right (write) start: African American language and the discourse of sounding right. *Teachers College Record*, 111(4), 973–998.

Makoe, P., & McKinney, C. (2014). Linguistic ideologies in multilingual South African suburban schools. *Journal of Multilingual and Multicultural Development*, 29(3), 186–199.

McKinney, C. (2017). *Language and power in post-colonial schooling: Ideologies in practice*. New York and London: Routledge.

Palmer, D. (2011). The discourse of transition: Teacher's language ideologies within transitional bilingual education programmes. *International Multilingual Research Journal*, 5(2), 103–122.

Volk, D., & Angelova, M. (2007). Language ideology and the mediation of language choice in peer interactions in a dual-language first-grade. *Journal of Language, Identity and Education*, 6(3), 177–199.

Woolard, K., & Schieffelin, B. (1994). Language ideology. *Annual Review of Anthropology*, 23(1) 55–82.

6
LANGUAGE TEACHERS' PROFESSIONAL LEARNING IN CHINA

Wen Qiufang

BEIJING FOREIGN STUDIES UNIVERSITY, CHINA

I have been a university English teacher in China for more than 40 years and have being doing research in the field of language teacher education (LTE) for about 30 years. Furthermore, I have successfully supervised 50 PhD students and over 50 Master's students. Almost all those who used qualitative research methods to investigate issues in LTE experienced great pains and frustration. Qualitative approaches are not taught as comprehensively as quantitative ones in graduate programs in China. The major reason is that the development of qualitative research methodology in China is about 20 years behind international trends (Wen & Lin, 2016). The common challenge postgraduates face at the start of their research is to select a suitable topic in LTE. In this chapter, I first propose two general strategies for topic selection and then propose five LTE-related topics based on my involvement in a large-scale project aimed at facilitating professional learning amongst college English teachers in China

Strategies for Topic Selection

The first strategy is to choose the topic by asking yourself a sequence of five questions:

1. What is the research area you are interested in?
2. What branch of the research area is your intended research object?
3. What type of participants do you want to choose?
4. What particular aspect of your selected participants do you want to study?
5. Is the topic worth researching?

The first question is for selecting a research area; the second one is for deciding the research branch within a particular area; the third is for choosing the relevant type of participants for the research; the fourth for determining your research focus; and the fifth question is for examining whether the selected topic is of significance.

The second strategy is to decide a theoretical perspective for your qualitative study. The perspective is just like a searchlight which helps people find a way in the darkness (Chen, 2000). I often use an analogy to show the importance of determining the perspective at the beginning of a qualitative study. Suppose there is a house with four windows facing four different directions. Now you are inside the house and asked to describe the outside view of the house. How do you do it? Most probably, you have to decide from which window you would like to observe the outside view. Surely, the outside views are different if you choose a window on the north side rather than the south side. The decision on a research perspective taken is like selecting a window. By choosing a window, you delimit your scope of observation but you do not know what you will see through the selected window. You are open to all the possible views through that window. Similarly, the researcher needs to have a perspective for deciding a direction for data collection and data analysis. For example, to study the professional development of a teacher, you might choose a cognitive perspective or a sociocultural one. These two contrasting perspectives would lead you to different aspects of the teacher. For the cognitive perspective, you need to collect data about the teacher's own cognition, while for the sociocultural perspective, you need to gather data on the visible interaction between the teacher and significant others (i.e., you–I interaction), and the invisible interaction between the participant and himself or herself (i.e., I–me interaction) (Wen, 2008). The decision on the perspective chosen should be clear from the start.

Research Topics

In the following section, I suggest five topics for research. These topics are based on my experience of being involved in a large project that aimed at developing an inter-university community of professional learning for university English teachers. The project lasted from 2011 to 2013. More than 50 English teachers from six different universities in Beijing participated in this project on a voluntary-basis in order to develop their teaching and collaboration competences, and conduct action research. The teachers varied in terms of age, teaching experience, education background, and research knowledge and skills. All the teachers participated in monthly meetings at which they engaged in various kinds of learning activities, such as critical reading of journal papers, watching video-recordings of community members, discussing their action-research plans, revising drafts of their action research papers, and so on. In addition, all the participants were required to write monthly reflective-journals, which were shared with community members via the internet. The participants also communicated using emails and WeChat from time to time. The project successfully ended with the publication of 18 action research papers and the production of 12 video-recordings of teaching, which were discussed and evaluated. In general, all the participants admitted in their journals that they made progress in professional learning and gave illustrative examples. From this project, various topics can be selected for research.

Novice English Teachers' Professional Development in an Inter-university Community

The first topic is related to different categories of participants. The study might aim to find out to what extent this kind of inter-university community is beneficial to the novice teacher's professional development. Furthermore, it could explore how these novice teachers seek help from others. Usually, novice teachers face more challenges and difficulties in teaching and research, and thus need more help, but they can also offer help themselves. Related topics could be developed by asking the same questions to different types of participants, such as highly motivated English teachers, experienced English teachers, or team leaders. Furthermore, a similar topic could be developed by making comparisons between two groups of participants in the project; for example, comparing experienced and less-experienced English teachers or higher academic degree and lower academic degree holders in this community.

Particular Aspects of Professional Learning

An example for this topic is to investigate the development of action research competence of the participants in this community. Here action research competence includes two sets of skills. One set of skills involves carrying out the research (i.e., problem identification, proposing an initial solution to the problem, implementing the proposed plan, and reflecting on the research), and another set of skills is writing a publishable paper based on the research. More topics related to professional learning within this community can be formed by shifting the focus from action research competence to collaboration competence or to teaching competence.

Emotional Challenges and Responses in an Inter-university Community of Professional Learning

The teachers involved in the project from six different universities did not know each other before the project started. Many of them felt uncomfortable or even embarrassed when their video-recordings or action research plans were discussed and evaluated by other community members. A research topic could focus on how this kind of community can develop an atmosphere of mutual trust and negotiate mutually beneficial cooperation to overcome the negative responses to such challenges. Thus, one topic would be how to meet emotional challenges in an inter-university community of professional learning, and another could explore variations in emotional responses within this community. Apart from emotional challenges, the teachers also experienced difficulties in professionally critiquing other community members. Discourse analysis of interaction among community participants would be one method to explore this topic.

Mechanisms for Developing an Inter-university Community of Professional Learning

Compared with primary and secondary school teachers, university teachers are more likely to prefer working individually than in groups. It is a daunting task to organize regular professional learning activities for such a large group of English teachers from different universities. Two related topics worth investigating include (a) examining how interdependent relations could be established in an inter-university community, and (b) the role of leadership in developing the inter-university community.

Sustaining the Effects of an Inter-university Community of Professional Learning

Very often the participants in the community are very active when the project is going on. However, it is unknown to what extent the effects of the project are sustained after the project has ended. Do participants continue their professional learning after the project has been completed? Specifically, the research topic would be the further effects of community learning on subsequent individual development.

Research Questions

1. What mediations do teachers rely on when they participate in meetings of the inter-university community? And how?

Question one is focused on the mediations evident in the participants' interaction (i.e., You-I dialogue). Sociocultural theorists believe that people's learning starts from social interaction and then moves to internalization through self-interaction and that the changes in mediations exhibited can well indicate the participants' progress in learning (Lantolf, 2000).

2. What do teachers write in their self-reflective journals with reference to 'you–I' interaction and 'I–me' interaction?

Self-reflective journals can provide the researcher with teachers' inner thoughts regarding what they have gained from social interaction and what is possible to be internalized.

3. What kind of contributions do teachers make to the inter-university community and to their own university community?

Question 3 helps the researcher obtain a more comprehensive picture of the community of professional learning.

4. What beliefs do teachers develop about teaching competence, action research competence, and collaboration competence?
5. How do they evaluate their development in teaching competence, action research competence, and collaboration competence?

Questions 4 and 5 are designed from a cognitive perspective as they aim to investigate the participants' cognition and their self-evaluation ability.

6. How do teachers feel when their video-recordings of teaching or drafts of their research papers are evaluated in the community?
7. How do they respond to any negative comments they might receive from community members?

These two questions aim to describe participants' emotional challenges and their responses to those challenges.

8. How are the teachers' relationships mutually constituted by the discourse in the community?
9. What roles do leaders play in developing the inter-university community?

Questions 8 and 9 attempt to find out how a community of professional learning can be established and developed.

10. To what extent does the project have subsequent effects on the participants' further professional learning?

This question aims at investigating whether the project has any sustained effects on the participants' professional learning.

References

Chen, X-M. (2000). *Qualitative methods and research on social sciences*. Beijing: Educational Science Press.
Lantolf, J. (2000). Second language learning as a mediational process. *Language Teaching*, 33, 79–96.
Wen, Q-F. (2008). On the cognitive-social debate in SLA for more than 20 years. *Foreign Languages in China*, 3, 13–20.
Wen, Q-F., & Lin, L. (2016). A comparative study of trends of research methods use in applied linguistics (2001–2015). *Modern Foreign Languages*, 6, 842–852.

7

THE IMPACT OF LANGUAGE TEACHER PROFESSIONAL DEVELOPMENT

Simon Borg

WESTERN NORWAY UNIVERSITY OF APPLIED SCIENCES, NORWAY

In recent years I have worked on several professional development initiatives (PDIs) for language teachers around the world. My role on these projects has often been to contribute to the design, conduct, analysis and reporting of impact studies and it is this practical experience I would like to draw on here in considering the kinds of topics that merit empirical attention as we seek to better understand what difference PDIs make to teachers. It is important that we do so not just for theoretical reasons but also for accountability given the substantial resources that Ministries and educational organizations worldwide invest in enhancing the competence of English language teachers.

The study of impact on PDIs is characterized by a tradition of quantitative work. There are clear reasons for this: quantitative data provide the kinds of 'hard' statistical evidence that funders and stakeholders often find more concrete and persuasive; numerical data are also typically more economical to collect and process than qualitative data; and success criteria for PDIs are also often framed in quantitative terms. Without in any way dismissing the role of quantitative work, here I will discuss how qualitative approaches – using various forms of observation, interviewing, reflective writing and visual methods (for the latter, see Margolis & Pauwels, 2011) – can play a greater role in the study of impact than they often, in my experience, currently do (see also Bell & Aggleton, 2016).

Strategies for Choosing a Topic

The focus of research on the impact of PDIs should be determined by the objectives a particular PDI has. These may vary but commonly address one or more aspects of teacher competence; this most obviously includes teaching competence (i.e., what teachers do in the classroom) but also encompasses a wide range of attributes such as knowledge, beliefs, attitudes, values, confidence, reflective capacity, and ability to work collegially (for a discussion, including of language teacher competency frameworks, see Borg, 2018). These diverse aspects of teacher competence are an obvious source of topics that can be studied qualitatively when the impact of PDIs is being researched.

Research Topics

Five research topics are discussed below, each representing an aspect of teacher competence that a PDI may seek to have an impact on.

Instructional Practices

PDIs often seek to bring about change in specific aspects of teaching. For example, a project I recently worked on in Azerbaijan (www.britishcouncil.az/en/english/project/teaching-for-success) aimed to help teachers develop their approach to teaching speaking. While its success in doing so was evaluated mainly using a quantitative classroom observation tool, this evidence was supplemented by qualitative observations with a sample of teachers: actual lessons were observed, detailed fieldnotes were made and these allowed for the construction of narrative accounts of these teachers' practices which provided insight into the impact that the project was having on their work. In addition to these observations, qualitative data were collected from interviews with teachers after their lessons and portfolios of materials and reflections which they compiled over several months. While the interviews provided further insight into what teachers were doing in the classroom and how far they felt the project was impacting teaching and learning, the portfolios provided a record of teachers' work over time. Another qualitative way of studying changes in teachers' work during PDIs is to ask them to write 'most significant change' stories (see Borg, Clifford & Htut, 2018). And, of course, the impact of what teachers do on student learning is another issue where qualitative analyses (for example, of students' language production) have much to offer.

Teacher Language Proficiency

Around the world, improving English language proficiency has increasingly become a focus of PDIs and understanding this element of language teacher competence is thus an important focus for research. There are various reasons for this increased attention to teacher's English; one, for example, is that the starting age for learning English has been lowered in many countries, meaning that generalist primary school teachers with little or no previous English study (linguistic or pedagogical) have had to teach the language. While the importance of good target language proficiency among English teachers is indisputable, making such teachers attend language improvement courses can be a very sensitive and controversial issue, particularly where teachers are formally tested.

Research into the development of teachers' English language proficiency often has a quantitative element (particularly where formal testing takes place), but extensive scope for qualitative research exists too. Relevant topics would be how teachers feel about their own English competence, the extent to which they feel it develops during a PDI, and, if it does, how their improved English (or their perception of improvement) impacts on how they feel about teaching English and how they go about doing so. The perspectives of trainers on such matters can also be studied qualitatively. Students too – for example, how far their feelings about learning English are affected by their perceptions of their teachers' English – provide further deserving avenues for qualitative study in relation to teacher language proficiency.

Teacher Knowledge

Teacher knowledge is a complex concept and the literature (for example, Verloop, Van Driel & Meijer, 2001) has posited many different kinds of knowledge that teachers have or need. One I will focus on here has been defined as propositional knowledge. In LTE, this includes the different levels of understanding teachers have of background theory related, for example, to second language acquisition, language teaching methodology and assessment. In the EfECT project (Borg, et al., 2018), teachers' theoretical knowledge was assessed via an exercise where concepts were matched with their definitions. In the Teaching Knowledge Test (TKT), such knowledge is assessed via a multiple-choice test. These are both quantitative measures. Qualitatively, though, interesting questions can be asked about the manner in which teachers' propositional knowledge develops during PDIs and about the role (if any) enhanced knowledge of this kind plays in teachers' pre-active and interactive decision-making, and in their professional lives more generally. It is often implied from the way PDIs are designed that propositional knowledge is first learned and subsequently applied in the classroom, but this assumption is also a legitimate focus for qualitative inquiry which seeks to understand – by observing teachers in professional development situations and in the classroom, and talking to them about their theoretical knowledge – whether this theory-to-practice model is actually viable. Teachers often describe professional development opportunities as 'theoretical,' and when they do, this is not normally a compliment! This suggests that there are problems not with theory itself and its relevance to teachers, but in the way teachers experience theory. Understanding such experiences and probing the thinking of teacher educators as they create opportunities for teachers to encounter theory are further issues that can benefit from qualitative inquiry.

Teachers' Beliefs

The study of teachers' beliefs is a major area of LTE research. Consensus exists on a number of conclusions about the nature of teachers' beliefs, how they affect teacher learning and their relationship to what teachers do in the classroom

(Skott, 2014). However, many of these conclusions are rather general – for example, that beliefs *tend to be* stable or that they *can* shape teachers' behaviors – and there remains ample scope, therefore, for the more fine-grained, highly contextualized and interpretive understandings of language teachers' beliefs that qualitative research can provide. This is not to rule out the value that carefully designed and critically interpreted larger-scale quantitative studies of teachers' beliefs can offer; but it is only qualitatively that we can develop deeper understandings of how teachers' beliefs are shaped during a PDI, how beliefs and behaviors interact during teaching, and how influential factors such as other cognitions (e.g., teacher knowledge) and the teaching context all feed into the equation to determine what happens in a classroom. Classroom observation will again be at the core of research into such issues, supported by additional qualitative insight into teacher learning, cognition and practice via reflective writing by teachers, document analysis (such as lesson plans and student work), interviews and visual artefacts such as drawings, which can be used as ways of enabling teachers to articulate beliefs.

Confidence

Teacher confidence (often discussed under the heading of self-efficacy) is an issue that has surfaced quite frequently in my recent work. While confidence – teachers' beliefs about their own abilities – on its own is not an indicator of competence, there are good reasons why boosting confidence might be an objective on a PDI. For example, teachers are more likely to invest effort in activities they feel they are capable of doing well (Tschannen-Moran & Hoy, 2001). It is also the case, though, that increased knowledge and self-awareness can actually reduce (at least initially) confidence. For example, in a study of Norwegian teachers of English on a one-year in-service course (Coburn, 2016), one conclusion was that while their confidence in speaking English in the classroom increased, they also felt (because they were more self-aware) less confident that they were good English-speaking models for their students.

Confidence can be studied quantitatively (for example, by asking teachers to rate their own competence on a numerical scale – see Borg & Edmett, 2018) but qualitative analyses can go beyond such measures and explore, including longitudinally during and beyond a PDI, how teachers feel about their own abilities, why they feel that way, what factors affect how they feel, and what role their confidence plays in the way they plan and teach. To add even greater complexity, it can be noted that confidence is not monolithic and that teachers will be more confident in certain aspects of their work than in others. Over 20 years ago, I was generally an assured teacher but I was once asked (in an institution I was fairly new to) to teach a lesson in a language laboratory and my limited knowledge of how to control the system meant I had little confidence in what I was doing during that lesson. My research has also highlighted how confidence can vary across domains of teaching, with one otherwise confident teacher feeling very uncertain when it came to explicit grammar work (Borg, 1999). There is extensive scope, therefore, for qualitative research which examines how confidence is affected by PDIs and how confidence relates to what teachers do in the classroom.

Research Questions

1. To what extent and in what ways does participation in a PDI that targets specific curricular domains (such as speaking) or skills (such as using technology) bring about changes in how teachers plan and teach in relation to those domains and skills?
2. What are teachers' perceptions of the ways in which taking part in a PDI influences what they do in the classroom?
3. What impact does being formally tested and/or required to attend a language improvement course have on teacher motivation at different stages of a PDI?
4. As a result of a PDI focusing on language improvement, to what extent do teachers have altered (more/less positive) views of themselves as professionals and, if they do, how far are such changes reflected in teachers' classroom practices?
5. What changes take place in teachers' propositional knowledge during a PDI and to what extent do any changes that occur influence how teachers plan, teach and think about their work?
6. How do teacher educators create opportunities for teachers to engage with theory during a PDI and what thinking underpins teacher educators' approach in doing so?
7. In what ways do PDIs influence teachers' beliefs about specific aspects of their work?
8. To what extent do any changes in teachers' beliefs that arise during a PDI impact how teachers teach English?
9. How is teacher confidence in relation to specific aspects of their work affected by participation in a PDI?
10. How do any changes in confidence that teachers report as a result of a PDI impact what they do in the classroom?

References

Bell, S., & Aggleton, P. (Eds.) (2016). *Monitoring and evaluation in health and social development: Interpretive and ethnographic perspectives*. London: Routledge.

Borg, S. (1999). Teachers' theories in grammar teaching. *ELT Journal*, 53(3), 157–167.

Borg, S. (2018). *Teacher evaluation: Global perspectives and their implications for English language teaching. A literature review*. Delhi: British Council.

Borg, S., Clifford, I., & Htut, K.P. (2018). Having an effect: Professional development for teacher educators in Myanmar. *Teaching and Teacher Education*, 72, 75–86.

Borg, S., & Edmett, A. (2018). Developing a self-assessment tool for English language teachers. *Language Teaching Research*. doi:10.1177/1362168817752543.

Coburn, J. (2016). *The professional development of English teachers: Investigating the design and impact of a national in-service EFL teacher education course.* Unpublished PhD thesis, Hedmark University of Applied Sciences, Norway.

Margolis, E., & Pauwels, L. (Eds.). (2011). *The Sage handbook of visual research methods.* London: Sage.

Skott, J. (2014). The promises, problems and prospects of research on teachers' beliefs. In H. Fives & M.G. Gill (Eds.), *International handbook of research on teachers' beliefs* (pp. 13–30). London: Routledge.

Tschannen-Moran, M., & Hoy, A.W. (2001). Teacher efficacy: Capturing an elusive construct. *Teaching and Teacher Education*, 17(7), 783–805.

Verloop, N., Van Driel, J., & Meijer, P.C. (2001). Teacher knowledge and the knowledge base of teaching. *International Journal of Educational Research*, 35(5), 441–461.

8

LANGUAGE TEACHER PSYCHOLOGY RESEARCH

Sarah Mercer

UNIVERSITY OF GRAZ, AUSTRIA

Like many of us who work in language teacher education (LTE), I started my career as a language teacher. This meant that for many years the focus of my research was on language learners. Their progression and wellbeing in my classes was my primary concern, and it was natural that I sought to combine my teacher/researcher roles by investigating my own work contexts. Several years ago, I moved over into language teacher education and took over running our pre-service teacher education program in ELT. Not surprisingly, my attention shifted from language learners to language teachers – in-service and pre-service. However, this shift was not only pragmatically driven. In my own work, I had found working with a complexity lens helpful in making sense of the messiness of real world language classrooms. In a complex dynamic system, the connections and relationships between parts of the system are key to understanding its character and development. I became aware that if I wanted to understand the teaching-learning process, then I needed to fully understand both key stakeholders involved – learners as well as the teachers.

Choosing a Topic

The first thing when entering a new field is to engage with the literature and see what has been done. This not only ensures I learn about the area, but it is also a great way to start identifying possible gaps, noticing those things that you want to find out about but are struggling to find sufficient literature on. I had spent many years working in the area of language learner psychology. This field had been dominated for a long time by research on motivation but, in recent years, it has seen much more diversification in terms of constructs and greater integration of different areas and perspectives. It was natural that with my shift to LTE I would look for many of the same topics and constructs. To my surprise, comparatively speaking, there appeared to be very little research conducted in language teacher psychology. There was a sizeable body of work to draw on in specific key areas such as identity and cognition, but many core aspects examined in learner psychology, such as emotions, motivation, attributions, mindsets, etc., appeared relatively under-examined with respect to teachers. This perception of a gap became a key drive for my colleague and I in bringing together a collection of papers on the topic, so I could learn from others and set out a possible research agenda for the future (Mercer & Kostoulas, 2018).

The other key source of inspiration for research comes from my own real world experiences and simply talking to and listening to others. In working with our students, I became aware of their concerns and their own needs as learners. I ensured I found ways to open dialogue with them in classes in written or oral form, so I could try to see the world a little better from their perspective. I critically examined our curriculum to see what was being taught and how closely this matched their perceived needs as well as key issues addressed in the literature. I also had the good fortune to be able to go out into language classrooms in schools and observe experienced language teachers. These were not formalized observations, but rather me simply asking to sit in on or join their classes to get a feel for language teaching in diverse classrooms. I have learned an enormous amount from watching them teach and interact with learners but also in individual conversations with them about their work, professional roles, and the daily challenges and joys of their jobs.

Current Research Topics

Through these discussions, my own experiences as a language teacher educator, and reflecting on the literature within our field but also beyond in general education, I have developed an interest in a number of areas that I believe are important and in need of further research.

Teacher–learner Relationship

Experienced language teachers know how important it is to ensure there is a good rapport with their learners. Not only does it help to reduce discipline problems, but it is also key to getting learners engaged and working actively. A good relationship with learners has been shown to be not only beneficial for their academic achievement, it can also make a teacher's experience of teaching much more positive. Yet, many student teachers frequently express concerns about how to build a good relationship with learners and, at the outset, they may struggle to navigate their positions in terms of relational closeness, friendliness, and strictness.

In language teaching contexts, relationships may play an even greater role, given the focus on personal, meaningful communication and the role of interpersonal skills needed for many communicative tasks and intercultural communication more generally. It is, therefore, surprising that there is relatively little empirical work on this. With my colleague, we have started to explore this area through the lens of teachers' socio-emotional competences (Gkonou & Mercer, 2017), but there are a great number of potential avenues to explore. These include investigating experienced teacher behaviors and perceptions about building rapport through interview, observation, or journaling. With student teachers, it would be useful to examine their perceptions of past positive or negative educational relationships and explore how these may connect to their future visions of themselves as language teachers. These would be exciting to explore through narratives and multimedia expressions of future selves.

Teacher Mindsets

Student teachers' beliefs about their skills in relationship building as educators link to my next field of interest. Do students believe that teachers with good interpersonal skills are naturally talented or are these skills that anyone can learn and develop? Mindsets refer to beliefs that a person has about how malleable or fixed a certain skill or competence is. These beliefs can either be fixed, meaning a person does not believe this skill, competence or trait can be developed in any way, or they can reflect more of a growth mindset in which the person believes their competences can be improved with effort, strategies, and a willingness to work on them.

In education, mindsets have been proposed as being a powerful contributor to learner achievement and motivation. It would, therefore, be reasonable to assume that the same types of beliefs could be influential for how pre-service teachers engage with their education courses. In language teaching, I am keen to explore the mindset beliefs of student teachers considering whether they hold more fixed or growth mindsets in respect to their own linguistic, didactic and pedagogical competences. In an initial study conducted using Q methodology (an approach to understanding subjective perspectives originating from factor analytic theory in which participants actively sort items known as the Q sort), we found that many of the socio-emotional competences of teachers, such as those implicated in rapport building, were aspects that the student teachers believed you could not really improve (Irie, Ryan & Mercer, 2018). Another term for mindsets is implicit beliefs, which refers to the fact they are often very deeply rooted and, in some cases, hard to articulate, making them difficult to research. An exciting dimension to the Q study was the use of interviews based around a card sorting activity of belief statements (the Q sort). This approach appears to reveal nuanced beliefs as well as those which are more difficult to consciously express.

Teacher Wellbeing

Another area that has become a key concern for me is language teacher wellbeing. In my dialogue with teachers at various stages of their career, I have become increasingly sensitized to the considerable pressure and stress teachers are under with weekends frequently disappearing and uncertain job prospects adding an additional strain. In language teaching specifically, further pressures can include language anxiety, managing multicultural contexts, and perceived low status for language educators. Across educational settings worldwide, there is an alarming increase in instances of teacher burnout and higher rates of attrition, in what can otherwise potentially be an incredibly rewarding job.

Finding an almost complete absence of empirical research or even discourse on this in language education is worrying. Teachers are key stakeholders in the teaching-learning process and, thus, their wellbeing should automatically be a primary concern. Research in general education shows clearly that high levels of teacher wellbeing are vital to effective, creative and engaging teaching, leading ultimately also to higher student achievement. If the teacher is not in a positive, motivated frame of mind, then they will have great difficulties in ensuring their learners are.

In our field, there is almost virgin territory with respect to empirical work on language teacher wellbeing. To begin with, research is needed to understand teacher perspectives on the stresses, strains, and joys of their work at all stages of their career from pre-service to third age. To do this, guided focus groups including counselling support might be useful. Not only could this generate valuable insights in a time-efficient manner (of concern for already busy educators), but potentially, in reciprocity terms, it could also give teachers something back from the process. Teachers at all stages could also be asked to keep a photo-journal to use as a basis for interviews to help capture some of the ongoing daily stressors and uplifts in their work inside and outside of the classroom.

Positive Language Teacher Education

My next concern is how to bring this issue of teacher wellbeing into teacher education programs. At present, quite naturally, many teacher education programs focus on basic didactic and pedagogical skills needed to teach language in very practical terms. However, if we are preparing teachers for a lifelong career as educators, they also need other skills that will serve them well throughout their careers. While critical reflection is one such skill that is common practice for many, I also feel teaching students socio-emotional competences, emotional regulation strategies, resilience techniques, and aspects of positive wellbeing should be a vital addition. In education more broadly, there has been an explosion in discourse about teaching twenty-first century life skills, which in many cases include explicit reference to mental and physical wellbeing. Surely, we should consciously be teaching these same skills to student teachers. In most cases, time constraints and pragmatic decisions about curricular priorities mean language teacher education programs rarely get round to teaching such life skills to help the teachers have long, sustainable and flourishing careers. Yet, there is already a large body of work from Positive Education (PE) and Positive Psychology Interventions (PPIs) to draw on in creating Positive Language

Teacher Education (PLTE) courses, modules or programs (see Mercer, Gregersen, MacIntyre & Talbot, 2018). What is now needed are empirical investigations of interventions designed to specifically promote wellbeing competences examining how language teachers respond, possibly using surveys and open-ended responses as well as evaluative journals.

Teacher Emotions

Finally, this takes me to the topic of teacher emotions. There has been growing acknowledgement of the fact that cognitions do not function independently of emotions and we need an understanding of both to support teachers effectively. Teaching is inherently imbued with emotions, and training as a teacher is a rollercoaster of emotions (Gkonou, Dewaele & King, in press). Understanding the function of these emotions, how they affect practices as well as ways of harnessing them through the effective use of emotional regulation strategies could provide further support for language teacher wellbeing. It is surprising how little is done explicitly to equip future language teachers with understandings of how emotions can enhance or inhibit the joy and effectiveness of teaching and how to manage emotions effectively for the benefit of themselves and their learners. A valuable window into teacher emotions could stem from the use of critical incident techniques and narratives in writing, multimodal or interview form.

Research Questions

1. What are the relational role models that student teachers draw on?
2. How are these connected with their own future vision of their relationships with learners?
3. What mindsets do student teachers hold about their own competences as language teachers or about language teaching competences in general?
4. In what ways could these mindsets be connected to discourses about teaching in their educational communities?
5. What are the positive stories of student teachers who flourish throughout their education?
6. What do student teachers perceive as threats to their wellbeing and what do they feel gives their wellbeing a positive boost?
7. What kinds of interventions for Positive Language Teacher Education (PLTE) can be developed that are perceived of as being effective from the student teacher perspective both immediately and long-term?
8. How can existing teacher education programs be adapted to include a dual focus on PLTE goals?
9. What are the dynamic emotional experiences of student teachers during their education?

10. What emotional strategies do student teachers use to manage negative and prolong positive emotional experiences?

References

Gkonou, C., & Mercer, S. (2017). *Understanding emotional and social intelligence among English language teachers.* London: British Council.

Gkonou, C., Dewaele, J-M., & King, J. (Eds.) (in press). *Language teaching: An emotional rollercoaster.* Bristol: Multilingual Matters.

Irie, K., Ryan, S., & Mercer, S. (2018). Using Q methodology to investigate pre-service EFL teachers' mindsets about teaching competences. *Studies in Second Language Learning and Teaching,* 8(3), 575–598.

Mercer, S., & Kostoulas, A. (Eds.) (2018). *Language teacher psychology.* Bristol: Multilingual Matters.

Mercer, S., Gregersen, T., MacIntyre, P., & Talbot, K. (2018). Positive Language Education: Combining positive education and language education. *Theory and Practice of Second Language Acquisition,* 4(2), 11–31.

9

EMOTIONS IN LANGUAGE TEACHER EDUCATION AND PRACTICE

Elizabeth R. Miller
UNIVERSITY OF NORTH CAROLINA AT CHARLOTTE, USA

Christina Gkonou
ESSEX UNIVERSITY, UK

Elizabeth's research has always relied on qualitative methods. Her early research used ethnographic and discourse analytic methods to explore issues such as power relations, language ideologies, learner identity and agency, and discursive positioning among adult immigrant learners of English in the US. Her more recent work with language teachers has relied primarily on narrative and thematic analysis in exploring teacher interviews. This work has included exploration of teacher identity work and ethical self-formation. Christina's research initially centered on language learner anxiety and how it is contextually and dialogically formed and understood. She then started looking at how teachers positioned themselves in classrooms with highly anxious learners, which led to more focused qualitative explorations of teacher emotions and how to foster socio-emotional competencies among language teachers.

Our collaborative research has explored the topic of language teacher emotions, the focus of this chapter. Working within this broader topic, we have explored teachers' emotion labor and agency, how language teachers orient to discourses of teaching-as-caring, and how they conceptualize the significance of 'critical incidents' in their professional development.

Strategies for Choosing a Topic

In reflecting on the strategies we have used to pursue particular research topics related to language teacher emotions, we recognize that potential topics often emerge when we are busily pursuing something else. For example, when we collaborated on a project that involved analyzing interviews with English language teachers working in Greece (Gkonou & Miller, in press 2019), our initial focus was on how these teachers dealt with anxious learners. However, as we read through the interviews multiple times, we began to notice the importance these teachers gave to demonstrating caring to their students, a practice which connected to the larger topic of teachers' emotion labor, and these two aspects of language teacher practice became the primary focus of our project. So one important strategy is for researchers to remain open to what their data show them. While qualitative data can be interpreted differently, depending on one's analytical tools and approaches, researchers' analyses are always data-driven and the data often lead to findings and insights that researchers do not anticipate.

This point leads directly to a second strategy, which is to read widely and across disciplinary boundaries. We have formulated topics and research questions related to language teacher emotions that developed from ideas we gleaned from general education research as well as work in psychology, sociology, anthropology, and cultural studies, among other fields. The cross-fertilization of ideas, findings, and methodologies from related disciplines often contributes to the seemingly serendipitous findings or insights from qualitative data that was noted in our first strategy. Third, we have found that our work with language learners and our familiarity with second language acquisition (SLA) research often helps us conceptualize topics related to language teachers. In the example noted above, it was while we were working with a focus on language learner anxiety, a well-established research topic in SLA, that we began to see the importance of examining the teachers' perspectives on these learners. A fourth strategy relates to examining evidence of what language teachers value or emphasize through analyzing important classroom artifacts such as syllabi and lesson plans. For example, we can understand and appreciate classroom priorities and teacher decision-making by analyzing qualitatively what goes into a lesson plan. Additionally, if we are to explore the perceived relevance and importance of language teacher emotions in teacher education programs, we can analyze the content and structure of internationally recognized teacher training courses such as the Cambridge CELTA or the Trinity Certificate in TESOL. This analysis could be supplemented by narratives collected by teacher educators, policy makers, and the scientific board of the awarding institutions.

Current Research Topics

Emotion Labor

One important topic that requires ongoing exploration is the interconnection between language teacher emotions and emotion labor. Benesch's (2017) interview study with language teachers demonstrated not only that emotions play a central role in their practice, but also that 'emotion labor' is a ubiquitous component of that practice. Working from a poststructuralist perspective, she defines emotion labor as the efforts by which "humans actively negotiate the relationship between how they feel in particular work situations and how they are supposed to feel, according to social expectations" (Benesch, 2017, pp. 37–38). In working to display and actually *feel* socially 'appropriate' emotions in the face of numerous challenges, such as tensions in working with students and colleagues, dealing with unfair or unrealistic educational policies, and/or coping with increased monitoring and accountability measures due to education reforms, language teachers risk feeling overwhelmed; this can lead to burnout, cynicism, and, sometimes, career abandonment. Language teachers often view their emotional stress as arising from their own personal inadequacies and thus work to 'fix' themselves.

Our research with language teachers in tertiary settings in the US and the UK, using interviews and online questionnaires, shows that even self-identified 'happy' and experienced teachers regularly undertake emotion labor (Miller & Gkonou, 2018). Examining teacher emotions from the perspective of emotion labor shifts the focus from the individual to the complex emotional ecologies, power relations, and social discourses that inform how language teachers often think they *should* feel. As such, further research is needed to understand more fully how language teachers in different contexts, with varying levels of experience are positioned by different social discourses and what emotion labor means and looks like in these diverse situations.

Agency

A related topic is the relationship between language teachers' emotions and their capacity to exercise agency. Teachers exercise agency as they undertake emotion labor and also as they critically examine those efforts. It is this latter point that Benesch's (2017) and our own work (Miller & Gkonou, 2018) emphasizes. More research is needed to explore how emotions themselves create capacities for language teachers to exercise agency by considering the question: What do emotions do? (see Benesch, 2017). That is, language teacher emotions and agency affect each other, and both can contribute to teachers' capacity to act and to assign meaning and relevance to particular practices or experiences, but this relationship is still not well understood. Interviews, teacher journals, visual collages, digital storytelling, among numerous other reflective practices, can engage language teachers in critiquing their emotional experiences and help them to consider how or whether to resist some forms of emotion labor and to reframe the pressures that contribute to that labor in terms of complex social, historical, and economic influences rather than as individual, internal emotional responses.

Identity

The intersection between emotions and identity is another topic that needs further research in order for us to better understand language teachers' professional development. Language teacher identity is now understood to be fundamental to teacher practice and growth as well as to social and political change more generally (Barkhuizen, 2017a). Research conducted in the broader field of education has furthermore demonstrated that teacher identities are nearly always formed in and through their emotional experience (Zembylas, 2005). In exploring how emotions help constitute teacher identities, researchers who adopt a dialogical and/or poststructural perspective will want to examine how teachers' accounts of their emotional experiences (emerging from one-on-one interviews, focus group discussions, or written reflections) intersect with a complex ecology of ideologies, histories, and daily interactions with others. Undertaking such research can help language teachers recognize the situated and contingent nature of their emotions and identities, allow them to position themselves differently, sometimes resist powerful norms, and even resignify what their teaching experiences mean.

Teaching as Caring

Another current research topic is the intersection between language learner and language teacher emotions, which often leads to an understanding of how language teachers enact teaching as caring. It is important to investigate how learners and teachers regulate their own emotions, but it is also worth examining how teachers help their students to regulate their emotions in class and how this process shapes and potentially impacts on teacher identity. In our own analysis of interview data from English teachers in Greece (see Gkonou & Miller, in press 2019), we found that the participating teachers put into practice several strategies for helping their learners to regulate their emotions. In rereading the interview transcripts though, we came across narratives of teachers in which they positioned themselves as aware and responsive to instances of language learner anxiety and worked towards consciously creating caring classroom environments to enable their learners to perform at their best. These discourses of teacher agentive action in response to high levels of learner anxiety also led to teacher emotion labor.

Critical Incidents

Analyzing teachers' accounts of critical incidents in their teaching practice and experience is another helpful way to understand the complexity of language teacher emotions. In producing narratives in response to researcher interview questions, teachers tend to tell stories, which might come from early in their careers or could be more recent, are self-reflective, and help them to interpret what happened retrospectively (Barkhuizen, 2017a, 2017b). Some of these stories could be classified as critical incidents due to their long-lasting effects, their high emotional impact and the fact that they are treated as leading to significant turning points in teachers' professional and often personal lives (Tripp, 2012). In our forthcoming research study of English teachers in tertiary-level settings in the US and the UK (Gkonou & Miller, forthcoming), we identified several critical incident stories in which emotionally charged discourse was employed and which revealed how teachers worked through ethical dilemmas and emotional challenges to experience emotional rewards. Conducting such research can help towards expanding our understandings of the complex nature of teacher emotions at different stages throughout their teaching journeys and of moments in their careers which defined their own professional identities.

Research Questions

1. How do teachers characterize their emotional experiences?

This open-ended question can help researchers to consider the role of teachers' emotion from a variety of theoretical and analytical perspectives.

2. What kinds of language do teachers use when describing their emotional experiences?

In examining teachers' linguistic choices in characterizing their emotions as somehow problematic or as desirable, researchers can gain insight into teachers' perspectives on their emotion labor or emotional rewards.

3. What kinds of emotions do teachers identify as most frequently experienced and in what situations?

This more focused question allows researchers to compare accounts produced by multiple teachers and/or to compare how emotions are assigned to diverse teaching situations.

4. In what way/s could teacher stories be used for the understanding of teacher emotions?

This question can help researchers to better understand the content and depth of stories that teachers produce with a view to learning more about teacher perspectives on changes in the emotional experience of teaching.

5. How do teachers describe or refer to changes over time in their emotional experience related to teaching?

From this question, researchers can gain insight into teachers' identity formation and professional development as well as their capacity to exercise agency.

6. What else or who else do teachers reference when giving accounts of their emotional lives?

Paying attention to these references can help researchers better understand the social, material, and political contexts in which particular emotions emerge.

7. How does the experience of different emotions translate into emotion labor?

This question can shed light on the possible link between different emotions and emotion labor, also showing how emotion labor can have a formative function for teachers and their practice.

8. What is the relationship between teacher emotions and teaching/classroom practice?

Through this more applied question researchers can look at how emotions work in practice and how they influence or interfere with the actual process of teaching.

9. How/to what extent could emotion-related input be incorporated into teacher education programs?

This exploratory question aims to elucidate how emotions could be directly and explicitly addressed in language teacher education.

10. How do teachers' accounts of emotion labor and agentive effort change when they have been introduced to poststructural or relational (or other theoretical) perspectives on emotions?

This kind of question can be used in teacher education courses or longitudinal research.

References

Barkhuizen, G. (Ed.). (2017a). *Reflections on language teacher identity research*. New York, NY: Routledge.
Barkhuizen, G. (2017b) Investigating language tutor social inclusion identities. *The Modern Language Journal*, 101, 61–75.
Benesch, S. (2017). *Emotions and English language teaching: Exploring teachers' emotion labor*. New York, NY: Routledge.
Gkonou, C. & Miller, E. R. (in press 2019). Caring and emotional labour: Language teachers' engagement with anxious learners in private language school classrooms. *Language Teaching Research*, 23(3).
Gkonou, C. & Miller, E. R. (forthcoming). Critical incidents in language teachers' narratives of emotional experience. In C. Gkonou, J.M. Dewaele & J. King (Eds.), *Language teaching: An emotional rollercoaster*. Bristol, UK: Multilingual Matters.

Miller, E. R. & Gkonou, C. (2018). Language teacher agency, emotion labor and emotional rewards in tertiary-level English language classes. *System: An International Journal of Educational Technology and Applied Linguistics*. https://doi.org/10.1016/j.system.2018.03.002.

Tripp, D. (2012) *Critical incidents in teaching: Developing professional judgment*. Abingdon: Routledge.

Zembylas, M. (2005). *Teaching with emotion: A postmodern enactment*. Greenwich, CT: Information Age Publishing.

10

RESEARCHING EMOTION IN LTE

Matthew T. Prior
ARIZONA STATE UNIVERSITY, USA

I am an associate professor of English at Arizona State University, where I teach and mentor students in applied linguistics, TESOL, second language acquisition, sociolinguistics, qualitative methods, and discourse analysis. My interdisciplinary research interests and publications focus on socio-psychological dimensions of second language learning and use, mental health and well-being, narrative and discursive-constructionist approaches to identity, and social interaction through the lenses of conversation analysis, discursive psychology, membership categorization analysis, and formulation analysis. A unifying thread that runs throughout my work is the topic of *emotion*, a fundamental feature of human life and language. Emotion (and associated terms such as *affect, feeling, mood, qualia*, and so on) can mean many things: a physiological response, a psychological process, a socio-cultural activity, an interpersonal resource for performing social action, an expression of identity, an agentive and moral force, and a means of experiencing and mediating the world. The complex and dynamic nature of emotion makes it an exciting and rewarding area of study and research.

Strategies for Constructing a Research Topic

Topic *construction* (not just selection) is a crucial, yet often challenging, part of all research. Personal inspiration or motivation can come from many sources: experience (e.g., as a teacher or student), a conversation, social media, a news report, or just a dilemma. To determine which topics are researchable and which questions are answerable, it is helpful to examine recent professional publications and conference programs; to consult other researchers, teachers, colleagues, and resources; and to familiarize yourself with potential data sources or research sites, when appropriate and available. It is also important to consider, among other things, what topics and approaches resonate with you; what data sources and research settings you can reasonably (and ethically) access; what skills, training, and background knowledge you have or require; and the resources, financial and otherwise, that may be needed. More than just a preliminary step before getting on with the 'actual' study, topic construction is an ongoing process of revision, reflection, and refinement (Flick, 2018). This adaptability is not only a core feature of qualitative research, it is one of its unique strengths, as it enables researchers to modify their studies to conditions or circumstances in the field that require or inspire innovation: to revise research questions, to decide upon new or alternative data sources, to choose a different research method or form of analysis.

When I approach a particular research topic or data set, I first aim to understand *what* is happening (e.g., Why do I/other people see this as interesting, important, puzzling, problematic, etc.?), so that I can get a rough sense of potential boundaries that the object of study might take, as well as to answer *why* and *how* it is or could be 'research-worthy' (Prior, 2016). This requires that I locate my research within larger disciplinary conversations: e.g., What has been studied about this topic? How has it been studied? Why? How might this study contribute to knowledge, regardless of research outcome? This also helps me find an entry point into inquiring about the topic. Following my interests in narrative, I view research as a creative act, and the researcher a story-teller, whose narrative is rigorously grounded in theory, methodology, and of course, empirical data. Because there are many ways to frame a topic – all shaped by experience, personal preferences, assumptions, beliefs, methodological choices, and professional alignments – I must consider what my particular 'story' of this topic might look like: Is it something I can or really want (or need) to tell? Am I the right person to tell it? Is this something other people will want to hear or read? After carefully weighing such matters, I find that I am better prepared to demonstrate how my study relates to other research stories on the topic and how it might contribute new insights or findings.

Current Research Topics

L2 researchers and educators have come to recognize that language teaching, learning, and use are not just cognitive or physical activities, they are also emotional and expressive encounters. I will discuss five contemporary, and often overlapping, emotion-related topics in L2 research that offer a rich array of research potential. Note, I use L2 here as a shorthand to refer to second/foreign/additional language research, learners/users, and teachers.

Anxiety

For well over four decades, *anxiety* remains one of the most enduring topics in L2 research (Gkonou, Daubney & Dewaele, 2017). As with many other emotion concepts, anxiety is notoriously difficult to define. However, there is general agreement that it is a response (e.g., tension, fear, vigilance, rumination, self-blame, reticence, loss of confidence, disengagement, avoidance) to a perceived threat. Researchers seek to understand how anxiety influences and is influenced (negatively *and* positively) by, inter alia, classroom pedagogy, learning experiences and outcomes, language use, self- and other-perceptions, and social participation. Foreign language anxiety (FLA), like classroom anxiety, test anxiety, and academic anxiety, is a form of performance anxiety associated with evaluation in a particular social and interactional context.

While the negative effects of high levels of anxiety on learning, performance, and perceptions of self-efficacy are well established (Horwitz, 2010), not all anxiety is harmful. Low levels of arousal can help learners focus their attention and mobilize strategies and resources to effectively respond to anxiety-inducing situations. Anxiety has often been investigated using quantitative measures and questionnaires, but introspective methods such as learner diaries, narrative inquiry, and interviews can help probe the conditions surrounding anxiety. They can also make us more aware of how learners perceive, experience, and talk about anxiety and what management strategies they employ.

Positive Emotions

In response to the prevalent focus on 'negative' emotions (e.g., anxiety, fear, sadness, shame, boredom) and associated pathological models of human behavior, researchers from diverse disciplines are turning to positive psychology to investigate how 'positive' personality factors and subjective feelings such as gratitude, hope, optimism, desire, love, happiness, enjoyment, contentment, belonging, empathy, 'flow,' spirituality, mindfulness, and so forth contribute to perceptions of well-being, success, competence, self-efficacy, and satisfaction. These matters are important for L2 research (e.g., MacIntyre, Gregersen & Mercer, 2016) because we want to know how language learning, teaching, and use can (and should) be personally meaningful and enjoyable – and how learners (and teachers) can become more resilient to various challenges and difficulties. In turn, we can examine how positive emotions may shape individuals' sense of autonomy and personal agency as well as their motivations, attitudes, identities, and social relationships. Questionnaires can be useful starting points, and personal narratives, interviews, and other in-depth approaches can help make visible learners' views on what kinds of environments and activities facilitate or inhibit their positive emotions.

Emotional Labor

The concept of 'emotional labor' (Hochschild, 2012), along with 'emotion work' and 'emotion management,' brings attention to sociocultural, sociopolitical, and other 'rules' that shape (i.e., reward and sanction) the expression and management (even 'faking') of emotions. In planning lessons, carrying out learning activities, and providing feedback, teachers regularly orient to their students (and themselves) as thinking *and* feeling persons. This involves closely attending to students' emotional states and needs and thus requires the ability to adjust instruction and the learning environment in ways that help support 'positive' feeling and participation states (e.g., calm, friendliness, enjoyment) while suppressing 'negative' ones (e.g., anxiety, frustration, anger).

There are, of course, a number of personal and professional costs (e.g., stress, burnout) and benefits (e.g., student satisfaction, continued employment) associated with this labor, but much of it goes unacknowledged and unexamined. It should be obvious that understanding *what* this emotion work is and *how* it is carried out is relevant to all areas of L2 education (Benesch, 2012, 2017), from teacher training and retention to materials design and classroom management. Qualitative methods are particularly useful for exploring how teachers recognize, manage, and experience the emotional dimensions of their work. By observing and documenting teachers' diverse activities at particular moments and over time (e.g., through ethnographic and/or case study approaches), we can examine how they engage in this emotional labor and what the various outcomes are.

Emotion Regulation

Equally deserving of attention is how learners manage their own emotions (or those of their peers) across their learning and communicative environments. For example, how do they deal with the frustration that arises from difficult activities or control their disappointment following negative feedback from teachers or other interactants? Emotion regulation thus refers to psycho-social processes that affect the intensity, duration, and type of emotions experienced and that influence personal well-being. Broadly speaking, emotion regulation consists of a four-part sequence (Gross, 2015): (a) a psychologically relevant situation, (b) attention to that situation, (c) appraisal of the meaning of that situation (based on beliefs, values, strategies, competencies), and (d) a behavioral and physiological response (e.g., fear, excitement). Types of regulatory strategies include: situation selection (avoiding certain people, places, activities, etc.; e.g., skipping class), situation modification (adjusting the situation to affect its emotional impact; e.g., sitting in the back of the classroom), attentional deployment (shifting attention to influence the emotions experienced; e.g., thinking about something else), cognitive change (adjusting or reframing how one thinks about a situation; e.g., seeing a test as an opportunity to show learning), and response modulation (directly influencing the experiential, behavioral, and/or physiological components of one's emotional response; e.g., eating, drinking, controlled breathing).

Because emotion regulation strategies can affect a learner's ability to direct attentional resources, use language, and participate effectively, we would want to know, for example, what activities and pedagogical practices (e.g., assessment, group work) cause particular emotions and what specific regulation strategies are effective (and teachable) over the long term. Experimental studies and surveys are common, but as with other emotion topics, qualitative interviews, focus groups, and observation can be helpful in documenting and explaining the temporal and situational dynamics of emotion regulation.

Emotion Discourse

Although emotions tend to be viewed as physiological and intra-psychological phenomena (i.e., as something individuals *have* or *experience*), L2 researchers are increasingly investigating how emotion may be verbally and nonverbally constructed and made relevant in interaction (i.e., as something people *do*). This interest in how emotion functions as a resource for interacting with others, describing experience, and managing identity opens up all language learning and use for study and analysis. This includes everyday conversation, institutional contexts (e.g., language classrooms, testing and assessment, research settings), various speech acts (e.g., greetings, invitations, requests, apologies, complaints), and other activities (e.g., storytelling, humor).

The approaches of conversation analysis and discursive psychology are particularly useful for analyzing how emotionality emerges at particular points in interaction, how it is interpreted or oriented to, and what the consequences are. While this area of research frequently requires audio-/video-recordings, interest in emotion in written (e.g., diaries, course papers) and digital texts (e.g., email, text messages, blogs, social media; including emoticons and emojis) is growing. By looking at the generic and context-specific forms and functions of emotion, we can investigate a wide range of multi-semiotic and multi-modal resources (e.g., talk, text, technologies, grammar, lexicon, semantics, language varieties and registers, prosody, gesture) and socio-pragmatic skills that L2 users develop and deploy to represent, share, organize, and comment on their own emotional lives and those of others.

Guiding Questions

1. What classroom activities increase, decrease, or have minimal effect on student anxiety?

This might focus on a learning *context* (e.g., study abroad, adult ESL, sheltered immersion), *mode* (e.g., written/spoken, productive/receptive), *channel* (visual, audio), and/or *participation format* (e.g., individual, pair, group, peer, teacher-student).

2. What strategies do L2 users rely on to regulate foreign language anxiety?

Which strategies are more/less effective? How are they learned? We might also examine specific sociocultural backgrounds and contexts of use.

3. In what ways do L2 users implicate emotions in their language-learning trajectories?

How are emotions described as initiators of actions as well as responses to events? How are specific 'turning points' framed in terms of emotion?

4. When retelling personal narratives, how do L2 users reframe or manage the emotional aspects of their experiences?

This question could examine, for example, how positive or negative experiences get reshaped or solidified over time, how narrative can be a 'therapeutic' or agentive resource, or how linguistic and other resources help (re)construct identity over time.

5. How do L2 users experience themselves as 'emotional' in their various languages?

This might look at emotion socialization, resources for emotive expression, self-perceptions of emotional competence, and so on.

6. Does practicing emotionally charged speech acts (e.g., arguing, complaining, expressing love) in instructed learning contexts increase student self-efficacy?

This may involve acting out situations and writing scripts or stories (based on real or hypothetical experiences, learner biographies, video clips, etc.).

7. Do L2 users perceive teacher feedback and language assessment as emotional value-judgments?

This would explore how 'objective' measures are 'subjectively' understood and experienced.

8. What strategies do L2 teachers use most frequently to manage students' 'negative' emotions (e.g., anger, sadness, fear, boredom) in the classroom?

How do these strategies influence student behavior, motivation, or participation?

9. How do novice and experienced L2 teachers perceive their roles in inducing or suppressing student emotions?

Do these teachers perform and understand this work in similar or different ways?

10. How do L2 teachers perceive the costs, benefits, and other consequences of their emotional labor? How does this affect their professional practices and personal well-being?

We might also explore students' perspectives on teachers' (or their own) emotion work.

References

Benesch, S. (2012). *Considering emotions in critical English language teaching: Theories and praxis*. London: Routledge.
Benesch, S. (2017). *Emotions and English language teaching: Exploring teachers' emotion labor*. London: Routledge.
Flick, U. (2018). *Designing qualitative research* (2nd edition). London: Sage.
Gkonou, C., Daubney, M., & Dewaele, J-M. (Eds.). (2017). *New insights into language anxiety: Theory, research and educational implications*. Bristol: Multilingual Matters.
Gross, J.J. (Ed.) (2015). *Handbook of emotion regulation* (2nd edition). London: Guilford Press.
Hochschild, A.R. (2012). *The managed heart: Commercialization of human feeling*. Berkeley: University of California Press.
Horwitz, E.K. (2010). Foreign and second language anxiety. *Language Teaching*, 43, 154–167
MacIntyre, P.D., Gregersen, T., & Mercer, S. (2016). *Positive psychology in SLA*. Bristol: Multilingual Matters.
Prior, M.T. (2016). *Emotion discourse in L2 narrative research*. Clevedon, UK: Multilingual Matters.

11

BELIEFS AND EMOTIONS IN LANGUAGE TEACHING AND LEARNING

Ana Maria F. Barcelos
FEDERAL UNIVERSITY OF VIÇOSA, BRAZIL

I have been a teacher of English in Brazil for the past 28 years, 26 of those as a professor teaching pre-service teachers of English. I teach at the same university where I was once, myself, a pre-service English teacher. In this long and interesting transition from a pre-service teacher to an English teacher and then a professor of English, my area of expertise research has been learners' and teachers' beliefs about language learning and teaching and, more recently, how this concept is related to their emotions, identities, and motivation. My work in the graduate school of languages involves advising students on this topic. My own research nowadays has focused more on teacher emotions and more specifically the emotion of love and how it is enacted by pre- and in-service teachers of English (or other languages). In this pursuit, working with language learning and teaching narratives has enabled me to understand these concepts.

Choosing a Research Topic

In my experience of becoming a researcher, choosing an LTE-related research topic happened quite naturally, but thinking about this in retrospect now, I suggest four strategies that new researchers can use to choose their research topics of interest:

1. *Be curious.* Pay attention to what is around you and be willing and give yourself permission to ask questions about the world, in this case about language learning and teaching. I used to pay attention to my colleagues' comments in learning English, such as "if I want to really learn English, I need to go abroad" among others, which struck me as intriguing at least, and which triggered my reflection on beliefs about language learning.

2. *Take formal courses.* My own topic of research was chosen during a graduate course I took. When the professor mentioned "culture of learning languages," I immediately associated it with what I had already been thinking and noticing about language learning. A light bulb went off and I decided right then what I wanted to know more about and investigate.
3. *Read.* After identifying the theme, of course, I went looking for material on it. What had been written on beliefs about language learning? In 1992, there was very little, especially in Brazil. So I stared a frenzied search for similar terms available at that time (without Web 2.0). Most of the literature was written in English. Thus, it is wise for researchers to know a second language to help read material in another language.
4. *Be chosen by the topic.* The second topic that I have been researching, emotions, chose me. That is, I was at a committee of a PhD dissertation and read this wonderful work that made this connection between beliefs and emotions. It caught my attention. In the meantime, in my own personal life, some personal changes were beginning to happen that would put me in contact with emotions that I had not experienced before. So, I can say that sometimes the topics choose us! We just have to be aware, alert and prepared to listen and follow the lead.

Current Research Topics

Identifying Teacher and Learner Emotions

Emotions are inextricably tied to teaching and learning. Besides this, they have an essential role in helping us understand teacher thinking, reasoning, learning, and change, as well as learners' ways of learning. According to Zembylas (2004, p. 198), "Emotions and teaching are deeply interrelated in complex ways, both epistemologically and constitutively." Zembylas (2005) defines teaching as "a way of *being* and *feeling*, historically, in relation to others" (p. 469). Thus, teachers and learners feel a range of emotions including positive and negative ones related to all aspects of the language learning and teaching process as well as contextual and socio-historical aspects that may, at times, influence whether teachers stay or leave the profession and whether learners persist with or give up language learning. Language teacher and learner emotions have usually been investigated by the use of written and visual narratives, interviews, diaries, classroom observation, and open-ended questionnaires.

Teacher Emotions and their Relationship to Action in the Classroom and to Student Learning

So far, just a few studies have investigated how teacher emotions are related to their actions in the classroom and to how they affect students' learning. We do know that emotions shape teachers' practices and interactions with colleagues, students and teaching. In addition, teachers feel a range of diverse emotions (both positive and negative) that may weigh in on how they teach and relate to students, thus influencing their motivation and beliefs about English learning. In this case, the methods most appropriate to use are those related to classroom observation or video-recording of lessons, which are then discussed later with teachers.

Relationship between Emotions, Beliefs and Identity

It has been suggested that emotions are intrinsically related to beliefs and identities (Barcelos, 2015; Kalaja, Barcelos, Aro, & Ruohotie-Lyhty, 2016). In other words, what we believe about language learning and teaching affects how we feel about it, and vice-versa. In addition, researchers (Day, 2004; Zembylas, 2004, 2005) have emphasized how emotions are inextricably tied to teachers' identities and play an essential role in understanding teacher thinking, reasoning, learning, and change. The ways in which teachers understand, experience, perform, and talk about emotions are highly related to their sense of identity (Zembylas, 2005). Teachers' identities are influenced by how they feel about themselves and their students. Their professional identity helps them position themselves in relation to students and make adjustments to their practice and their beliefs in order to engage with students (Day, 2004). To investigate this topic visual and written narratives, interviews and class observations would be appropriate.

Emotions and Teacher Development/Learning

As key elements of teaching and learning, what role do emotions play in teacher development and learning? According to some studies (Barcelos & Ruohotie-Lyhty, 2018; Wolff & De Costa, 2017; Song, 2016), emotions are an important aspect of teachers' careers and development, shaping what they do in class as well as their relationship with colleagues, students and the profession itself. As Golombek and Doran (2014) have stated, emotions are essential to understanding the kinds of decisions teachers make in the classroom. Despite this fact, until recently the role of emotions in learning to teach has been largely ignored (Golombek & Doran, 2014). But this has begun to change and some studies (Rodrigues, 2015) have focused on how student teachers' beliefs about teaching, in Brazil for instance, have triggered emotions of frustration and sadness, but also that with positive experiences these emotions and beliefs could be re-shaped. I believe language teacher education could include instruction on how to prepare student teachers to deal with the reality shock once they enter the profession, help them deal with the duality of their role (of being teacher and students at the same time) in addition to trying to apply the theory they learn in sometimes adverse contexts. In this case, visual and written narratives and interviews would help with understanding how teachers have developed and learned about teaching.

Emotions and Beliefs as a Component in Language Teacher Education Courses

How will this become a topic in language teacher education curricula? Beliefs probably are already a topic in language teaching courses, but emotions are probably not. Since teaching is an emotional activity, how can emotionality be included in language teacher education programs to start raising future teachers' awareness of the role emotions play in the process of teaching and learning languages? First, language teacher educators need to include specific courses on language teachers' and leaners' emotions. Second, in these courses, student teachers would be involved in exercises aimed at developing awareness of their own as well as of learners' emotions, how they are displayed in discourse, the strategies to manage emotions and, most importantly, how social context and power structures influence emotions. In this case, a document analysis of the curricula of different language teacher education programs would help to diagnose what is already included in the curriculum and how the study of emotions could be included.

Research Questions

1. What kinds of emotions do language teachers experience?

We still know very little about the kinds of emotions that teachers feel and the kinds of factors that triggers these emotions in them.

2. Do they experience attentive/pedagogical love in their practice? If so, what is this love related to?

It is believed that love is an essential part of an effective teacher (Day, 2004). But there are not many studies in applied linguistics about love in language teaching.

3. How are teacher emotions related to their practices?

Although we do have some few studies on teacher emotions, there is very little written on how teacher emotions relate to their practices. Are their practices congruent with their emotions?

4. What teaching practices are more conducive to positive or negative emotions?

We know that teachers have positively and negatively experienced emotions related to students, colleagues, and so on. But we know very little on the kinds of practices or triggers that affect their emotions.

5. What kinds of emotional support are there for in-service language teachers to help them deal with their emotions?

As emotions permeate teachers' work, we need to understand if they are offered any support and, if so, what kind of support, and how it helps them in their practice.

6. What kinds of strategies do teachers use to deal with uncomfortable emotions?

In other words, are teachers able to deal with the complexity of emotions in their work? How?

7. What is the relationship between teachers' and students' emotions?

We know students' emotions can be a huge source of positive and negative emotions in teachers. But are their emotions similar or different? How do their emotions relate to each other?

8. How do emotions relate to teacher learning and student learning processes?

In which ways do emotions affect how teachers learn to become teachers and how students learn the language?

9. How are teachers' beliefs about students and teaching related to the kinds of emotions they feel?

We know emotions are intrinsically related to beliefs. Thus, it is important to know how these beliefs influence the kinds of emotions teachers feel.

10. How can language teacher educators provide a safe space for student teachers to talk about and reflect on their emotions in a way that will help them deal better with their emotions in the classroom?

References

Barcelos, A.M.F. (2015). Unveiling the relationship between language learning beliefs, emotions, and identities. *Studies in Second Language Learning and Teaching*, 5(2), 301–325.

Barcelos, A.M.F., & Ruohotie-Lythy, M. (2018). Teachers' emotions and beliefs in second language teaching: Implications for teacher education. In J.D. Martinez Agudo. (Ed.), *Emotions in second language teaching: Theory, research and teacher education* (pp. 109–124). New York: Springer.

Day, C. (2004). *A passion for teaching*. London: Routledge/Falmer.

Golombek, P., & Doran, M. (2014). Unifying cognition, emotion, and activity in language teacher professional development. *Teaching and Teacher Education*, 39, 102–111.

Kalaja, P., Barcelos, A.M.F., Aro, M., & Ruohotie-Lyhty, M. (Eds.) (2016). *Beliefs, agency and identity in foreign language learning and teaching.* Basingstoke: Palgrave Macmillan.

Rodrigues, N.N. (2015). *Relationships between pre-service teachers' emotions and beliefs about learning and teaching English.* Unpublished doctoral dissertation. Viçosa, Universidade Federal de Viçosa, Brasil.

Song, J. (2016). Emotions and language teacher identity: Conflicts, vulnerability and transformation. *TESOL quarterly*, 50(3), 631–652.

Wolff, D., & De Costa, P.I. (2017). Expanding the language teacher identity landscape: An investigation of the emotions and strategies of a NNEST. *The Modern Language Journal*, 101-S, 76–90.

Zembylas, M. (2004). The emotional characteristics of teaching. *Teaching and Teacher Education*, 20, 185–201.

Zembylas, M. (2005). Emotions and teacher identity: A poststructural perspective. *Teachers and Teaching: Theory and Practice*, 9, 214–238.

12
LANGUAGE TEACHER IDENTITIES IN TEACHER EDUCATION

Bonny Norton

UNIVERSITY OF BRITISH COLUMBIA, CANADA

Peter De Costa

MICHIGAN STATE UNIVERSITY, USA

A pleasure and privilege of academic life is the opportunity to collaborate with like-minded colleagues on research topics of mutual interest. Our collaborative work began in April 2010 when Peter and his fellow graduate students invited Bonny to give a plenary address at a graduate student conference at the University of Wisconsin. Since then, our shared interest in identity, language learning, and language teaching has led to a number of productive collaborative projects, which have greatly enhanced our respective research programs. Three of our collaborative publications on identity have laid the foundation for this chapter on research topics in language teacher identity (LTI): Our co-editorship of a special issue of *The Modern Language Journal* on 'Transdisciplinarity and language teacher identity' (De Costa & Norton, 2017), a co-authored chapter on research agendas for the future in the *Routledge handbook of language and identity* (De Costa & Norton, 2016), and a co-authored article in *Language Teaching* on 'Research tasks on identity in language learning and teaching' (Norton & De Costa, 2018).

Language teacher identity research has gained much ground in language teacher education, and this trend looks promising for future research. Apart from the special issue of *The Modern Language Journal*, noted above, recent research includes the special issue of *TESOL Quarterly* on language teacher identity in multilingual settings, edited by Varghese, Motha, Trent, Park, and Reeves (2016) and edited collections by Barkhuizen (2017) and Cheung, Said, and Park (2015). As we author this chapter, a recent call has gone out for a 2019 special issue of *TESOL Journal* that takes an identity-oriented lens to the lives of TESOL teachers.

Strategies for Choosing an LTI Research Topic

In choosing or constructing a research topic on language teacher identity, scholars would need to become familiar with the existing literature on language teacher education in general and language teacher identity in particular. They would then determine what research topics would contribute to stimulating debates in these areas, while balancing this determination with a level of personal interest in their chosen topic. Interest in LTI research has been relatively recent, and there is much potential for advancing this area of research.

In this chapter, we identify five research topics that invite further research on language teacher identity across multiple domains. In identifying these five areas, the strategies we adopted were to first determine exciting areas of current debate in language teacher education, and then determine to what extent they had a bearing on language teacher identity. Further, we asked ourselves what theories might enhance the development of research topics on language teacher identity. The areas we identified range from postcolonialism, social class, and race to the digital revolution and the methodological turn in language teacher education. In the context of this wider educational landscape, we suggest that LTI research can be undertaken at global, national, institutional, or interpersonal levels. The five research topics below, while interrelated, offer a range of areas that invite vibrant and productive research on language teacher identity.

LTI Research Topics

Postcoloniality and LTI

There is now increasing research on language teacher education in diaspora and postcolonial sites where multilingualism is the norm. Such research responds to calls to restore agency and professionalism in periphery communities and gives due recognition to local vernacular modes of learning and teaching. Such challenges have been taken up by emerging scholars who explore ways in which globalization is impacting language teacher identity in tertiary language education programs. A special issue of the *Journal of Multilingual and Multicultural Development* (Norton, 2014) grapples with the ways in which language learners and teachers in African communities are navigating complex identities in changing times. Two particularly active sites of research are South Africa and Uganda, where interest in language teacher education raises important questions about the relationship between educational policies and language teacher identity. Future LTI researchers might wish to explore how language-in-education policies in particular impact the professional identity development of language teachers.

Social Class and LTI

New conceptions of social class are emerging in our neoliberal era, in which globalization is shifting traditional conceptions of class as determined by socio-economic status. Much identity work on social class in the field of language education draws on Bourdieu's constructs of capital and habitus (e.g., Darvin & Norton, 2015), which conceive of class as relational and emergent. Kanno and Vandrick (2014) have edited a special issue on social class in the *Journal of Language, Identity, and Education*, which seeks to broaden debates on social class in the field. The contributions provide a lens through which scholars can examine how language learning and teaching can either reproduce or disrupt economic and social inequities. While the emergence of the neoliberal post-industrial work order renders traditional labels of 'middle class' and 'working class' defunct, important research topics remain on the research agenda, including an examination of language learners who inhabit a transnational habitus (Darvin & Norton, 2015) and navigate the world both physically and virtually. Work on this group of learners and their teachers will be significant because it highlights the material conditions of globalization and its structures of inequality.

Race and LTI

Debates on the legitimacy of the non-native speaking language teacher have much relevance for research on language teacher identity. In the field of English language education, for example, the identity of nonnative English speaking teachers (NNEST) is of central interest to debates on the ownership of English. The use of the label NNEST itself inevitably constructs an identity defined by being Other (non) to a standard (native) along racialized lines. While the label acknowledges the existence of a periphery, it can also perpetuate the marginalization of the accents, professional qualities, and competencies of speakers whose first language is not English, thus promoting 'native speakerism,' which often serves as a proxy for whiteness. Cheung, Said and Park's (2015) volume on language teacher identity examines how the disempowering discourses of NS superiority can shape feelings of inadequacy and professional illegitimacy among NNESTs. While the binary debates of the 1990s between native speakers and non-native speakers have become more nuanced and textured, there is still much to explore, especially as debates on legitimacy and ownership in English teaching worldwide intersect with race and emotions.

LTI in a Digital World

In the field of language education, there is much interest in the ways in which our increasingly digital world is impacting learning and teaching (Darvin & Norton, 2015). In the virtual world, the ability to construct functional selves through digital interaction is becoming increasingly common as multilingual learners and teachers draw on a wide range of semiotic resources to project new global identities. Recent identity research has started to explore the connections between learner and teacher identities. The research of Toohey, Dagenais, and Schultze (2012) is a case in point. In an innovative video-making project with school children in India, Mexico and Canada, Toohey et al. found that the making of videos offered language learners opportunities for meaning-making that extended beyond their particular second language capabilities. Such research has important implications for language teachers, who will need to examine their professional identities as they navigate their teacher identities in virtual classrooms and in computer assisted language learning (CALL).

LTI Methodological Issues

A robust LTI research agenda needs to be consistent with a rapidly expanding interest in the diverse ways LTI issues can be investigated both systematically and rigorously. There has thus been increased discussion on what methodologies can be adopted in order for LTI research to be effectively conducted in an ethical, respectful, and non-intrusive way both within the domains of the physical and virtual classroom. To date, methodologies such as action research, case study, narrative inquiry, conversation analysis, and critical discourse analysis have been adopted to examine identity (De Costa & Norton, 2016; Norton & De Costa, 2018). However, as observed by Darvin (2019), we need to expand this methodological foundation to ensure that identity studies will continue to be a rich and productive research area in applied linguistics. The need for such a foundation has become all the more important given the rise of digital learning and teaching, a phenomenon that has spawned new methodologies like online ethnography and enabled 'big data,' including teacher data, to be investigated across larger and multiple contexts. Methodologically, the emergence of digital research tools and new online platforms for instruction could potentially herald a new era of mixed method-oriented LTI research. From an ethics perspective, such research needs to take into consideration the vulnerability of language teachers who decide to become research participants in LTI studies.

Research Questions

1. With reference to two schools with contrasting socioeconomic resources, how do language teachers navigate the digital literacy practices of their classrooms?
2. With reference to a multiracial group of native and/or non-native teachers of English, to what extent is race implicated in teacher experiences of legitimacy as English language teachers?

3. With reference to a collaborative transnational study of language teachers in two different regions of the world, what cultural practices are deemed most salient to successful language teaching?
4. As children's digital storybooks move from the Global South to the Global North, how is language teacher identity in the Global North implicated?
5. With reference to a study of first year language teachers in a rural and urban school, respectively, what cultural practices impact language teacher identity?
6. With reference to a longitudinal study of a language teacher education program, to what extent does language teacher identity shift over time?
7. How can we explore the ways in which language-in-education policies influence language teacher identity development at the micro- (classroom), meso- (school), and macro- (national) level?
8. Given that language teaching involves emotional labor, to what extent do the emotions teachers encounter impact their identity development?
9. How do language teacher identity researchers negotiate the ethical dilemmas that emerge when working with teacher participants?
10. What new insights does the application of quantitative research methods yield, and how can they be used effectively with qualitative methods to extend the LTI research agenda?

References

Barkhuizen, G. (Ed.) (2017). *Reflections on language teacher identity research.* New York: Routledge.

Cheung, Y.L., Said, S.B., & Park, K. (Eds.) (2015). *Advances and current trends in language teacher identity research.* Oxford: Routledge.

Darvin, R. (2019). Identity. In A. Phakiti, P.I. De Costa, L. Plonsky & S. Starfield (Eds.), *The Palgrave handbook of applied linguistics research* (pp. 777–792). London: Palgrave Macmillan.

Darvin, R., & Norton, B. (2015). Identity and a model of investment in applied linguistics. *Annual Review of Applied Linguistics, 35,* 35–56.

De Costa, P.I., & Norton, B. (2016). Identity in language learning and teaching: Research agendas for the future. In S. Preece (Ed.), *Routledge handbook of language and identity* (pp. 586–601). Abingdon, Oxon: Routledge.

De Costa, P.I., & Norton, B. (Eds.) (2017). Transdisciplinarity and language teacher identity (Special issue). *The Modern Language Journal, 101* (S1).

Kanno, Y., & Vandrick, S. (Eds.) (2014). Social class in language learning and teaching (Special issue). *Journal of Language, Identity, and Education, 13*(2).

Norton, B. (Ed.) (2014). Multilingual literacy and social change in African communities (Special issue). *Journal of Multilingual and Multicultural Development, 35*(7).

Norton, B., & De Costa, P.I. (2018). Research tasks on identity in language learning and teaching. *Language Teaching, 51*(1), 90–112.

Toohey, K., Dagenais, D., & Schulze, E. (2012). Second language learners making video in three contexts. *Language and Literacy, 14*(2), 75–96.

Varghese, M., Motha, S., Trent, J., Park, G. & Reeves, J. (Eds.) (2016). Language teacher identity in multilingual settings (Special issue). *TESOL Quarterly, 40*(3).

13

UNDERSTANDING LANGUAGE TEACHER IDENTITIES

Conceptualizations, practices and change

Maria Ruohotie-Lyhty

UNIVERSITY OF JYVÄSKYLÄ, FINLAND

I have been a foreign language teacher and language teacher educator for 15 years. These years have included happy, joyful, hilarious, surprising, boring, emotional, sad, and frightening experiences with my students and colleagues – experiences that have challenged my beliefs about language teaching and made me rethink my teaching and my identity as a teacher. Today, as a language teacher researcher and teacher educator, my priority is to better understand these processes of change that every teacher has to go through in developing their identities and language teaching practices. I believe these processes are of great importance for the development of language teaching at large. This has resulted in me focusing on language teacher identities and especially on the study of narratives that capture the emotional richness of human experience. To me, listening to practitioners' stories of their professional lives provides me with the opportunity to understand what the essential questions of language teaching are. To reach an understanding of the identity development process as a whole, I have studied both pre- and in-service language teachers' identities and identity development. I have also developed pedagogic models to support these processes. In this chapter, I present some new approaches and questions in language teacher identity research that could facilitate a better understanding of the work of language teachers, and as a consequence help teacher educators to support them in that work.

Choosing a Research Topic

I believe that good research topics should somehow be connected to our life-histories and lived experiences. In addition, a research topic should be one that we really want to explore and invest our time and effort in. We should ask ourselves which phenomena interest us. For me, as a beginning researcher the first people I decided to go to were other newly qualified teachers. I wanted to better understand my own and their experiences of struggling with the challenges of teaching. Their views helped me to build my understanding of the difficulties and potentialities of the beginning phase of teaching languages, and they also led me to discover my major research area. As a consequence, researching in-service language teachers' experiences also made me reconsider teacher education practices from the point of view of identity development. I became active in developing practices that organized learning differently to support identity development. This cycle of research has continually inspired even more questions.

In addition to the above, I would suggest a researcher first take time to consider what has been problematic, odd, or interesting for him/her as a language learner and/or teacher. Emotions provide good ways of finding topics that are worth investigating. Negatively experienced emotions challenge us to better understand ourselves and others. Choosing a topic can also be guided by our future hopes for a career. If interested in university teaching, for example, a topic might be found in this area. Good research topics are often quite near to us. Whose stories would you like to hear? Who would you like to understand? A good topic addresses a problem that other people also often recognize. In addition to being personally significant, we should therefore consider the value of the topic in a broader context. Research in education is always about solving real life problems connected with learning and teaching.

Current and Future Topics

Conceptualizations of Language as Part of Language Teacher Identities

During the past decades, the understanding of language has changed considerably, from being a system to a resource for participation and learning. Despite this considerable change, and the consequent changes in the content of the academic study of language, little research has focused on language teachers' conceptualizations of language as part of their professional identities. This is surprising in the light of the vast literature on language learner and teacher psychology. From a practical perspective, these conceptualizations are, however, at the very center of language teacher identities. The central role of language as both the goal and medium of instruction makes language teaching different from teaching other subjects. This relationship between teachers' conceptualizations of language and their identities mediates the professional practice of teachers in significant ways. Teachers are considered to be gatekeepers in the classroom. Their ways of understanding language have a significant impact on building learning environments and learning itself (Borg, 2006). No change can permeate schooling and language teaching practices unless it is considered meaningful and worth investing in by practicing teachers. By understanding teachers' ways of conceptualizing language as part of their professional identities, it would also be possible to design better teacher education and in-service training for teachers. To study this topic, interviews, visual or written narratives might offer a possible starting point.

Language Teachers' Identities and Practices

In addition to being constructed in talk teacher identities are also enacted in teaching practices (Varghese, Morgan, Johnston & Johnson, 2005; Trent, 2014). The studies on language teachers have until now mostly focused on narrative forms of data enabling the exploration and understanding of discourses. However, not much attention has been paid to the study of classroom practices in the field of teacher identity research. In our attempts to understand more thoroughly the identities of language teachers, I believe a focus on their practices would be crucial. It would complement our understanding based on teacher narratives in significant ways.

To connect the narrative study of language teacher identities to the study of teaching practices, think-aloud protocols and stimulated recall methods would be valuable tools. Also, teacher blogs, that have to some extent already being introduced in teacher research projects (Golombek & Doran, 2014), could help to gain a more day-to-day perspective on the phenomenon. Ethnographic methods including classroom observation and artefacts, portfolios, and teaching materials could also help in understanding the connection between identities and practices.

Teacher Identities in the Midst of Change

Language teacher research has shown that periods of change play an important role in identity development (Kalaja, Barcelos, Aro & Ruohotie-Lyhty, 2016). Transitions and changes in the contexts and contents of work cause individual teachers to reconsider identities and practices. In the field of general teacher research, several studies have addressed the significance of transition phases and changes in curriculum for teacher identities and beliefs. The study on language teachers has until now shown less interest in the significance of contextual and societal changes for language teacher identities. However, there has been some research on the significance of teacher education and transition to full-time teaching for language teacher identity development (e.g., Kayi-Aydar, 2015). In the midst of micro and macro level educational and societal change an understanding of the subsequent change in language teachers' work and its relationship to teacher identity development could offer a valuable perspective needed to develop teaching and learning of languages in different contexts.

This kind of research often necessitates a longitudinal perspective. Studying teacher identities in transition periods needs to take into account not only their immediate reactions to change, but the long-term significance of the change for language teacher identity development. Conducting interviews both individually and in groups could be a valuable data collection method. A more participatory method in the form of discussion groups for teachers during a change could also provide institutional insights into the different phases of the process.

Language Teacher Identity Development across the Career Span

As indicated above, some language teacher research has already focused on the processes that are significant in beginning language teacher development (e.g., Kayi-Aydar, 2015; Ruohotie-Lyhty, 2013). In contrast, the development of teacher identities after the induction period has received less attention. Previously, it has been assumed that experienced language teachers have remained relatively stable in their ways of teaching. The understanding of individual teacher development has, however, changed to recognize the need and possibility for continuous development in teachers' identities and practices (Kalaja, Barcelos, Aro & Ruohotie-Lyhty, 2016). Until now, however, we have little understanding of the ways in which this development takes place after the beginning phase. To me, this kind of research would help us to see the processes involved in teacher development more holistically.

For this kind of study life-history narratives could offer a useful approach. Teachers could be asked to draw a timeline of their past and present experiences. Another perspective could be offered by group interviews with teachers of different ages or longitudinal case studies that would follow individual teachers' development over a longer period of time.

Supporting Language Teacher Identity Development

In my previous suggestions for language teacher identity research, I have concentrated on topics that increase our understanding of identity development. As my last research topic, I would like to challenge researchers also to engage in developing teaching practices, tools and methods to support pre- and in-service teachers in their identity development. I believe our research should be connected to real educational problems. For this kind of research action research provides a suitable framework. By developing research-based language teacher education, we can support the development of teaching and learning of languages.

Research Questions

1. In which ways do language teachers conceptualize language in relation to their professional identities?
2. In which ways are these conceptualizations significant in their everyday practices as language teachers?
3. In which ways are these conceptualizations linked to larger societal discourses on teacher identities?

4. Which identities are drawn upon when language teachers make sense of their own practices?
5. To what extent are language teachers' identities compatible with their classroom practices?
6. What other phenomena become important in language teachers' practices in addition to their narrated identities.
7. How do language teachers conceptualize *change* as part of their work?
8. How is the change significant in language teacher identity development?
9. In which ways do language teachers' identities develop in different phases of their careers?
10. How can language teacher identity development be supported in pre- and in-services education?

References

Borg, S. (2006). *Teacher cognition and language education: Research and practice.* London: Continuum.

Golombek, P., & Doran, M. (2014). Unifying cognition, emotion, and activity in language teacher professional development. *Teaching and Teacher Education*, 39, 102–111.

Kalaja, P., Barcelos, A.M.F., Aro, M., & Ruohotie-Lyhty, M. (2016). *Beliefs, agency and identity in foreign language learning and teaching.* Basingstoke, UK: Palgrave.

Kayi-Aydar, H. (2015). Teacher agency, positioning, and English language learners: Voices of pre-service classroom teachers. *Teaching and Teacher Education*, 45, 94–103.

Ruohotie-Lyhty, M. (2013). Struggling for a professional identity: Two newly qualified language teachers' identity narratives during the first years at work. *Teaching and Teacher Education*, 30, 120–129.

Trent, J. (2014). Innovation as identity construction in language teaching and learning: Case studies from Hong Kong. *Innovation in Language Learning and Teaching*, 8(1), 56–78.

Varghese, M., Morgan, B., Johnston, B., & Johnson, K. (2005). Theorizing language teacher identity: Three perspectives and beyond. *Journal of Language, Identity, and Education*, 4(1), 21–44.

14

RESEARCHING LTE THROUGH A VYGOSTKIAN SOCIOCULTURAL THEORETICAL PERSPECTIVE

Paula R. Golombek

UNIVERSITY OF FLORIDA, USA

Some 40 years ago, I began working with English as a second language (ESL) students, a volunteer tutoring experience with refugees in Buffalo, New York, for which I was ill-prepared but enthusiastic. I learned to teach, reflect, theorize, and conduct research through my experiences as an ESL teacher while and after studying for a master's degree in teaching English as a second language (MATESL). Being engrossed in praxis de-stabilized my epistemological understandings of language teachers and teaching – so much so that I felt compelled to pursue doctoral work addressing language teachers as theorizers in their own right through the construct of personal practical knowledge. My 30 years engaging as a language teacher educator – mainly with novice ESL teachers in an MATESL program and in an undergraduate certificate program – has inspired my research in language teacher education. My practices as a teacher educator and my research, both grounded in a Vygotskian sociocultural theoretical approach (SCT), work in concert as I investigate such topics as the roles of language teachers' narrative inquiry (Johnson & Golombek, 2002; Golombek & Johnson, 2017) in professional development (PD), of narrative and emotions in PD, including teacher identity, and of the quality and consequences of language teacher educator mediation in PD.

Choosing a Research Topic

Research topics concerning language teacher education (LTE) emerge in and through social interaction. This is, not surprisingly, an inherently Vygotskian idea. Fruitful social interactions that intimate research questions include the varied activities and conversations associated with language teaching. Simply put, when we talk to teachers about their teaching – their goals, interactions with specific students, challenges, and success – research questions may emerge. When we critically discuss lesson plans with teachers, work through an instructional activity or approach, read through and comment on their teaching journals, or dialogue with them as we watch their teaching videos, research questions can emerge. Yet, we need, as Dewey notes (1933), to exhibit certain dispositions during these interactions to free us from habitual actions and thinking; by questioning the taken-for-granted in our interactions through attitudes of open-mindedness, responsibility, and wholeheartedness, questions can emerge and eventually materialize into well-founded research questions. Ideas for research often emerge when we experience discomfort and ambiguity of contradictions, which can open up spaces of transformation (Vygotsky, 1978). By externalizing our feelings of discomfort and puzzlement connected with teaching through talking or writing, they become objects to explore.

We talk and write – to ourselves or with others – into research questions organic to what we do as teachers and teacher educators by making connections between theory and practice. When you talk to a teacher or respond to their journals, try to explain to yourself what happened or why you did what you did (talking or writing to yourself or others) through relevant concepts of a theory (ies) that guides your thinking. For example, I used Vygotsky's concept of *perezhivanie* to help me understand my emotional reaction to teachers with whom I have worked. Talk to a colleague with whom you share an intellectual interest. Yet, an uninformed friend or partner can be equally helpful because you must explain your ideas in a way that they can understand. Audio-record yourself with your phone as an idea comes to you while you are walking home or driving in your car. When you read theory, which you must do, illustrate the theory in the margins (or wherever you take notes) with examples from your practice. Yes, make concept maps. My favorite strategy is to draft an email to my writing buddy (have a writing buddy!) detailing my confusion but then typically not sending it. I usually write myself into a clearer idea through the process.

Research Topics

Greater Attention to LTE Pedagogy

Preparing English language instructors has become increasingly complex as they teach in diverse economic, educational, institutional, political, and sociocultural contexts. The professional preparation of teachers for such varied instructional settings requires us to consider not only the traditional two-year, university-based teacher education programs, but short-term, on-line programs/certificates, and governmental attempts to re-train local teachers of other subjects or re-certify teachers trained in other countries. There is much to explore in terms of the pedagogy of LTE: What do we do, why do we do it, and what are the effects of what we do? This includes the theory, goals, and intentions underlying the learning-to-teach activities specified in a program and the kinds of teacher educator mediation provided in response, as well as the consequences of these activities and mediation on teacher learning. This could involve a variety of approaches, such as ethnography, case studies, narrative inquiry, and practitioner research. Longitudinal research on teacher development is needed to go beyond the six-month study typical of much research. For Vygotsky, pedagogy was a form of research, so using research to ground and change teaching in LTE would be welcome.

Relationship of Influence

A persistent but largely understudied area in LTE involves the relationship between what teachers do and what students learn, described as a *relationship of influence* (Freeman & Johnson, 2005). Documenting such a relationship is challenging because it conceptualizes teacher learning and student learning as dialectically shaping each other, and as such, it is a methodologically challenging relationship to study. It involves tracing the internal activity of teacher professional learning as it is unfolding. This includes descriptions of the people, activities, and tools (mediational means) that shape teacher learning, and how and why teachers take up these mediational means to develop their conceptions and practices of teaching. It also involves tracing the unfolding of what and how students learn and how. One methodological approach advocated to do this is through language teacher self-inquiry, especially through narrative, that documents the dialectic of teacher–student learning, offering an insider's view into this relationship of influence (Johnson & Golombek, 2018b). Teacher's self-inquiry also suggests other data collection procedures, the products of which can be interconnected, for example think aloud protocols by teachers evaluating student essays and linguistic analysis of subsequent student essays; and think aloud protocols by teachers talking through a lesson plan, video of the lesson being enacted, and any concrete products constructed by students (e.g., written products such as essays, blogs or journals, and oral products captured through audio/visual means such as presentations or skits).

The Social Turn

In theory, research in LTE has embraced the 'social turn' (Johnson, 2006), that is, we conceptualize language teaching as interpretive and socially-culturally situated activity, and language teachers as historical, theorizing, feeling, intentional, and goal-directed agents. Yet, research in LTE embracing the social turn remains vulnerable to treating the social as a separate variable, or the social and the individual in binary terms. From a Vygotskian perspective, the individual and the social are viewed as being in a dialectic. Researching this means deconstructing the present to find its preconditions in the past (how it came to be as it is), to project its likely future (what it could be), asking what is happening now that allows us to imagine the future. Vygotsky illustrated this through a description of a water molecule: It contains hydrogen and oxygen, which are distinct entities, but they are transformed, or unified, when they come together. Narrative inquiry is an appropriate methodology for researching the unity of the individual/social in LTE as it provides for temporal dimensions, anemic perspective, varied sources of data, and rich descriptions.

Emotion/cognition as Dialectic in Teaching/Learning and Teachers/Learners

Researching teacher and student emotions has become an increasingly popular LTE research topic. As with any trend, we need to go beyond simply cataloguing emotions and to theorize more fully about the nature and interrelationship between emotion/cognition, the role of emotion/cognition in language teaching/learning, the relationship between teacher and learner emotion, and the role of language and language learning in emotion/cognition self-regulation. This idea of emotion as integral to teaching/learning is likewise embedded within the 'relationship of influence,' as well as the 'social turn.' Researching the consequences of teacher and student emotion, thus, is appropriate for research within a qualitative/narrative paradigm, particularly as we are looking to expand our understandings rather than make causal inferences. Emotions are typically captured through narratives, so multiple elicitation tools and prompts would be useful to capture oral, written, and visual narratives, retrospective and in-the-moment narratives, and autobiographical and critical incident narratives. Phenomenological approaches can provide insights into how teachers and learners experience events.

Ecologies of Teachers' Inner Lives

Recently, Kubanyiova and Feryok (2015) suggested that a more productive way to think about teacher cognitions is the concept of *ecologies of teachers' inner lives*, an all-encompassing, emergent, situated, distributed, and embodied characterization of teachers as whole persons taking action in the social world. This concept enables us to address each of the themes addressed in this chapter. Conceiving of language teaching as *emerging sense-making in action* pushes us to think beyond the often retrospective teacher accounts of what they did and why, how their understandings were being shaped, and consider ways to account for this in-the-moment. Understanding teacher cognitions as distributed obliges us, again, to go beyond thinking as residing in the individual but in activity systems (SCT) or nodes (complexity theory). And conceptualizing teachers as taking action in the social world obliges us to consider the moral issues involved in language teaching and language teacher education. How we address each of these concerns involves both typical and innovative methodological approaches. Finding ways to capture emergent sense-making has been done through narrative inquiry, talking through concepts/instructional practices with a researcher, and think aloud protocols.

Conversation analysis, or other discourse analytic techniques, can be a way to capture thinking in-the-moment rather than retrospectively. Gathering data beyond the individual and their personal history is necessary, including teaching/learning cohorts, students, administrators, and parents.

Research Questions

1. How do the practices of a particular language teacher education program/professional development workshop meet the needs of the language teachers in this sociocultural, historical, political context?
2. How do the practices and interactions of this language teacher education program or professional development workshop provide intentional and systematic pedagogies designed to support the development of language teacher expertise?

Exploring the intentions and consequences of our practices as language teacher educators is necessary to ensure that language teacher education programs matter (Johnson & Golombek, 2018a).

3. In what ways does student engagement with activities/assignments of a particular class shape their understandings of specific subject matter (for example, nominalization) and how does students' engagement shape teacher understanding of that subject matter?
4. When students do not understand a particular concept (or subject matter), how does the teacher respond in terms of student feedback or re-presenting the concept to the class?

Language teacher learning and student learning needs to be understood as shaping each other.

5. How does the mentor teacher/co-teacher/colleagues/teacher educator influence the teacher's conceptualization and practices of teaching in the practicum?
6. How do the values, policies, and practices of an institution shape the teacher's conceptualization and practices of teaching?

The social must be conceptualized as integral to the individual teacher and not as an added variable.

7. How does the teacher find out about the emotional experience (*perezhivanie* in a Vygotskian sense) and integrate it into the learning environment?
8. What forms of language teacher mediation can assist beginning teachers to regulate their emotions in their initial learning-to-teach experiences?

Teacher and student emotions are lenses through which they experience and interact in the language classroom.

9. How does a teacher's moral concerns shape their *emergent sense-making in action*?
10. How does student engagement with X (some concept, for example, modals and hedging in making a request or modals and stance in academic writing) shape a teacher's *emergent sense-making in action* concerning X?

The concept of *ecologies of teachers' inner lives* provides an all-encompassing construct through which we can explore language teacher cognitions.

References

Dewey, J. (1933). *How we think*. Chicago: Henry Regnery.
Freeman, D., & Johnson, K. E. (2005). Towards linking teacher knowledge and student learning. In D.J. Tedick (Ed.) *Language teacher education: International perspectives on research and practice.* (pp. 73–95) Mahwah, NJ: Lawrence Erlbaum Associates.
Golombek, P.R., & Johnson, K.E. (2017). Re-conceptualizing teachers' narrative inquiry as professional development. *Profile*, 19, 15–28.
Johnson, K.E. (2006). The sociocultural turn and its challenges for L2 teacher education. *TESOL Quarterly*, 40(1), 235–257.
Johnson, K.E. & Golombek, P.R. (2002). (Eds.) *Teachers' narrative inquiry as professional development*. New York: Cambridge University Press.
Johnson, K.E. & Golombek, P.R. (2018a). Informing and transforming language teacher education. *Language Teaching Research*. Advance online publication. https://doi.org/10.1177/1362168818777539.
Johnson, K.E. & Golombek, P.R. (2018b). Making L2 teacher education matter through Vygotskian-inspired pedagogy and research. In J. Lantolf, M. Poehner, & M. Swain (Eds). *The Routledge handbook of sociocultural theory and second language development* (pp. 443–456). New York: Routledge.
Kubanyiova, M., & Feryok, A. (2015). Language teacher cognition in applied linguistics research: Revisiting the territory, redrawing the boundaries, reclaiming the relevance. *The Modern Language Journal*, 99(3), 435–449.
Vygotsky, L.S. (1978). *Mind in society: The development of higher psychological processes*. (Eds., M. Cole, V. John-Steiner, S. Scribner, & E. Souberman). Cambridge, MA: Harvard University Press.

15

CONTEXT IN SOCIOCULTURAL THEORY

Anne Feryok

UNIVERSITY OF OTAGO, NEW ZEALAND

Places have always been important for me, so much so that they identify the times of my life. Perhaps this is because I have taught in different language learning situations where students had different language learning goals, in the United States where I was born and in Haiti, Senegal, Poland, Armenia, and New Zealand. I gained my doctorate at the University of Auckland in 2004, and I have been teaching applied linguistics and supervising research students at the University of Otago since 2007. Most of my research is in sociocultural theory (SCT), which holds that higher cognitive functions are socially and culturally mediated (re-formed), and in language teacher cognition and development. Many of my research students share my interests, although some have worked in other theories and topics. Whatever they do, I urge them to pay attention to the context and how it has mediated teacher and learner development.

Strategies for Choosing a Research Topic

My research choices arise through a fairly slow process. Sometimes I am curious about something, usually potential participants and how they 'fit' a theoretical issue. However, I often don't clearly articulate the specific topic until quite late, when I'm analyzing data or even initially drafting findings. This approach may sound vague but it is based on a practical strategy that I strongly recommend to all novice qualitative researchers: Think about potential topics 'in context' from the perspective of a situation in which you have experience and where you have found willing participants. There is a powerful negative reason for this strategy: No topic becomes a research study if no one agrees to participate. Potential participants are more inclined to entertain the ideas of someone in whom they recognize an affiliation than someone who is 'out of context,' especially if the researcher is a novice without significant experience in the topic and context.

I implemented the negative strategy and then discovered a positive strategy in my PhD (Feryok, 2004). I initially decided that my study would take place in the two-year TESOL Certificate program in which I had taught in Armenia. First, I want to emphasize that this practical decision did not guarantee success. In fact, even though I had my own institution's approval, I was not granted access to the institution in which the program was taught because of concerns about me delivering part of the program from which participants would be recruited. What would I do? I was angry and frustrated and felt hopeless all at once. However, because I was familiar with the context itself, I realized that I could directly approach graduates of the program whom I personally knew and through them negotiate access to their teaching sites. 'All' I had to do was redesign my study! This meant that my topic had to change.

Instead of looking at my topic solely through my understanding of the research literature, which had led me to look at the relationship between theory and practice in TESOL programs, I started looking at my topic through the eyes of the people I could ask to participate. This came about as I started thinking about the graduates of the TESOL program. I had already realized that for many of these teachers, their two-year certificate was their *second* teaching qualification, on top of a five-year teaching qualification. But why were they interested in yet more study, especially if they had teaching experience? I thought about how a major historical event, the break-up of the Soviet Union in 1989, had not merely disrupted but irrevocably changed their lives. How had this affected them personally and professionally? I soon realized that the disappointment of being denied access to my original research site was actually a lucky break: I had almost ignored the richness of the participants' everyday reality from their own perspectives. The positive strategy, therefore, is that qualitative research topics should have ecological face validity – the participants should be able to recognize and understand why the topic is relevant to their context. That happens because the researcher has a good idea about the issues that concern potential participants – not just the issues in the literature.

Topics

Formation of New Beliefs and Practices in Context

One of the best documented areas in language teacher education research in SCT has been the formation of new beliefs and practices, in part thanks to research from Karen Johnson and her colleagues (e.g., Johnson & Dellagenlo, 2013). This research offers powerful evidence of how language teacher education can have a positive impact on language teachers. It uses sociocultural theoretical concepts, such as the zone of proximal development and perezhivanie (see below) in language teacher education. Because sociocultural theory is philosophically committed to the idea that society, culture, and language influence thought, there is considerable room for further research in other contexts. It is important to understand that even though descriptive studies have been done in SCT, SCT is actually about transformation, so an SCT study should involve purposeful efforts to transform the beliefs and practices of the participants using SCT concepts. New beliefs and practices can also arise spontaneously, and although they cannot be determined in advance, planning a curriculum, syllabus, or lesson is fertile ground for such concepts emerging (see Feryok & Oranje, 2015). Although Feryok and Oranje's study uses complex dynamic systems theory instead of SCT, it uses an SCT research method, microgenetic analysis, which captures new formations as they emerge in real time.

Linking Teaching to Learning in Context

The aim of teaching is learning, but establishing that teaching actually leads to learning is notoriously difficult. However, SCT has a tool for establishing that link, the zone of proximal development (ZPD), which examines how teachers establish an intersubjective space in which they support learners through collaborative interaction aimed at making meaning in the language. This topic, therefore, extends the previous topic by examining how already formed teacher beliefs and practices contribute to student learning, and how those beliefs and practices continue to develop through classroom teaching. In particular, the influence of contextual factors on how classroom teaching and learning is organized and how teachers and learners experience it is under-researched (see Al-Murtadha & Feryok, 2017, for its impact on learners). However, finding a convincing way to document contextual (as opposed to solely interactional) influences is a real challenge. Activity theory, which is closely related to SCT, can be a useful framework for systematically understanding the different aspects of contextual influences, especially if historicity is directly considered (see Cross, 2010).

Agency in Context

Although use of the term agency in language teacher education has dramatically increased in recent years, most accounts still look at agency as the individual exercise of power. Within sociocultural theory, agency involves the conscious intention to act in a self-regulated or controlled way. However, because sociocultural theory assumes that many cognitive functions are socially mediated, these criteria are necessary but not sufficient for agency. The social sources of agency and their transformation into individual agency must be identified within the context by examining the complex relationships among people, the prevailing beliefs and attitudes of society, and the organization and use of power. (Because of these contextual issues, a post-structuralist approach to agency is also effective.) The development of agency is particularly important to research so that those learning to teach are well equipped for classroom reality; however, research on how in-service teachers manage to maintain their agency in the face of modern threats is equally important (see Feryok,

2012). Methodologically, a historical approach is needed: agentive activity needs to be defined, identified, and its development traced backward, and then presented in chronological order.

Commitment in Context

Commitment (see Moodie & Feryok, 2015) is an under-researched area in language teacher education. It includes both the dedication and resilience needed to meet personal language teaching goals and the retention of language teachers to maintain an effectively functioning teaching system. Both areas of commitment are crucial to sustaining successful learning. A parade of changing teachers disrupts the continuity that teachers need in order to discover who their learners are and how they learn. It also prevents institutional knowledge from being developed and transmitted, disrupting both novice and experienced teachers as they constantly have to reinvent the wheel. Teachers may struggle to fulfil their commitments because of challenging social, political, and economic situations. In such contexts, inspiring teachers are worthy of study for many reasons, not least of which is how they sustain their commitment. Research is also necessary to understand why language teachers are difficult to recruit and retain. Both areas have implications for second language teacher education by attending to the personal qualities that teachers need to draw on over their careers. In qualitative research narrative inquiry has been used to explore the life stories of such teachers, and it is possible to take a sociocultural perspective on narrative data by using the historical approach mentioned above.

Perezhivanie in Context

One recent topic to attract attention in sociocultural theoretical approaches to second language teacher education is perezhivanie (singular; perezhivanija, plural). Perezhivanie is difficult to easily translate into English; it can be thought of as the 'interface' between people's responses and the challenging situations they face. It includes both situational features (what they pay attention to in the situation) and personal features (the characteristics that shape their responses). Understanding both sets of features requires attention to the larger context. Although perezhivanija have an emotional component, they also involve cognition and can stimulate or stifle motivation. Different people, situations, and periods in a person's life may elicit different perezhivanija. Methodologically, it might be wise to focus on another research topic (such as commitment or policy reforms) and be prepared for the possibility that perezhivanija might emerge. Identifying these features could help a researcher understand how to help a language teacher cope more effectively, such as by learning to understand and control emotional responses (see Golombek, 2015). However, clearly articulating how perezhivanie can be identified is a challenge.

Research Questions

Below I have provided research question frames that need to have the italicized words specified. For example:

- a *language* might be a first or target language
- *language concept* might be specified by a language feature or function (e.g., tense, cohesion, politeness, asking questions)
- *context* might be a country, institution, program, or specific situation (e.g., single or mixed gender classes)
- *social identity* might be gender, sexual orientation, ethnicity, religion
- an *intervention* might be a teaching or learning method, technique, or objective
- *contextual factors* might be historical, political, economic, social or cultural (e.g., war, new government, gender separation)
- a *policy* might be a national or local policy (e.g., assessment)
- an *opportunity* might be a teaching or learning goal (e.g., providing feedback, participating in groups)
- a *challenge* might be a goal (e.g., implementing a new curriculum) or a problem (e.g., classroom discipline).

1. How do experiences about learning a *language concept* in *context* mediate the development of pre-service teacher beliefs and practices about teaching that *language concept* in *context*?
2. How do non-native speaker in-service teachers of a *language* in the *language-speaking context* respond to concept-based instruction on a *language concept*?
3. How do changing norms in *context* mediate how language teachers' *social identities* influence the classroom participation opportunities of language learners of different *social identities*?
4. How does an *intervention* in the activity systems of *language* teachers in *context* mediate their students' language development?
5. How do *contextual factors* mediate the development of agency in pre-service teachers in *context*?
6. How does the implementation of a *policy* mediate the agency of teachers in *context*?
7. How do personal beliefs about *context, contextual factors* or *policy* mediate the development of personal commitment in language teachers in *context*?
8. How do first-year teaching experiences mediate the commitment of teachers to continue teaching in *context*?
9. How do the perezhivanija of a teacher in differing *contexts* or under differing *sociocultural factors* mediate the provision of *opportunities* to learners?

10. How are the perezhivanija of teachers facing a *challenge* in *context* influenced by their personal characteristics?

References

Al-Murtadha, M., & Feryok, A. (2017). Studying English in Yemen: Situated unwillingness to communicate in sociohistorical time. *Innovation in Language Learning and Teaching*, 11(3), 230–240.

Cross, R. (2010). Language teaching as sociocultural activity: Rethinking language teacher practice. *The Modern Language Journal*, 94(3), 434–452.

Feryok, A. (2004). *Personal practical theories: Exploring the role of language teacher experiences and beliefs in the integration of theory and practice.* Unpublished doctoral dissertation. University of Auckland, New Zealand.

Feryok, A. (2012). Activity theory and language teacher agency. *The Modern Language Journal*, 96(1), 95–107.

Feryok, A., & Oranje, J. (2015). Adopting a cultural portfolio project in teaching German as a foreign language: Language teacher cognition as a dynamic system. *The Modern Language Journal*, 99(3), 546–564.

Golombek, P.R. (2015). Redrawing the boundaries of language teacher cognition: Language teacher educators' emotion, cognition, and activity. *The Modern Language Journal*, 99(3), 470–484.

Johnson, K. E., & Dellagenlo, A. (2013). How 'sign meaning develops': Strategic mediation in learning to teach. *Language Teaching Research*, 17(4), 409–432.

Moodie, I., & Feryok, A. (2015). Beyond cognition to commitment: English language teaching in South Korean primary schools. *The Modern Language Journal*, 99(3), 450–469.

16

ACADEMIC WRITING
Linking Writers, Readers and Text Content

Rosemary Wette

UNIVERSITY OF AUCKLAND, NEW ZEALAND

My first professional experience as a second language teacher was as a teacher of German, but in the early 1980s I moved into teaching English as a second and foreign language to both children and adults. More recently, I've been involved in second language (L2) teacher education and advanced academic literacy. My interest in researching academic writing grew out of my work designing and teaching undergraduate and postgraduate courses, largely for L2 writers. This interest has resulted in a number of research projects over the past five years, both in my own classes and those of colleagues and peers. My publications on aspects of academic literacy instruction and skill development include process-product blends in the classroom practices of writing teachers, the use of textual and collaborative modeling, the development of ability in writing using sources in academic writing and disciplinary courses, the benefits of concept or mind maps in genre based courses, and the academic literacy challenges faced by international graduate students entering English-medium universities as well as the coping strategies they develop.

Choosing a Research Topic

Although a careful reading of the research and scholarly literature is essential before any topic is selected, my own research is always grounded in themes about which I have at least some professional knowledge and experience. All were initiated from aspects of my teaching practice that I thought I needed to know more about – either because they were problematic, or because I could see possibilities for further exploration of the topic area. It can take time to develop a research topic, and at some stage I might make written notes of the questions and ideas I've come up with, and then discuss these with other colleagues who teach academic writing courses.

However, in order to progress my personal thoughts to the next stage, it is important to study book chapters and articles in quality journals on the theme I'm interested in. I look for what authors have to say about its significance and current interest value, the aspects that have already been thoroughly examined, as well as those that have been given less research attention. It may be that the topic has already been investigated, but by using different types of participants or methods of data collection and analysis to the ones I intend to use. Topics may have been fully investigated with L1 writers, but further research with L2 writers is needed to explore the extent to which findings are applicable to their particular needs.

I also have a careful look at the conclusion sections of articles and chapters where authors recommend directions for future research. If I find a topic area that two or more researchers note as worthy of further investigation, this boosts my confidence that I'm not wasting my time on a 'So what!' or 'Who cares?' topic, but exploring one that others in the field consider worthwhile. At this stage, my approach to developing a topic involves repeated broadening and narrowing moves: Reading out into the literature, and then going back to my own thinking and emerging ideas about whether the study is practicable within available time and resource constraints, as well as within my own skills and experience as a researcher.

Current Research Topics

Disciplinary Differences

Over the past 20 years, a number of research studies and scholarly texts (e.g., Hyland, 2000) have informed us about the disciplinary differences in discourse practices that inexperienced academic writers need to become aware of. These include differences in assignment types and tasks, in how written assignments including citation practices are assessed, in the degree of emphasis on conciseness and precision, and in how academic arguments are constructed. Insights from this research have led to re-examination of the value of generic or 'common core' writing skills courses, and many universities now include discipline-specific tuition embedded in or adjacent to content-based lectures and tutorials. Studies of the effectiveness of this tuition have collected data from questionnaires (using Likert scale and open-ended responses) and interviews with students and faculty in order to ascertain students' language and learning needs, as well as the most useful aspects of the tuition. Looking ahead, further research on the implications of disciplinary differences for the teaching of academic writing would be of value: longitudinal case studies of how novice students develop proficiency during their undergraduate studies (through narrative frames or reflective diaries, and/or textual analysis and text-based interviews), or interviews with faculty about their expectations and the abilities they require of students at the beginning and end of their undergraduate studies.

Writing Using Sources

The concept of *intertextuality* emphasizes the interconnectedness of all texts, and the fact that all writers are indebted to the authors of previous texts on the topic. Writers can represent other texts through direct quotation in the words of the original author, or through paraphrase or summary citations composed in the writer's own words. While deliberate unacknowledged copying or plagiarism is unacceptable, patchwriting (partial paraphrase of source content) is now regarded as a legitimate stage of development for novices. Research interest has shifted from the extent to which students' citations are (il)legitimate to studies that explore the numerous challenges of writing using sources, and how instruction can help develop proficiency. Suggestions for research include exploring students' cognitive processes while working with sources, and collecting data from think-aloud protocols or 'google docs' to virtually observe how participants construct and edit their citations from sources. Text-based interviews could be used to stimulate participants' recollections of their citing decisions. For an intervention study, questionnaires, focus group interviews and/or text-based interviews could be used to explore students' understandings before and after instruction, preferably over multiple iterations. Longitudinal studies with post-tests and further questionnaires and semi-structured interviews over two to six semesters would allow for the tracking of skill development, while comparative studies would facilitate discussions of disciplinary and task differences.

Synthesizing and Integrating Multiple Sources

It is acknowledged that composing citations from multiple sources calls for the interplay between reading and writing as writers select content and weave it into their own texts as citations. Summarizing involves transformation of the source text (Bereiter & Scardamalia, 1987), which requires knowledge of the text's content, proficient reading skills, adequate lexical and syntactic resources for identification and compression of selected content, and the ability to integrate this content into the writer's argument. Being able to consider ideas from multiple source texts before deciding on an appropriate synthesis is another skill requirement, and inexperienced writers find mastery of this skill set particularly challenging (Wette, 2017). As yet, we know relatively little about why experienced writers choose particular source content and how it is blended with other sources, or about how the skill can be taught. Virtual observation of how novice and experienced writers compose summary citations and how they work with multiple sources to create syntheses of source content could be useful, and intervention studies would allow for skill development to be examined by analyzing texts that students produce before and after instruction. To the fullest extent possible, research needs to be done using authentic disciplinary texts and tasks.

Stance and Engagement

The term *stance* describes how writers convey their interpretations of particular arguments and evidence, while *engagement* describes how writers relate to their readers (Hyland, 2005). The term *metadiscourse* refers to the range of text features that help the writer to convey their attitudes to text content, and to negotiate relationships with readers. Neither stance nor engagement strategies feature in texts by inexperienced writers, who tend to use citations for attribution purposes only and to show little awareness of the needs of readers (Wette, 2017). Cross-cultural differences between emphases on 'writer-responsibility' and 'reader-responsibility' can intensify the challenges of conveying appropriate stance and engagement for L2 writers. Many studies to date have used corpora to report on disciplinary or novice-expert differences in the use of these features; however, there is a need for research that includes text-based interviews to elicit students' and disciplinary instructors' perspectives, and for longitudinal case studies using interviews and diaries to follow stages of skill development. Pre-and post-tests could be used to collect information on the effectiveness of instruction.

Models as Textual Mentors

Genre-based instruction, with its emphasis on text analysis and explicit teaching of text characteristics, is now the leading approach in L2 writing instruction. Scholarly texts recommend that instruction blends textual, cognitive and disciplinary dimensions of genres as well as providing extensive practice and feedback. The value of models and imitation for scaffolding learning has long been acknowledged (Cope & Kalantzis, 1993), as has the need for teachers to advise novices not to regard models as reproducible templates, but guides that need to be transformed in the texts that they themselves produce (Bereiter & Scardamalia, 1987). Strategies that may help students develop confidence and proficiency include analysis of well-written texts, observation of the teacher's writing processes, working with the teacher as a group to construct text exemplars, and collaborative composing with peers (Wette, 2014). Audio or video recording of classroom discourse could be used to show how particular modeling strategies are enacted in teacher-led or group discussions. Questionnaires, interviews, diaries and stimulated recall would be other suitable ways of investigating how students use models in their writing.

Research Questions

1. How do undergraduate students develop the knowledge and skills to produce texts appropriate for their disciplines?

This question calls for longitudinal studies using introspective data, and analysis of texts produced for disciplinary courses.

2. What skills and strategies can be advanced through instruction in discipline-specific writing practices?

This question requires examination of students' abilities before and after discipline-aligned courses that develop proficiency using authentic texts and tasks.

3. How do writers locate and use source texts in their written assignments in different disciplines for different task types?

Interviews, diaries and virtual observations (using 'google docs') would gather useful data.

4. How can instruction or disciplinary support assist students to transition from plagiarism to patchwriting, and from patchwriting to the ability to compose legitimate summaries and paraphrases of sources?

Combinations of interviews with faculty, observation of tutorials and lectures, and textual analysis could be used to answer this question.

5. Are differences in faculty views of plagiarism influenced by disciplinary norms, by students' experience of university study, or are they fundamentally idiosyncratic?

This question would require text-based interviews with faculty responsible for assessing undergraduate assignments.

6. How do students summarize (a) from single sources or (b) multiple sources with different and possibly conflicting information? What knowledge and strategies do they use?

This question calls for virtual observation and text-based interviews with students.

7. How can instruction in disciplinary contexts help students to develop the integrated reading and writing skills they need in order to compose citations from multiple sources?

This question requires examination of students' abilities before and after discipline-aligned instruction that uses authentic or near-authentic texts and tasks.

8. How can direct instruction that includes analysis of exemplary text models, extensive practice opportunities and feedback from teachers and peers assist students to use metadiscourse strategies appropriately?

This question requires an examination of students' level of ability before and after discipline-aligned instruction using authentic texts and tasks.

9. How does proficiency in the use of metadiscourse affect the quality of texts produced by undergraduate students?

This question calls for text analysis and interviews with instructors who grade the work of undergraduate students.

10. What uses do students make of models, and what gains in their ability to construct these genre exemplars can be found as a result of using models of various kinds as instructional tools?

Data could be collected from observations, introspective methods and pre-and post-instruction comparisons.

References

Bereiter, C., & Scardamalia, M. (1987). *The psychology of written composition*. Hillsdale, NJ: Erlbaum.
Cope, B., & Kalantzis, M. (1993). Introduction: How a genre approach to literacy can transform the way writing is taught. In B. Cope & M. Kalantzis (Eds.), *The powers of literacy: A genre approach to teaching writing*, (pp. 1–21). London: Falmer Press.
Hyland, K. (2000). *Disciplinary discourses*. Harlow: Longman Pearson.
Hyland, K. (2005). Stance and engagement: A model of interaction in academic discourse. *Discourse Studies*, 7, 173–192.
Wette, R. (2014). Teachers' practices in EAP writing instruction: Use of models and modeling. *System*, 42, 60–69.
Wette, R. (2017). Source text use by undergraduate post-novice L2 writers in disciplinary assignments: Progress and ongoing challenges. *Journal of Second Language Writing*, 37, 46–58.

17

ENGLISH L2 WRITING IN INTERNATIONAL HIGHER EDUCATION

Jim McKinley

UNIVERSITY COLLEGE LONDON, UK

English L2 writing in an international higher education context has been a central research focus throughout my career. In my early days teaching on a TESOL master's program, I found students struggling to shift from formulaic, basic, grammatically accurate writing, to university writing requiring original contributions to knowledge, and an original voice. After many, many years of contemplation, I produced a conceptual piece on contrastive rhetoric (McKinley, 2013). My thinking on the topic then moved to a consideration of how a social constructivist paradigm (McKinley, 2015) and awareness of metalanguage in argumentative writing (McKinley, 2018) might help to understand university English L2 critical argument and writer identity. As a PhD program director and supervisor of many master's and doctoral projects in TESOL, I've found that students succeed when they write about a familiar topic, questioning everything they believe to be true about it, and challenging these beliefs using knowledge gained in their higher degree studies. It is the higher education context that will serve as the general area from which I situate my recommendations for L2 writing research in this chapter.

Choosing a Research Topic

Master's students of TESOL need to be practical when choosing their topics. They need to be realistic: the dissertation is short, and the time to conduct the study and write the dissertation is short. Simple is best. The topics, and their questions, need to lend themselves well to appropriate research designs. Far too often I come across master's dissertations where the topic and questions are ill-formed, and the study, involving interviews with a handful of friends, shows little to no evidence that the student understands research and is deserving of the degree. Also frustrating is when students offer implications for 'better teaching,' 'improvements' or 'fixing' the programs students came from, before the study even takes place. A good topic is based on a problem the student has experienced, but the process of the inquiry needs to reflect a holistic perspective.

These same considerations are also important at the doctoral level. While doctoral students have a longer period of time to undertake a more substantial piece of work, they need to work within the finite time and word limitations available to them. A doctoral study should be seen as an exercise in research, where candidates demonstrate their ability to conceive, design, conduct and report on an original contribution to knowledge. It does not need to achieve the dramatic impact that is more typically achieved over a larger body (sometimes a lifetime's worth) of work, which can be continued after graduation as they embark on independent research careers.

While the previous paragraphs address master's and doctoral students, the ideas apply to all researchers. Novice and experienced researchers alike must consider what is achievable in any given study, taking into consideration time, resources, and due process (not to offer sage advice without the evidence to back it up). For researchers at all levels, choosing the right topic is a reflexive process. First, a good topic will be familiar – one from experience. This topic will also be filled with questions about *how* and *why*. It can be based on either a language teaching or learning experience, or both. Next, the topic needs to be questioned in a way that does not produce answers. These are the answers to 'discover' through research inquiry. Assumed outcomes of the study need to be reformulated into questions. Good questions will avoid 'fixing' a perceived problem, and instead explore the possibility of a problem. Such questions lend well to qualitative inquiry. Finally, the topic should be socially situated, taking into consideration contextual factors that will impact the research design.

Of utmost importance in consideration of topic choice is recognizing that a qualitative study does *not* mean the study must involve human participants. A good topic will lend itself well just as easily to interviews and observations as it would to other qualitative approaches, such as systematic reviews of literature, document analysis, or corpus studies.

Current Research Topics

While socially-situated English L2 writing education has been explored in great depth in thousands of studies, less research has been done on the impact of the international higher education context on the phenomenon. And in our increasingly globalized world, international uses of English are on the rise in academic writing, putting into question native speaker standards and norms (see McKinley & Rose, 2018), which handily problematizes the entire research area. The five research topics below all consider English L2 writing from an international higher education perspective that challenges much of what we may have understood about this area.

Standards and Norms in English L2 Writing

Academic writing is generally considered less amenable to variation and change than spoken language. But when it comes to *English* academic writing, as an academic lingua franca with a large majority of writers using L2 English, we are currently witnessing substantial challenges to the standards and norms that have been maintained as synonymous with native fluency. In a study of the author guidelines of academic journals (McKinley & Rose, 2018), the guidelines were often found to position L2 writers as deficient in relation to 'native' standards. The study demands a discussion surrounding the need to decouple good academic English writing from concepts such as nativeness. We are at a time now where it is unethical to maintain so-called 'native speaker norms.' We need to encourage all authors to write using an English that can easily be understood by a broad, heterogeneous, global, and multilingual audience. This topic draws into question both teaching and assessment practices involving English L2 writers in international higher education, particularly in relation to deficiency models of such writers.

Social Constructivism in English L2 Writing Education

If we understand academic writing to be socially situated, we should consider, then, in what ways knowledge is socially constructed through English L2 writing education. We should consider how the interrelationship between the elements of cultural practices in academic discourse and writer identity is influenced by the sociocultural values of academic discourse. We have an opportunity to problematize the interrelationship by viewing English L2 writing through a social constructivist lens, inquiring into how thinking processes are shaped by awareness of the social nature of academic discourse, and how this thinking arises from a writer identity that fits in with the culture of English academic writing. Using social constructivism as an analytical framework for English L2 writing (e.g., McKinley, 2015), this topic targets the context of learning at the classroom, university, as well as broader cultural level, raising questions regarding the impact of context at these different levels on English L2 writers' identity development.

Critical Thinking and/or Pragmatics in English L2 Writing

L2 learners' critical thinking in academic writing has been challenged in the literature. The questions draw on issues related to contrastive rhetoric, as well as studies in pragmatic competence. In a conceptual paper on contrastive rhetoric (McKinley, 2013), it is argued that criticisms of English L2 writing learners' ability to think critically are misguided, and suggestions are offered for positive development of critical thinking that serve as ideal points to challenge through studies in other contexts. On pragmatics in English L2 writing, still little research has been done in this area, as most pragmatics studies target speaking. Zhao and Kaufer's (2013) study investigating the use of a pragmatic assessment tool in L2 writing classroom challenges criticisms of English L2 writers' pragmatic competence by targeting discourse-level pragmatic behaviors in L2 writing. While their study incorporated significant quantitative data, their analysis suggests potential in conducting qualitative research in this area. Furthermore, research development in the area of English as a lingua franca has put the relevance of studies in pragmatics at risk, making it an especially current topic of inquiry.

Use of Metalanguage in Supporting English L2 Writing

English L2 writing teachers and students may benefit from being provided with explicit metalanguage for the social construction of writer identities. Support for this is found in the hundreds of studies that have used Hyland and Tse's (2004) framework for identifying such metalanguage. In my own study developing a framework for this purpose (McKinley, 2018), the findings suggest that struggles students face to meet their teachers' expectations of their writing could potentially be alleviated if both teachers and students were aware of the metalanguage used by student writers in establishing their writer identities, and by teachers when assessing students' writing. Such a suggestion requires further inquiry, to investigate the impact of an awareness of this language on both students and teachers. The idea of explicitly addressing writer identity in English L2 writing education has been contested in the literature as unhelpful for learners who need to stay focused on the basics of academic writing.

Assessment and/or Washback in English L2 Writing Education

Research into assessing English L2 writing has focused a great deal on different types of, and attitudes toward, feedback, especially grammar correction. Assessment is often a major concern for students and teachers alike, and as the assessment of writing is notoriously vague, subjective, and difficult to quantify, it is a valuable topic for qualitative inquiry. In exam-based educational cultures, concerns about feedback are secondary to the bigger issues of 'teaching to the test,' known as the washback effect (see McKinley & Thompson, 2018). Because assessment is such a major concern, teachers might find themselves teaching exam preparation over the development of sustainable skills, known as negative washback. There is also positive washback, when teaching to the test leads to the development of sustainable skills. Especially in international higher education, the impact of testing and assessment is one worth exploring, as research into international uses of English have problematized the area even further.

Research Questions

1. How open are learners and teachers to non-standard uses of English in L2 writing?

This question targets attitudes of key stakeholders toward Englishes in written modes of communication.

2. How do attitudes to non-standard Englishes vary across types of writing?

This question builds on the first research question by exploring differences between specific registers and genres of written communication.

3. How could standards and norms of English writing be challenged in language curricula to reflect global uses of English?

This question requires action research, field research, or teacher/learner narratives to uncover classroom practices that succeed in delivering a global perspective of English use.

4. How socially situated is English L2 writer education, and what influence does this have on learners' writer identity?

As education is highly contextualized, there is a need to explore the influence of various classroom environments and pedagogies on L2 writer development including writer identity.

5. What influences (both positive and negative) does the L1 have on L2 writing development?

This research question targets contrastive rhetoric and the role of the L1 in L2 writing development, investigating linguistic and cultural differences between the two languages.

6. How is pragmatic competence developed in English L2 writing education?

Pragmatic competence in L2 writing has been less explored. There is opportunity to consider English as a global lingua franca, which challenges relevance of native-benchmarked pragmatic competence.

7. How can awareness of metalanguage support English L2 writing teachers' feedback?

This research question requires analysis frameworks or systems to identify metalanguage for L2 writing teachers to better understand students' intentions in their writing.

8. How can English L2 writing students and teachers use metalanguage to understand writer identities in appropriate and effective written arguments?

This question focuses on using metalanguage to make instruction explicit about L2 writer identities. This idea has been contested in the literature, making it a worthy area of inquiry.

9. How do assessment practices influence English L2 writing education?

This is a valuable area for qualitative inquiry as the subjective nature of writing assessment makes it difficult for students to understand why they receive the scores they do.

10. How is evidence of a washback effect dealt with in English L2 writing education?

The washback effect of testing in ELT is an area of great debate, and investigating the effect in English L2 *writing* education provides a useful framing of the issue.

References

Hyland, K., & Tse, P. (2004). Metadiscourse in academic writing: A reappraisal. *Applied Linguistics*, 25(2), 156–177.

McKinley, J. (2013). Displaying critical thinking in EFL academic writing: A discussion of Japanese to English contrastive rhetoric. *RELC Journal*, 44(2), 195–208.

McKinley, J. (2015). Critical argument and writer identity: Social constructivism as a theoretical framework for EFL academic writing. *Critical Inquiry in Language Studies*, 12(3), 184–207.

McKinley, J. (2018). Integrating appraisal theory with possible selves in understanding university EFL writing. *System*, doi:10.1016/j.system.2018.07.002.

McKinley, J., & Rose, H. (2018). Conceptualizations of language errors, standards, and norms in English for research publication purposes: An analysis of journal submission guidelines. *Journal of Second Language Writing*, 42, 1-11.

McKinley, J., & Thompson, G. (2018). Washback effect in teaching English as an international language. In J.I. Liontas (Ed.) *The TESOL Encyclopedia of English Language Teaching*. Project Editor: M. DelliCarpini; Volume Editor: S. Abrar-ul-Hassan. Hoboken, NJ: Wiley.

Zhao, H., & Kaufer, D. (2013). DocuScope for genre analysis: Potential for assessing pragmatic functions. In N. Taguchi & J.M. Sykes (Eds.) *Technology in interlanguage pragmatics research and teaching* (pp. 235–260). Amsterdam: John Benjamins.

# 18

ACADEMIC WRITING

The Human Side

Pat Strauss

AUT UNIVERSITY, NEW ZEALAND

My area of research interest was originally second language teacher education in the context of the South African educational system. Then I moved to New Zealand and took up a position as an academic writing advisor in a student learning center. The work was demanding – I was overwhelmed with students, primarily English second language speakers, needing help with their academic writing. Many returned over and over again, unable, it appeared, to transfer my advice to their assignments. Quite simply, the students needed to learn how to help themselves. While the work of English for Academic Purposes (EAP) researchers was very helpful, the academic literacies approach resonated more strongly with me. EAP focuses on the academic texts students need to master, that is, it tends to adopt a pragmatic approach, while the academic literacies approach argues that it is not sufficient simply to look at these texts. We need to examine the broader sociolinguistic contexts in which these students and their teachers work. Importantly, we need to consider agency and identity in our examination of academic writing. Students should not have to lose their voice to gain a place in the academic world. My interests are how language, particularly academic language, affects the people who use it and how the language, in turn, is affected by the environments in which it is employed. In this chapter, I focus on the challenges facing both second language students as they attempt to contribute in their own way to the academy and the academic staff who endeavor to assist them.

Choosing a Research Topic

Be passionate about it: My first piece of advice would be make sure you are really interested in what you are proposing to research. It's often a great idea to draw on your own experiences and challenges. What do you feel strongly about?

Make sure it's feasible: Can the research actually be done? A PhD student of mine wanted to investigate ways in which he could improve the teaching of academic English to his Palestinian students. Unfortunately, the political situation in the Middle East meant that there was no guarantee that he would be able to enter or leave Palestine when he needed to. Researchers might not have a situation quite as dramatic as this one but they have to be pragmatic.

Be flexible: The PhD student mentioned above had to be prepared to change his original topic. He had invaluable experience working with his Palestinian students whose first language is Arabic, so when his original proposal proved impossible to implement he rethought it and changed his PhD topic to an investigation of the academic challenges students from Arabic speaking countries face when they enroll in undergraduate courses.

Play to your strengths: Are you bi- or multilingual? Do you have in-depth knowledge of another country? If you wish to understand research participants' perspectives on aspects of teaching or learning academic English it's always a great advantage to be able to do so using the person's first language. English teachers who are not first language speakers of English might also prefer to be interviewed in their first language. This approach often yields rich data. Sharing a cultural and linguistic background with participants often means they will respond in ways they would not with an outsider.

Current Research Topics

What We Don't Know (but Need to) about the Academic Writing Challenges Facing L2 Student Cohorts

The massification of higher education means that we have students from all over the world coming to tertiary institutions in New Zealand to study through the medium of English. Many of the students have either learned English as a second or a foreign language, and some of them have been educated through the medium of English. However, this variety of English is often quite different from that required by New Zealand universities. The students often find that what was considered acceptable academic English in their own countries is not viewed as such at their new universities. We will be better able to meet their academic writing needs if we have a greater understanding of their backgrounds. For example, research could be conducted in students' home countries and could explore how students are prepared for the demands of international study. English teachers at schools and universities in students' home countries could be interviewed, textbooks, English language syllabi and language assessments could be reviewed, and classroom observation could be carried out. Students who are planning to study at an English medium university could be asked about their expectations and assumptions. This type of research could also be carried out in bridging programs offered in the countries where students plan to study.

The First Years of Study – How Do L2 Students Adjust to the Demands of Academic Writing?

We need to understand more about how L2 students transfer (or don't) what they have learnt about academic writing prior to their entry to tertiary institutions. Students might have received instruction in academic writing at school level, or in bridging programs offered at universities, polytechnics or private language schools either in their home countries or in New Zealand. Are students able to take what they have been taught on these programs and successfully transfer this knowledge to the writing of assignments? As Skyrme (2018) points out, L2 students may go from a position of having a great deal of input and advice about their writing to very little. There are also L2 students who have not had exposure to any such teaching. It is widely recognized that L2 students need help during the entire period of their studies, and often under-resourced student learning centers are not in a position to offer sufficient support. L2 students need to develop their own strategies to cope, and many use the numerous academic writing sites on the internet or ask their L2 peers for assistance. They might also seek advice from their discipline faculty. It is important that we investigate the efficacy of these strategies and how effective they are in helping students cope with the writing demands of their courses.

The Positioning of L2 (Thesis) Writers

Although this topic can be explored at all levels it is possibly most relevant at postgraduate level, simply because at this level it is expected that students will be able to write well and at considerable length. Being a postgraduate student involves more than just collecting and analyzing data and writing up the findings. Casanave (2008) points out that thesis and dissertation students become involved in "a variety of practices within disciplinary communities heretofore unknown to them even if they are familiar with the disciplinary subject matter" (p. 17). Often the most complex issue is L2 students' relationships with their supervisors who often have very different sociolinguistic backgrounds to those of the students they supervise. It is apparent from the literature that supervisory relationships play a major role in postgraduate student success (Lee, 2008; Strauss, 2012). What is also acknowledged is that this relationship is located in an unequal power structure and that particularly L2 students might find themselves at a considerable disadvantage. They might find it difficult to exercise their agency with regard to the writing of their thesis. In order for the thesis writing experience to be a positive one students need to be able to negotiate with their supervisors to ensure that the voice heard is one that the students wish to own.

Discipline Faculty and Academic Writing

Discipline faculty do not always have a clear understanding of what makes good academic writing. Turner (2011) points out that while many academics have a tacit understanding of what good writing is they are unable to explain this to their students. Often, they tend to focus on superficial features such as spelling, punctuation and grammar, while neglecting concepts such as argument and structure (Lea & Street, 1998). In addition, many faculty believe that because students have gained entry to their courses they have mastered the academic language required. However, many international students enter Western universities familiar only with examination style assessments. They are unaccustomed to producing assignments that involve essay and report writing. To exacerbate matters writing instructions for assignments are often vague and of little real help. Assignment briefs will note that spelling and punctuation need to be accurate and stress the importance of correct referencing and in text citations, without dealing with structural requirements. In addition, faculty are often at odds as to how the writing, as opposed to the content, should be assessed, and while they profess that students' ability to write well is important, their assessment of this writing is often confusing for their students (Skyrme, 2018; Strauss, 2017).

The Role of Academic Writing Teachers

There is a great deal of scope to explore the role and status of academic writing teachers. In New Zealand, academic writing courses are offered at private training establishments, polytechnics, and universities. The majority of these courses, often called bridging or foundation studies, are offered prior to enrolment on degree or diploma programs. What we need to know is how well this support prepares students for the writing they will be expected to do. To find out it is necessary to examine the roles, status and practices of those involved in teaching at this level. Unfortunately, it is widely recognized that academic writing tutors often do not receive the support and recognition they deserve for their work with students which, as Turner (2011, p. 31) notes, demands "intellectual rigour and arduous labour." This is because the technicist perspective that views academic language as something mechanical that can be easily fixed is the institutionally dominant one. Academic writing teachers are frequently viewed as servants of the discipline masters. Not only does this diminish their sense of self-worth but it also sidelines and disempowers them. They are effectively prevented from raising issues around academic writing and its importance for learning.

Research Questions

1. How do the assumptions about academic writing of a specific language group (e.g., Arabic-speaking students) impact on their English academic writing proficiency?
2. How might the ability of L2 students from a particular country or cultural group to cope with English academic writing at tertiary level be improved before they leave their own country to study abroad?

3. How do L2 students cope with the academic writing demands of their discipline courses during the first years of study?
4. How well do generic academic writing courses prepare L2 students for the academic writing demands of their discipline courses during the first years of study?
5. How might tertiary institutions better support the academic writing development of L2 students *during* their mainstream studies?
6. How do supervisory relationships impact on L2 students' sense of agency and identity in the writing of a thesis or dissertation?
7. What are the expectations of discipline faculty of the academic writing of their students (e.g., first year) and how are these expectations conveyed to the student cohort? What support is given to help L2 students reach the required level of proficiency?
8. How does the wording of assignment briefs and the feedback given by faculty on the language L2 students use in assignments influence students' academic writing development?
9. How do tutors on preparatory academic writing courses view their role in preparing L2 students for tertiary study?
10. How do academic writing support teachers at polytechnics and universities view their role in supporting students in the writing demands they face during their years of study?

References

Casanave, C. (2008). Learning participatory practices in graduate school: Some perspective-taking by a mainstream educator. In C. Casanave & X. Li (Eds.), *Learning the literacy practices of graduate school. Insiders' reflections on academic enculturation* (pp. 14–31). Ann Arbor, MI: University of Michigan Press.

Lea, M., & Street, B. (1998). Student writing and staff feedback in higher education: An academic literacies approach. *Studies in Higher Education*, 23(2), 157–172.

Lee, A. (2008). How are doctoral students supervised? Concepts of doctoral research. *Studies in Higher Education*, 34(3), 276–281.

Skyrme, G. (2018). Learning to write in the University after the writing course is over: What helps second language writers? *Higher Education Research and Development*. doi:10.1080/07294360.2018.1477741.

Strauss, P. (2012). 'The English is not the same': Challenges in thesis writing for second language speakers of English. *Teaching in Higher Education*, 17(3), 283–293.

Strauss, P. (2017). Caught between two stools? Academic writing in 'new' vocational disciplines in higher education. *Teaching in Higher Education*, 22(8), 925–939.

Turner, J. (2011). *Language in the academy: Cultural reflexivity and intercultural dynamics.* Bristol, England: Multilingual Matters.

19
CRITICAL QUESTIONS IN ENGLISH FOR ACADEMIC PURPOSES

Gregory Hadley

NIIGATA UNIVERSITY, JAPAN

Language teacher education (LTE) represents a dynamic maelstrom of personal beliefs, historical forces, and sociopolitical dynamics, which are further intensified through constant social interaction. Researching LTE represents a multidimensional act evoking both the emotions and intellect as one seeks to construct critically aware questions about what is taking place in their second language classrooms and educational institutions. A critical perspective, one that is "concerned in particular with issues of power and justice in the ways that economy, matters of race, class, and gender, ideologies, discourses, education, religion and other social institutions, and cultural dynamics interact to construct a social system" (Kincheloe & McLaren, 2000, p. 281), can shed light on the pedagogical premises supporting the status quo, and open doors of new discovery regarding the nature of areas such as English for Academic Purposes (EAP) in the twenty-first century. Especially given the way in which university-level EAP is being transformed around the world as a result of national policies advocating a neoliberal approach as a means of restructuring their societies (Ding & Bruce, 2017; Hadley, 2015), the need for asking critical questions about EAP has taken on a greater sense of urgency.

For 15 years, I taught and managed an undergraduate English language program that was designed to enable and encourage Japanese students to further access academic materials and to expand their opportunities for participating in university-sponsored short-term overseas study programs. Partly to stay abreast of developments in EAP, I also taught several summers on EAP pre-sessional programs in the UK. These sojourns to the UK allowed me to witness steady and significant changes in the way that EAP was being approached by teachers and coordinators and how it was being reshaped by new administrative managers, many of whom had only recently been hired from the world of business and finance. In this chapter, I suggest strategies, potential areas of exploration, and critical research questions for studying LTE as it relates to EAP.

Research Strategies

Because a critical perspective centers on problems of power, inequality, orientation, and indoctrination, it might be tempting, especially for new researchers, to simply go out into the field with, for example, a questionnaire aimed at exploring such concerns. The problems with this strategy is that starting out with an exploratory questionnaire, the researcher may simply find answers to the questions asked, but miss the more pressing concerns of the research participants. Granted, the use of questionnaires early on as a research strategy may be an unavoidable risk, especially if access to the people or venues in their study is limited, or if they are restrained by their Institutional Research Board (IRB). In this case, the strategy one should take is to first engage in a deep reading of relevant research literature before attempting to enter the field. However, if the researcher has greater academic freedom, and if they have long-term and unfettered access (often because they are embedded within the social arena), then a more effective strategy is to begin by observing the people, places, and things within one's area of research interest, and to take detailed notes of what one sees, hears, and reads from public documents such as office posters, administrative announcements, advertisements, and so on. This strategy would provide the researcher with deeper insight, which would enable them to develop more effective questions for subsequent in-depth examination. But in order to avoid the urge to observe and record everything, the following are possible topics and questions that might aid in tightening one's critical focus.

Topics

I believe the following five topics are both pertinent and current for LTE as it relates to EAP situated within universities that have adopted policies that strengthen autocracy, and encourage neoliberal practices. While presented as providing personal choice and stimulating healthy competition, these practices are damaging to language pedagogy and the humanistic aspirations of many language teachers.

International Students

Over the past 20 years, the number of international students going to the Anglophone world for university education has skyrocketed. International students make significant economic contributions to universities and national economies, though many feel shortchanged when it comes to truly participating in the life of the university community. Studying the lived experiences of international students would be a rich area of critical investigation. Other related areas of interest would be the social and communicative interactions of international students on campus, with a focus on the experience of 'otherization' through 'becoming foreign.' Phenomenological approaches focusing on student narratives, ethnography, and mixed methods approaches would all be appropriate for this type of research.

EAP Pedagogy

Much of what is taught in EAP is ostensibly focused on enabling learners to successfully access the university and succeed in their field of study. However, critical voices have questioned the tenets behind the materials taught to students and also on the way that certain forms of discourse are privileged over others (Haque, 2007; Harwood & Hadley, 2004). From a critical discourse perspective, a study of the language used by those wielding the most (and the least) power in the EAP program would yield interesting discoveries about the underlying values and premises guiding teachers, students, and policy makers. Focusing upon who says what, to whom, where, and why, would also be enlightening. Additionally, a study of the curriculum, especially who creates it, who administers it, and how it is actually deployed in the classroom, would be helpful to many in EAP. Such research would likely require one to be a participant observer, and a case study methodology would be the most advisable approach to take.

EAP Teacher Identity

The notion of teacher identity has long been an interest in LTE. In recent years the question of teacher identity has increasingly become controversial, as members of university communities struggle for who has the right to determine a person's professional identity (Varghese, Morgan, Johnston & Johnson, 2005). Studying how EAP teachers ideally see themselves and what they feel they should be doing, and positing this with the conflicting views of others within the university, would help to document the momentous changes currently taking place in the profession. Studies of conflicting and complementary perceptions of teachers' roles, of agency, EAP teacher professionalism, collegiality, as well as investigations into the life-world of the EAP teacher, would be certain to make an impact among educators. Observations followed by extensive interviews, together with a study of teacher narratives, would all serve as appropriate ways for identifying critical themes.

EAP Management

Another area requiring the critical gaze is that of EAP administration. Questions as to who manages EAP, who gets promoted, what is valued and rewarded, and how EAP is evaluated, would reveal much about the current situation of EAP today. A focus on gender, race, and class would also stimulate questions concerning the current status quo, in terms of who has power and how it is used.

Investigating as well the activities of people who are disempowered or undervalued, and a search for those whose voices are not being heard, would further reveal new perspectives on LTE. This would require a considerable number of interviews and observation tasks, which admittedly would be difficult, since many university elites can hide behind the notion of 'ethics' and 'ethical review' as a pretext for shielding themselves from exposure and accountability. Nevertheless, more insider accounts of this area of EAP are needed.

EAP in Context

A wider view of how EAP has reached its current condition would help to contextualize it within the broader social, political, and economic currents affecting the Western University as a social institution. This sort of study could be carried out as a case study of one particular EAP program and would begin as a historical study of EAP at that university, which would shed light on its current position within the institution. By tracking the particular history of the unit, one could then spread out to explore curricular trends and the trajectory of different waves of international student groups based on nationality, gender, socioeconomic status, and political relationship with the host country. The researcher would also seek to study broader sociopolitical and economic trends that were prevalent during the time of such developments. All of this would foster a deeper understanding of EAP within the greater scheme of things, as multiple points of commonality from the case study of one particular EAP unit could be made to other EAP units at universities within the same country, and beyond. Studies such as these would entail a considerable amount of archival research, but the results would allow for a greater understanding of who presently pulls the strings in EAP, who is being marginalized, and where EAP is likely to head in the foreseeable future, if collective action is not taken to encourage peaceful and positive change.

Research Questions

1. Interview up to ten international students who have recently entered the university EAP program. What are the common problems they encounter as a result of their status as outsiders? What strategies do they use that result both in failure and success?
2. Follow the lives of three international students who have recently entered the university EAP program. Following their trajectories, how do race, gender, nationality, and class affect their trajectories?
3. Conduct interviews with three different focus groups – students, EAP teachers, and administrators – connected in some way to the EAP unit. How do they believe EAP should be taught in the classroom? Pay attention to key words and phrases suggesting conflict as well as convergence.

4. With race, class, nationality, and gender as a backdrop, who and how does one become an EAP teacher? Pay particular attention to key 'turning points' that led them to the present. Who is underrepresented as an EAP teacher, and why?
5. From either a gendered or queer perspective, how do EAP teachers become 'feminized' or 'stigmatized' within the neoliberal university system, and how does this process contrast with the dominant masculinity implicit in university management roles?
6. Conduct a series of interviews with people who have been tasked with the management of EAP. How did they get 'raised up' to a management position? Who gets into management, who doesn't, and why? What are the implications for EAP teachers and international students?
7. Interview EAP managers and others tasked with administrating some aspect of EAP. What are some of the common problems that they face on any given day with the EAP program? What issues and concerns are absent in their narratives?
8. Conduct a historical study of the EAP program in your institution. How does your current EAP program compare to when it began? What does what you find reveal about the current ideologies intended to guide the EAP program?
9. Study the progressive waves of major international student nationality groups that have come to your EAP program over the past twenty years. How have the changes complemented certain political, economic, or social trends during each period up to the present?
10. In what ways do international students and EAP teachers either engage in or support their own oppression and marginalization on campus?

References

Ding, A., & Bruce, I. (2017). *The English for academic purposes practitioner: Operating on the edge of academia*. Cham, Switzerland: Springer.

Hadley, G. (2015). *English for academic purposes in neoliberal universities: A critical grounded theory*. Heidelburg, New York, and London: Springer.

Haque, E. (2007). Critical pedagogy in English for Academic Purposes and the possibility for 'tactics' of resistance. *Pedagogy, Culture & Society*, 15(1), 83–106.

Harwood, N., & Hadley, G. (2004). Demystifying institutional practices: Critical pragmatism and the teaching of academic writing. *English for Specific Purposes*, 23(4), 355–377.

Kincheloe, J., & McLaren, P. (2000). Rethinking critical theory and qualitative research. In N. Denzin & Y. Lincoln (Eds.), *Handbook of qualitative research* (2nd edition) (pp. 279–313). Thousand Oaks, CA: Sage Publications.

Varghese, M., Morgan, B., Johnston, B., & Johnson, K. (2005). Theorizing language teacher identity: Three perspectives and beyond. *Journal of Language, Identity & Education*, 4(1), 21–44.

20
RACE IN CRITICAL RESEARCH

Ryuko Kubota

UNIVERSITY OF BRITISH COLUMBIA, CANADA

As a female professor originally from Japan, engaging in research and teaching in applied linguistics and language teacher education, I have been working in institutions of higher education in North America since the early 1990s. My research can be broadly defined as critical applied linguistics, and includes theoretical and empirical research that sheds light on various topics from critical perspectives. Specifically, my primary interest has been to expose how discourses, ideologies, policies, and practices in language education reflect and shape unequal power relations that privilege or marginalize different languages and language users, and to explore how the status quo could be transformed. The ultimate vision is praxis – committed reflection and action for social transformation through questioning and reconceptualizing taken-for-granted assumptions and critiquing how power produces social injustices (Kubota & Miller, 2017).

My empirical studies have mostly been concerned with learners or users of an additional language. For instance, I have investigated the cultural dimension of second language writing from a critical perspective, the effect of teaching about linguistic diversity, the ideological and affective meaning of learning English in non-formal settings, and the contradictions in the ideology of English through examining transnational workplace communication. Many of these topics, as well as my theoretical writings on culture, race, critical multiculturalism, neoliberal ideology, and critical pedagogy aim to improve language teaching. In this chapter, I will focus on race in critical qualitative research, though my scholarly engagement with race has mostly been theoretical.

Choosing Research Topics

There are multiple ways in which inquiry topics are chosen for research. In my case, concrete experiences often motivate me to conduct research. For instance, my doctoral dissertation research on critical contrastive rhetoric, which investigated rhetorical structures of L1 and L2 essays written by Japanese students compared with L1 essays written by their Canadian counterparts, was motivated by my own experience of teaching Japanese in a graduate program in the United States. Previously, I had learned about cultural difference in written discourse organization and accepted the claim that English texts are organized logically, linearly, and deductively, whereas L2 English texts written by Asian students tend to be non-logical, circular, and inductive. However, in teaching Japanese to native speakers of English, their L2 writing did not fit the accepted expectations for L1 English writers. This prompted my doctoral study. Years later, my interest in reconceptualizing issues of culture in second language teaching led to a scholarly debate with another scholar, eventually encouraging me to explore theoretically the idea of race.

Another example is my current study on language choice and communicative experiences among transnational Japanese workers in Asia. I decided to pursue this topic based on a previous study on Japanese adults learning English in non-formal settings in rural Japan. In this study, local business managers I interviewed expressed intriguing views that contradicted the government's promotion of advanced English skills for global business. With funding availability, I decided to expand this research by focusing on both Japanese and South Korean multinational corporations and overseas work contexts.

Before pursuing this topic, I struggled with potential ethical consequences. As I have discussed elsewhere (Kubota, 2017), I had initially explored the possibility of investigating culturally and linguistically minoritized students learning Japanese as an additional language in Japan. Although this topic would address important issues of marginalization and resistance in an under-explored context, I began asking myself who would benefit from my *studying down* in the power hierarchy. In the end, I decided to *study up* by shedding light on elite multinational corporate workers' workplace communicative experiences and their implications for language-in-education policies. (Note: *Studying across* is another category of research in which, for instance, an indigenous scholar studies their own community.) In making this decision, I did not intend to devalue the lives of marginalized learners; rather, the feeling of uneasiness about my potentially becoming the main beneficiary of the study shifted my topic.

In sum, being curious and reflexive about what I observe in the local and wider communities has helped me find socially relevant and critically significant topics. At the same time, potential ethical implications have also influenced my topic choice.

Research Topics

Race in language teaching and learning raises important questions for critical research. Along with other identity categories, such as gender, class, language, and sexuality, it can be studied critically in language teacher education. However, it is important to note that these categories or any other topics alone do not constitute criticality (Kubota & Miller, 2017). Moreover, defining what is critical and what is not is contentious. Pennycook (2001) argues that although critical applied linguistics must foreground critiques of social injustices and underlying politics, prescribing the definition should be avoided in light of the postmodern skepticism toward epistemological fixity and essentialism. Simultaneously, we should constantly reflect on the veracity of the link between our critical research and the realization of social transformation (Kubota & Miller, 2017). With these caveats in mind, I offer five broad research topics regarding race in language teacher education. These topics give rise to a number of inquiry foci depending on the context (e.g., geographical location; learning space/context; program type; institutional type; learner's age), language (e.g., foreign language; second language; heritage language), and institutional policies (e.g., curriculum; assessment; student placement; hiring of teachers). Research topics need to be selected with a concrete focus. Also, these five topics interact with each other and shape multiple discourses and human experiences, requiring us to recognize this complexity.

In studying the idea of race, it is important to note that race is a socially constructed category. Difference among groups of people is not determined biologically but produced by the social and discursive practices of racialization. Racialization sometimes leads to racism, negatively affecting people individually, institutionally, and epistemologically. Furthermore, the negative connotation attached to the idea of race often causes other concepts, such as culture, language, and religion, to become a proxy for race. Another important issue to keep in mind is that race intersects with other categories, such as gender, class, language, nationality, and sexuality, forming complex beliefs, experiences, and social systems. Exclusively focusing on race would only paint a partial picture of human experiences. The suggested topics need to be investigated in conjunction with other identity categories.

Race and Learner Beliefs or Subjectivities

The idea of race impacts learner beliefs or subjectivities. A research study can investigate the processes and consequences of the construction of learners' beliefs or subjectivities. The participants can be racially minoritized students, who might be marginalized, resisting, or discovering a new identity, as seen, for example, in ethnographic research on African American university students learning Portuguese during study abroad in Brazil (Anya, 2017). Racially majority students' subjectivity construction can be a topic of investigation too. For example, through conducting an ethnography in a US high school, Bucholtz (2011) investigated the ways in which white students performed their racial identities.

Race and Teacher Beliefs or Subjectivities

Similar to the above topic, one can study the ways in which pre-service or in-service teachers (re)construct their beliefs or their sense of self. Though race is not her central focus, Park (2015) demonstrated how race, as implied in nonnative speakerness, marginalized pre-service East Asian teachers of English in the United States. Focusing on in-service ESL teachers in US schools, Motha (2014) revealed how these teachers' racial identities emerged from group conversations over afternoon tea during the school year.

Race-based subjectivities and ideas held by both learners and teachers can be investigated via ethnography, case study, and narrative inquiry. Data can come from observations, interviews, content or discourse analyses of autographical narratives and journal entries, and more. Counter-storytelling, as a type of narrative inquiry, is also a common methodology of critical race theory.

Race and Classroom Interaction

Classroom interaction is generated by a teacher's instruction or peer talk. In these discursive spaces, racialization or racism may get produced overtly or subtly. For instance, Talmy (2010) conducted an ethnography using critical discourse analysis and revealed how racial hierarchies among ESL students in a Hawaiian high school were constructed. A researcher may also want to conduct participatory action research to work collaboratively with teachers to implement an anti-racist curriculum in language studies.

Race and Learning Materials

Learning materials, such as textbooks and audiovisual resources, can construct particular meanings for racialized groups via various images and discourses. One can analyze foreign language textbooks and conduct a critical discourse analysis of texts and images to expose racial representations. Yamada (2015), for instance, conducted a critical discourse analysis to examine widely used junior high school English textbooks in Japan, whereas Taylor-Mendes (2009) conducted interviews with students and teachers of English in Brazil to elicit their interpretations of racialized visual images in the textbooks they were using.

Race and Education Policies

Language-in-education policies as demonstrated in policy documents, curricula, program/institutional policies, and assessment systems may convey subtle meanings of racialization and racism. These meanings may be reflected in the placement of students in a special class/program, the hiring of teachers and administrators, and the selection of instructional materials and approaches.

These issues can be analyzed by conducting critical discourse analyses of policy documents or interviewing stakeholders about how they interpret, enact, or resist the policies (Motha, 2014).

Research Questions

In constructing research questions, it is important to integrate the three question words: *what, who,* and *where*. The *what* is obviously the topic, whereas the *who* is the target participants (if the study involves human subjects), and the *where* indicates where the data are collected or in which context the study is situated. In the following research questions, the *where* should be filled in by the readers according to their own interest or circumstances. The first five questions address the five individual topics listed above, whereas the next five combine two of these topics.

1. How do racially minoritized Asian students in a secondary school negotiate their subjectivities through learning English as a second language?
2. What racial subjectivities do pre-service teachers develop in a teacher preparation class focused on anti-racist education?
3. How are racialized meanings reflected and produced in high school students' peer interaction in the classroom?
4. How are racialized groups represented discursively in the textbook?
5. How do language teachers interpret, enact, or resist institutional language policies in relation to issues of race?
6. How do the visual images in language textbooks influence the understanding of the racialization of the *self* and the *other* among elementary school students?
7. How do language and literacy assessment policies and practices in a high school create an institutional racial hierarchy and affect students' subjectivities?
8. How do teachers use teaching materials for anti-racist education and how does the instruction influence the students' beliefs about racialized groups?
9. What anti-oppressive visions and policies does a language teacher education program embrace and how do they influence the experiences of minoritized teacher candidates in the program?
10. How do in-service teachers create and implement an anti-oppressive foreign language curriculum and how does the experience influence the teacher's racial subjectivity?

References

Anya, U. (2017). *Racialized identities in second language learning: Speaking blackness in Brazil.* New York, NY: Routledge.

Bucholtz, M. (2011). *White kids: Language, race, and styles of youth identity.* Cambridge, UK: Cambridge University Press.

Kubota, R. (2017). Studying up, down, or across?: Selecting who to research. In J. McKinley & H. Rose (Eds.), *Doing research in applied linguistics: Realities, dilemmas, and solutions* (pp. 17–26). Abingdon, UK: Routledge.

Kubota, R., & Miller, E. R. (2017). Re-examining and re-envisioning criticality in language studies: Theories and praxis. *Critical Inquiry in Language Studies*, 14, 129–157.

Motha, S. (2014). *Race and Empire in English language teaching: Creating responsible and ethical antiracist practice*. New York, NY: Teachers College Press.

Park, G. (2015). Situating the discourses of privilege and marginalization in the lives of two East Asian women teachers of English. *Race, Ethnicity and Education*, 18, 108–133.

Pennycook (2001). *Critical applied linguistics: A critical introduction*. Mahwah, NJ: Lawrence Erlbaum Associates.

Talmy, S. (2010). Becoming 'local' in ESL: Racism as resource in a Hawai'i public high school. *Journal of Language, Identity, and Education*, 9, 36–57.

Taylor-Mendes, C. (2009). Construction of racial stereotypes in English as a foreign language (EFL) textbooks. In R. Kubota & A. Lin (Eds.), *Race, culture, and identities in second language education: Exploring critically engaged practice* (pp. 64–80). New York: Routledge.

Yamada, M. (2015). *The role of English teaching in modern Japan: Diversity and multiculturalism through English language education in globalized era*. New York, NY & London, England: Routledge.

21
GENDER AND LTE

Harold Castañeda-Peña

UNIVERSIDAD DISTRITAL FRANCISCO JOSÉ DE CALDAS, COLOMBIA

I was born in Colombia (South America). Thinking about gender and language learning in my country is a challenging task. I have related to this topic as materials writer, teacher educator and researcher (Castañeda-Peña, 2008). My story begins some decades ago when I wrote materials for preschool students who were learning English. In these learning materials, I introduced, against the odds, ideas of gender drawing on discourses of equity and diversity that were obviously not shared by the publishing house. My life as a teacher educator and researcher is also part of this story. For several years, I taught an undergraduate course titled *Gender, Identity and Language* until this was prohibited by one school authority at that time. I, however, have kept researching, with graduate and undergraduate students, topics related to gender and the teaching and learning of English. In terms of LTE we have explored narrative experiences of English teachers with non-normative sexualities. We have also investigated the social representations of gender identities in language textbooks and the social and educational practices associated with such representations. We have investigated the language-learning narrative experiences of gay, lesbian and heterosexual students. Finally, we have ascertained English language teachers' professional development drawing on gender topics (Mojica & Castañeda-Peña, 2017). The road has been stony and full of difficulties, but it is also full of achievements. In this chapter I describe three strategies for choosing a research topic related to gender and LTE, strategies that may appear to be very obvious but that we sometimes overlook. I also describe topics that I believe can be part of a contemporary research agenda and, finally, I list some questions that can inspire future research for those who are interested in the interconnection between gender and LTE.

Choosing a Researchable Topic

Examining one's own assumptions and warrants about gender. As a researcher I always try to examine my own assumptions and warrants (Swann, 2002) to pose a researchable problem. Sometimes we believe that situations that are derived from gender are not important or are not researchable because gender is not apparently involved. The natural presence of men and women or people with non-normative sexualities does not necessarily lead to a situation to investigate from a gender perspective if we do not use warrants. This strategy means reflecting on the geopolitical perspective from which we position ourselves and to investigate a topic that we are passionate about.

Finding 'absences' in gender specialized literature: Sometimes it is common for us to feel that everything has been researched in a particular area that we are passionate about (e.g., gender, identity, and LTE) and that we have nothing new to say about it. However, a good strategy that could work for some is to review what has been written about and problematized in the specialized literature. This could help to find 'absences' or gaps; that is, aspects of the researchable topic that have not been considered before or simply neglected.

Scrutinizing social practices that might make gender invisible: Researchable problems related to gender, identity and LTE are not problems on their own but are related to the social structures in which they are located, that is, schooling and language learning and teaching, among others. Therefore, a helpful strategy might be carefully observing social practices and to question whether such situations make you feel uneasy and why. Asking oneself such questions could lead to the development of a research topic.

Current Research Topics

Gendered Identities in LTE

It is important to think about the sexual fluidity of humans and their gender variability in the context of LTE. "I do not know what to do with male students who are/act feminine in my English class" or "His notebook is neat" (with a tone of despair or disappointment), is what one commonly hears from in-service language teachers. Additionally, little is known about gay/lesbian/transgender language teachers (Lander, 2018). Therefore, considering sexual and gendered identities in LTE becomes paramount. Understanding this could result in educational policies at a general level helping teachers at a particular level (e.g., English language lessons) to make more gendered discourses available for language learners. Most discourse studies and narrative methodologies could work towards achieving this goal.

Gendered Discourses (Educational and Non-educational) in LTE

It is important to continue exploring gendered discourses from different angles aiming at understanding how LTE is seen, lived and discursively constituted from a gendered identity perspective. In my personal view, there are colonial mechanisms that have historically framed the discursive production of LTE. These discourses have apparently been rooted historically in mechanisms such as patriarchalism and misogyny, in which school life and language learning are anchored. As a consequence, harmful ideologies normalize language teachers' and language learners' identities. This means there is perceived to be only one way of being a language teacher or a language learner. There seems to be epistemological and ontological violence against discursive expressions of sexual, romantic and gendered identities in language learning. Such violence is garishly entangled together with the production and legitimation of discursive processes in LTE that: (a) police language teachers' and language learners' bodies, (b) favor urban second/foreign language centered education as a norm that excludes identities of English language teachers and students who belong to rural, indigenous, gypsy and other communities, and (c) associate language teachers' and language students' identities with racialization processes denying multiplicity. Qualitative discourse approaches could be used to ascertain language learning and teaching experiences in dialogue with narrative perspectives.

Gendered Representations (in Language Learning Materials and Media)

As evident in specialized literature "discourses crucially exist in constellations, networks or 'orders' of related discourses ... raising the alternative possibility of discoursal colonization" (Sunderland, 2004, p. 45). This holds true for graphic and textual gendered representations in language textbooks and media where gendered discourses and identities tend to be normalized and become canonical. However, consumers of textbooks and media (e.g., language teachers and language students) construct their own ideological gendered interpretations when engaging with learning and visual texts, which may resist or legitimize the discursive representations. It is thus worth exploring teachers' and students' talk around such representations (see Sunderland, Cowley, Rahim, Leontzakou & Shattuck, 2002). Consequently, representations could be addressed using multimodal discourse analysis and content discourse analysis. Teachers' and students' talk about these gendered (identity) representations could be studied using conversation analysis, elements of critical discourse analysis, and FPDA (Feminist Poststructuralist Discourse Analysis).

Gendered Classroom Interaction in LTE

Language teachers seem not to be fully aware of how their pedagogical planning for language teaching could result in social practices disadvantageous for some of their language learners. This could happen because implementing lesson plans also establishes power relationships among students. Power issues might have positive or negative consequences for some learners when they interact virtually or in face-to-face encounters. For example, Edward, a gay male language learner documented by Rondón (2012, p. 84), claims that "he does not consider [language learning] as a way to personal expression; he actually does not perceive an existential issue in the language learning process since he is detaching his sexual identity from his self in the [language classroom]." This might happen because he has to interact in a scripted way where he has to blur out his identity to avoid social consequences due to his gay identity. Discourse, narrative, and conversation analysis approaches could enable understanding of the interactional processes and experiences in LTE.

Gendered Teacher Education

Indisputably, "researchers have assembled evidence about particular practices that help teachers develop the kinds of teaching expertise necessary to assure that all children learn" (Darling-Hammond & Baratz-Snowden, 2005, p. 41). Additionally, traditions and approaches supporting teaching language teachers have been identified (Díaz-Maggioli, 2012). However, little is known about how language teachers address sexual and gender identities inside and outside classrooms. Themes to be explored within this trend include: (a) teachers' knowledge and experiences relating to discourses of language learning within a gender framework, (b) the gendered symbolic meanings teachers associate with the act of teaching languages, and (c) the discursive construction of gendered subjectivities teachers either favor or resist in their language teaching practices. Ethnographic, discursive, and narrative perspectives could be useful to investigate gendered teacher education.

Research Questions

I hope that the following set of questions can contribute to decentering the ideologies behind gender (identity) scholarship in LTE. Exploring these (newer) questions privileges the idea of acknowledging that there exist emergent social and cultural conditions strengthening 'other' sexualities and 'other' genders in language teaching and learning. Acknowledging such 'otherness' constitutes one way (perhaps not the only one) to restore a less normalized and more diverse field of study.

1. What gendered colonial mechanisms operate contemporarily in LTE?
2. What discoursal colonization practices have been enforced gender-wise by LTE scholarship work?
3. What other sexual and gender identities evident in language classrooms contribute to explain language learning?
4. What discursive construction of gendered subjectivities are favored or resisted by language teachers?

5. How does this discursive construction relate to language teaching and learning?
6. What social practices are shaped by representations of sexual and gender identities in language learning materials and media?
7. What new gender-based principles underpinning processes of LTE could be incorporated into initial teacher education and language teachers' professional development programs?
8. What language learning experiences are narrated by language learners who hold non-normative sexual and gendered identities?
9. What language teaching experiences are narrated by language teachers who hold non-normative sexual and gendered identities?
10. What classroom interactional patterns could be fostered to support a healthy language learning environment inhabited by language learners who hold non-normative sexual and gendered identities?

References

Castañeda-Peña, H. (2008). Interwoven and competing discourses in a pre-school EFL lesson. In K. Harrington, L. Litosseliti, H. Sauntson & J. Sunderland (Eds.), *Gender and language research methodologies* (pp. 256–268). Basingstoke: Palgrave Macmillan.

Darling-Hammond, L., & Baratz-Snowden, J. (Eds.) (2005). *A good teacher in every classroom: Preparing the highly qualified teachers our children deserve*. San Francisco: Jossey-Bass.

Díaz-Maggioli, G. (2012). *Teaching language teachers: Scaffolding professional learning*. Lanham, MD: Rowman & Littlefield Education.

Lander, R. (2018). Queer English language teacher identity: A narrative exploration in Colombia. *PROFILE: Issues in Teachers' Professional Development*, 20(1), 89–101.

Mojica, C. P., & Castañeda-Peña, H. (2017). A learning experience of the gender perspective in English teaching contexts. *PROFILE: Issues in Teachers' Professional Development*, 19(1), 139–153.

Rondón, F. (2012). LGBT students' short range narratives and gender performance in the EFL classroom. *Colombian Applied Linguistics Journal*, 14(1), 71–90.

Sunderland, J. (2004). *Gendered discourses*. Basingstoke: Palgrave McMillan.

Sunderland, J., Cowley, M., Rahim, F., Leontzakou, C., & Shattuck, J. (2002). From representation towards discursive practices: Gender in the foreign language textbook revisited. In L. Litosseliti & J. Sunderland (Eds.), *Gender identity and discourse analysis* (pp. 223–255). Amsterdam: John Benjamins.

Swann, J. (2002). Yes, but is it gender? In L. Litosseliti & J. Sunderland (Eds.), *Gender identity and discourse analysis* (pp. 43–67). Amsterdam: John Benjamins.

22

RESEARCHING ENGLISH AS AN INTERNATIONAL LANGUAGE

Heath Rose

UNIVERSITY OF OXFORD, UK

Before moving into academia, I worked for 15 years as a language teacher – both as a Japanese language teacher in Australia and an English language teacher in Japan. These early professional experiences shaped my interests as a researcher and inspired me to seek ways to teach language according to students' ever-changing needs. When I was teaching on one of the very first bilingual business degree programs in Japan, I became particularly sentient to the fact that there was a mismatch between the curriculum, which embodied American English centrality, and my students' needs, which centered on doing future business in English with predominantly non-native speaking neighbors such as Korea and China. This spurred me to examine more closely the proposals and challenges surrounding the teaching of English as an international language. These earlier experiences led me to become an avid researcher of Global Englishes, which examines the growth of English as the world's foremost global lingua franca (see Galloway & Rose, 2015; Rose & Galloway, 2019). The spread of English as a global language impacts many facets of language teaching education and many contexts where language teachers work. Therefore, there is tremendous scope to explore issues at the nexus of Global Englishes research and English language teaching, which is where the bulk of my own research lies.

Strategies for Choosing a Topic

When my postgraduate students first consult with me about choosing a topic, I usually ask them two key questions:

1. What are you interested in?
2. Who (or what) do you have access to for research purposes?

I do this to highlight the fact that not only do students need to have a vested interest in their topic, but they also need to have access to a suitable population or data set to carry out original research. Sometimes what they have interest in will be methodologically informed, such as an interest in action research. In this case, the question of who they have access to (i.e., their own students) may help to inform their topic. For example, if they are currently teaching an academic reading class, then reading-oriented action research might be a good starting point. From this point they can begin to explore the relevant reading literature to help inform the cycles of their action research.

A more targeted strategy is to get students to skim recent editions of LTE-oriented journals such as *ELT Journal, TESOL Quarterly*, the *Language Learning Journal*, or *Foreign Language Annals*, and locate a study that is interesting to them. Using this as a basis, I encourage them to design a replication study (in the case of masters-level research), or a study where they extend knowledge in either new areas or contexts (in the case of doctoral-level research).

Finally, if a student is really unsure, I encourage them to select a topic that directly connects to their supervisor's research area. Choosing a topic closely related to their supervisor's research expertise not only allows students to benefit from expert knowledge of the methodologies needed during data collection and analysis, but the supervisor will also likely be able to give the student a timely topic and direct them to good resources to help them develop their topic knowledge. For example, as my area of interest lies in Global Englishes, I am in a good position to advise students on what would be valuable to research within the realm of teaching English as an international language.

Research Topics

Evaluation of the Curriculum for Global Englishes Content

Numerous researchers point to a lack of materials as being a major barrier to innovating English language teaching practices (Galloway, 2017). As ELT materials remain undoubtedly oriented around 'native-speaker' norms, research is needed to understand how Global Englishes can be integrated to challenge these norms. Considering the vital role that ELT materials play, we simply need more research into materials evaluation and analysis of how key Global Englishes constructs (the target interlocutors, role models, norms, cultures, ELF strategies) are construed in textbooks. While some exists (e.g., Syrbe & Rose, 2018; Rose & Galloway, 2019), further research into how these materials are used (and what they communicate to learners about language norms) is needed to ensure that current practices are effective in preparing learners to use English in global contexts. Analysis should ideally take the form of qualitative text analysis, sometimes called qualitative content analysis, where materials are analyzed through a framework that delineates key constructs of Global Englishes, including: representations of target interlocutors;

exposure to varying types of English use; representations of global, local, and glocal (globalized in local contexts) English-using cultures; and representations of ownership of English. There is also methodological scope within this topic to explore the experiences of teachers and students using these materials.

Approaches for Teaching English as an International Language

A second key research topic surrounds a need for classroom-based research into the effects of Global Englishes' innovations on student learning. While some in-depth work has been done (see Galloway 2017 for an overview), more is needed. It is particularly important to investigate students' perceptions, reactions, and reflections towards learning to use English as an international language. This could be done via a number of methods that tap into student experiences throughout a learning period, including: learner diaries; learner narratives; reflective accounts; interviews; and focus groups. Teacher narratives, auto-ethnographies or duoethnographies are also useful in communicating practices within professional circles (see Rose & Montakantiwong, 2018). To examine the effect of an innovation on learning outcomes, action research or classroom-based field research is needed so that contextualized data can be collected before, during and after innovative changes in the curriculum. See Galloway (2017) for ideas of what intervention could look like.

Attitudes of Learners towards Variation in English

Language attitudes are important as they underpin the way we think and feel about languages in society, and ultimately influence our behaviors towards language users. All people, whether consciously or unconsciously, make daily inferences about other people based solely on the language they use, including one's dialect, accent, vocabulary and grammatical choices (see Galloway & Rose, 2015; Galloway, 2017). In the realm of English as an international language, we are particularly interested in exploring teacher and learner attitudes associated with so-called 'non-standard' Englishes, which make up the majority of the English used globally. Historically, the field has relied on indirect methods such as the matched guise technique and verbal guise technique, where participants are asked to evaluate pre-recorded speakers on an attitude-rating scale. By limiting attitudes to the static varieties used in the recordings, these methods do not accurately account for the complexities of how English is used in global and local contexts, where plural, ever-changing, fluid forms of language are used. Thus, there is tremendous scope to explore attitudes via in-depth qualitative methods to delineate what underpins teacher and learner attitudes. Such research gets to the core of understanding how educators can positively influence attitudes to prepare English learners to become global language users.

Challenges Associated with English Medium Instruction

The world has seen a boom in English medium instruction (EMI), which is defined as "the use of the English language to teach academic subjects (other than English itself) in countries or jurisdictions where the first language of the majority of the population is not English" (Macaro, et al., 2018, p. 37). Language teaching and learning in EMI contexts needs more research attention in terms of how English language education facilitates the use of English as an academic lingua franca. As EMI continues to grow as an educational model around the world, we need on-the-ground research on the unique language-related challenges associated with EMI, so that English language educators can better prepare students to use English as an academic lingua franca. This research – at the nexus of TESOL and EMI – must be context specific to capture the intricacies of learner, teacher, program and discipline-specific challenges. An in-depth qualitative approach that explores EMI experiences via case studies will help policy makers to better understand the contextualized challenges of learning content through a second language.

Multilingualism in EMI and ELT Classrooms

The use of English in a global educational context raises questions about *what English* should be used in EMI, thus reconceptualizing the 'E' in EMI (Rose & Galloway, 2019), as well as the 'E' in ELT. Policies guiding the implementation of English language within education are often motivated by political ideologies that insist on English-only or English-always use in the classroom, despite arguments against such practices. As multilingualism is embraced in language teaching education as an important pedagogical tool (and a natural feature of multilingual communication), there is tremendous opportunity to explore how other languages are used in the classroom vis-à-vis codeswitching or translanguaging. Researchers could take a plurality-perspective of Global Englishes by exploring global orientations within educational contexts, such as McKinley's (2018) evaluations of program-level transitions from English as a foreign language to English as a lingua franca. Researchers could also explore how English is being used alongside other languages in EMI and ELT classrooms. This would be an excellent opportunity to tie the research with contemporary 'hot topics' in applied linguistics related to the multilingual turn (see May, 2014).

Research Questions

1. How, if at all, are Global Englishes represented in English language textbooks?

This will provide needed research into whether current materials are underpinned by appropriate ideologies to teach English as an international language.

2. How do students and teachers react to (and interact with) globally oriented teaching materials?

It is important not only to evaluate current materials for their shortcomings, but to build on this knowledge in the creation of globally oriented materials and (importantly) to report on their use in classes.

3. How can the 'Global Englishes Language Teaching' proposals (see Galloway, 2017; Rose & Galloway, 2019) be integrated into English language classrooms?

Research on this topic will help to bridge a long-observed theory-practice divide by reporting on-the-ground pedagogical innovations via practitioner-led research.

4. What are the context-situated challenges of teaching English as an international language?

This research question aims to explore the various barriers that teachers may face when trying to innovate their own curricula to teach English as an international language.

5. What are students' attitudes towards non-standard varieties of language?

A contextualized, qualitative examination of student attitudes is necessary to counter-balance the compartmentalized (dialect-specific), quantitative research that has typified language attitude research.

6. How do beliefs and experiences underpin learners' attitudes towards the flexibility and plurality of Englishes?

As language attitudes underpin people's beliefs, feelings and behaviors, this research question aims to delineate the influences of attitudes to better understand how teachers may positively influence them.

7. What language-related challenges do students experience when studying content via the medium of English?

As the world is experiencing a boom in EMI, it is imperative that contextualized fieldwork is conducted to accurately capture language learning issues so that research keeps pace with policy implementation.

8. What English is used in English medium content courses?

This research question aims to critically challenge native-speaker hegemony in EMI educational contexts. By understanding uses of non-standard Englishes in EMI we can better capture diversity in the use of English by all L2 users (both teachers and learners).

9. How are languages other than English used in EMI and ELT?

This research question explores the functions of translanguaging and codeswitching within English language teaching, which may help to inform practices that embrace languages alongside English within language pedagogy.

10. How can EMI stakeholders move towards a hybrid and plural perspective of English (including use of languages other than English) in EMI contexts?

This question combines two research topics by exploring the teaching of English as an international language within EMI.

References

Galloway, N. (2017). *Global Englishes and change in English language teaching*. Abingdon: Routledge.
Galloway, N., & Rose, H. (2015). *Introducing Global Englishes*. Abingdon: Routledge.
Macaro, E., Curle, S., Pun, J., An, J., & Dearden, J. (2018). A systematic review of English medium instruction in higher education. *Language Teaching*, 51(1), 36–76.
McKinley, J. (2018). Making the EFL to ELF transition at a Global Traction University. In A. Bradford & H. Brown (Eds.), *English-medium instruction at universities in Japan: Policy, challenges and outcomes* (pp. 238–249). Bristol: Multilingual Matters.
May, S. (2014). Introducing the 'Multilingual Turn.' In S. May (Ed.), *The multilingual turn. Implications for SLA, TESOL and bilingual education*. (pp. 1–6). New York: Routledge.
Rose, H., & Galloway, N. (2019). *Global Englishes for language teaching*. Cambridge: Cambridge University Press.
Rose, H., & Montakantiwong, A. (2018). A tale of two teachers: A duoethnography of the realistic and idealistic successes and failures of teaching English as an international language. *RELC Journal*, 49(1), 88–101.
Syrbe, M., & Rose, H. (2018). An evaluation of the global orientation of English textbooks in Germany. *Innovation in Language Learning and Teaching*, 12(2), 152–163.

23

MULTILINGUALISM IN (FOREIGN) LANGUAGE TEACHING AND LEARNING

Anne Pitkänen-Huhta
UNIVERSITY OF JYVÄSKYLÄ, FINLAND

I am an applied linguist who considers language learning to be a socially constructed practice. In fact, I would rather talk about applied language studies than applied linguistics, as I understand this area of inquiry to include any language-related research that bears a strong connection to societally significant phenomena. In that broad palette of research, my own work would be placed at the interface of the areas of language learning and teaching, on the one hand, and discourse studies and sociolinguistics, on the other. I have always worked with students who wish to be language teachers. Over the years, I have seen hundreds of students entering working life that is in constant turmoil. My principal interest, therefore, is in the changing conditions of language learning, in the diversity of learners, and in the societal and personal push and pull forces under which teachers and learners have to create meaningful practices.

A note on the terminology I use in this chapter is needed here. I am fully aware of the complexities of placing languages into the categories of mother tongue, first, second, foreign, and so on, as language use keeps taking new shapes in the changing world. I will, nevertheless, use here the term *foreign language* when I talk about the languages that are typically learnt and taught in classrooms and which people use to varying degrees in work, study and leisure contexts, since our educational systems still categorize languages as school subjects with specific labels such as mother tongue or foreign languages.

Strategies for Choosing a Topic

When thinking about how I have identified my research topics, I realize that the processes are, in fact, a great mystery to me. It is impossible for me to give a good recipe for finding and choosing topics, but what I can do is to suggest a few ingredients that seem to work for me and that sometimes have resulted in a very interesting meal. I will briefly discuss four ingredients that work for me. I do not present the ideas in any order of importance or preference.

Team work has always been the core of my research activities. I have had the pleasure of having very resourceful and invigorating colleagues with whom to share and create wild ideas. This might be a cliché but I still firmly believe that the best and most innovative ideas for research are born in informal discussions in coffee rooms and corridors. I therefore encourage people to engage in idle talk around societally interesting and topical issues that may lead to important research questions.

Cross fertilization is something that arises from team work when you build on the coffee room discussions in a more organized way in seminars and conferences, both in your own organization as well as in national and international gatherings. New ideas often arise from the most unexpected combinations of research areas.

Media is an excellent source of ideas; follow the current discussions and debates on issues related to language. As an example, one could mention the concern in Finnish media over the lack of diversity in Finland's language reserve. Fewer and fewer school children choose to study languages other than English and thus proficiency in languages often means proficiency in English only. Experts, especially from commerce and manufacturing, are making worrying statements about Finns losing the edge on international markets because of a lack of skills in languages other than English. So, this kind of discussion gives researchers plenty of topics for research from different angles.

None of the above work unless you practice constant critical *self-reflection*. Observe your own teaching or a colleague's teaching, relate your observations to changes in the world, read research literature beyond SLA, language learning, teacher education, and analyze your own experiences.

Current Research Topics

Increasing multilingualism has important repercussions for (language) education (e.g., Cenoz & Gorter, 2011; Douglas Fir Group, 2016; May, 2014). In Europe, in particular, classrooms have become more and more multilingual and multicultural in recent decades. This area is, however, also relevant in contexts where multilingualism has always been present. Research has focused on second language learners or on heritage language maintenance in second language contexts, but what has been almost completely ignored are foreign language contexts. There have, however, been some concerned voices about the neglected area of the relationship between multilingualism and foreign language learning and teaching (e.g., Kramsch, 2014; Lo Bianco, 2014) but very little empirical research.

Multilingual Learners in Foreign Language Classrooms

The increasingly diverse linguistic repertoires evident in classrooms makes foreign language learning a complex matter. Therefore, the relationship between learners, teachers, and the languages present in the classroom needs to be examined. Learners' cultural and linguistic backgrounds have an effect on how they relate to the foreign language being taught. The language in question may have quite a different sociolinguistic status in the lives of different learners, and the learners' experiences may also differ in relation to the language. Teachers, on the other hand, may struggle with how to recognize, acknowledge, and make use of all languages present in the classroom.

In researching this topic, it is crucial to get insight into the lived experiences of learners and teachers, and therefore to adopt methods that help researchers unravel the inner feelings of the research participants. The experiences and feelings could be captured through verbal and visual narratives, for example, that would prompt the participants to share their experiences (e.g., Kalaja & Pitkänen-Huhta, 2018).

Teaching Practices in a Multilingual Group

Very often learners in the foreign language classroom are assumed to be monolingual speakers of the same language. Although this is not the case anymore, it is still often considered that the learners' linguistic backgrounds do not have consequences for how the foreign language is taught. If problems are encountered, the solution is to resort to monolingualism, that is, to use the target language only. As with the previous topic, it is important to study both teacher and learner perspectives. The most direct way to study teaching practices is to observe classrooms. To connect observation to teacher and learner experiences, it would be beneficial to engage in collaborative work with both teachers and learners during data collection as well as data analysis.

Teaching/Learning Materials for Multilingual Groups

Learning materials play an important role in shaping classroom teaching and learning practices, and therefore it is crucial to study materials as well. Materials have typically been designed with the assumption that all learners share the first language. An example from the European context are textbooks in Finland. Finland has very strong markets for textbooks. They are generally very good, and they are expected to reflect the National Core Curricula. But still today, the foreign languages are taught mostly through Finnish. Students need to know Finnish to understand the instructions in tasks, and wordlists have translations in Finnish. Those whose Finnish skills are not up to the level of first language are at a disadvantage. For this research topic the most appropriate method would be textbook analysis, but I would suggest that it would be complemented with teacher and student interviews. This would give more insight into how materials are used in the classroom. One possible extension of these methods would be to initiate research on learning materials in teacher training and thereby involve future teachers in materials development.

Discourses of Multilingualism/Monolingualism in Policy Documents

Policy documents such as curricula form the basis of teaching and learning in the classroom. It is therefore crucial to examine what kinds of explicit and implicit conceptualizations of multilingualism (or perhaps monolingualism) they hold. What the crucial documents are depends on the context of a particular study. It might be national curricula, school specific curricula and policies, individual classroom policies, assessment guidelines, teaching materials, or media discussions on schools and teaching. The appropriate research method for this topic depends on the kinds of discourses that are relevant to study. It could be textual and (critical) discourse analysis of documents, observation, interviews, and so on.

Teacher's Conceptualizations of Language vs. Their Teaching Practices

What the teacher does in the classroom is crucial for their learners to learn, and what the teacher does is based on her/his understanding of the goal and means of teaching, i.e. *language*. It is important to approach this topic from several angles, as it is vital to understand what the conceptualizations are, where they come from, and how they are enacted in classroom practices. The methods could include teacher interviews, focus group interviews, questionnaires, visual and verbal narratives, and visualizations as prompts for further discussion. These would have to be contrasted with observed (video-recorded) classroom practices and teacher reflection on the observed practices.

Research Questions

1. How do teachers recognize and acknowledge multilingual learners in their foreign language classrooms?

To create meaningful practices for all learners in the classroom, teachers would need to know their students' cultural and linguistic backgrounds and make use of the potential of multilingualism in their classrooms.

2. How do learners see their multilingualism in relation to learning a foreign language? Is it beneficial for learning? Does it hinder learning?

It is equally important to know how learners themselves recognize their cultural and linguistic backgrounds and how they are able to connect that to the learning of new languages.

3. How do foreign language teachers take multilingual learners into account in their teaching practices?

Taking multilingualism into account in classroom practices is a very complex issue, and therefore we need to know if teachers do this in practice and how they do it.

4. How do 'monolingual' or the majority language speakers in foreign language classrooms benefit from teaching practices that take into account multilingual learners?

It should be self-evident that adopting classroom practices that are culture and language sensitive are beneficial for all learners, but how exactly this takes place in foreign language learning is not known.

5. How is multilingualism evident in foreign language learning materials?

As materials are often the primary gatekeeper in the classroom, it is paramount to know if and how different foreign language learning materials take multilingualism into account.

6. How do teaching materials support multilingual learners?

As a follow-up to the previous question, this question would take a closer look at the mechanisms of support in the materials.

7. How does multilingualism feature in specific policy documents related to language education?

This question connects grassroots practices to broader societal structures and examines how ideas of multilingualism are spread from the top down.

8. How do teachers understand the concept of language?

If we find an answer to this question, we will better understand how languages are taught in classrooms.

9. What are the sources of teachers' conceptualizations of language?

Teachers formulate their conceptualizations from different sources, including their own experiences, their education and teacher training, policy documents, materials, and the media. To be able to improve teacher education, we need to know what these sources are.

10. How do conceptualizations of language reflect the teaching practices of specific teachers?

This question combines the two previous questions and delves deeper into the relationship between conceptualizations and actual classroom teaching and learning practices.

References

Cenoz, J., & Gorter D. (2011). A holistic approach to multilingual education: Introduction. *The Modern Language Journal*, 95(3), 339–343.

Douglas Fir Group.(2016). A transdisciplinary framework for SLA in a multilingual world. *The Modern Language Journal*, 100S, 19–47.

Kalaja, P., & Pitkänen-Huhta, A. (2018). ALR special issue: Visual methods in applied language studies. *Applied Linguistics Review*, 9(2–3), 157–176.

Kramsch, C. (2014). Teaching foreign languages in an era of globalization: Introduction. *The Modern Language Journal*, 98(1), 296–311.

Lo Bianco, J. (2014). Domesticating the foreign: Globalization's effects on the place/s of languages. *The Modern Language Journal*, 98(1), 312–325.

May, S. (Ed.). (2014). *The multilingual turn: Implications for SLA, TESOL and bilingual education*. New York and London: Routledge.

24

ENGLISH LANGUAGE TEACHING IN MULTILINGUAL CONTEXTS

Christa van der Walt

STELLENBOSCH UNIVERSITY, SOUTH AFRICA

I started my career as a high school English language teacher. As I became more interested in language learning and teaching, specifically English second language learning and teaching, I started postgraduate studies. After three years I moved into university teaching where I once more taught second language students how to improve their proficiency. One of my classes involved teaching English to students who needed the class for their professional programs; mostly law and education. I started questioning the content of the class, but more importantly, I started questioning the very practice of teaching English in our multilingual context. One of my doctoral advisers pointed out that to expect multilingual students to reach 'native-like proficiency' was ridiculous, and he introduced me to the World Englishes concept. As I moved into language teacher education, my interest in multilingualism developed into my current field of expertise, which is multilingual education, particularly at higher education level. This was also the point at which I started turning away from purely quantitative research and started using qualitative research methodologies.

Choosing a Research Topic

My own research projects inevitably emerged from my context and the problems I observed there. Before I started my doctoral studies, I took time to 'find' a topic. In the humanities and social sciences, students often choose their own topic, based on their interests. In these cases it is important to choose wisely. I wanted to investigate a particular feature of my students' writing, but I realized that I didn't have the linguistic knowledge to do a comprehensive analysis of learner English. However, I did have the sociolinguistic knowledge, which led me to a topic that focused on the ways in which politeness manifests in teachers' English.

I would recommend that prospective researchers think about the following when they choose a topic, bearing in mind that "there are numerous decisions to be taken at various points in the inquiry and making an injudicious choice may have ethical implications, contaminate the data, prolong the inquiry or, at worst, invalidate the findings" (Evans, 2010, p. 85):

1. How much do you know about the topic or problem? Have you read about the problem you want to investigate? If you need to start a separate study in an entirely new field as a result of your initial reading, you may need to reconsider your topic by possibly limiting the scope of your enquiry. We all need to do extensive reading for our projects, but we also need to be realistic. When I started my doctoral studies, I did not know much about Brown and Levinson's work on politeness, but I knew enough about the discipline that I could make sense of what they were saying. Talk to an academic who is working in the field and read a few articles before you decide on the *scope* of your topic.
2. If you are going to collect data from students or fellow teachers or government institutions, do you have access to such people? If not, how do you propose getting access to them? It is often difficult to enter, for example, a school environment without any contextual knowledge. This does not mean that you should only do research in a context where you are known, but you need to consider this aspect before you finalize the topic.
3. Doing qualitative/narrative research usually requires intensive and sustained contact with research participants and the 'data' that they give you. Will it be possible for them to make time for you? Could the questions you ask or the observations you plan intrude in a space that they might not want to share? Although you cannot prevent participants from withdrawing from your study, considering the possibility from the outset could result in changes to the topic.

Current Research Topics

Multilingual Language Teachers' Linguistic Knowledge over Time

Longitudinal studies on second language teachers' insight into and mastery of linguistic knowledge, particularly pedagogical content knowledge (PCK), over a number of years are rare, mostly because there is much pressure on researchers to either finish a PhD or get results that can be published. A topic like this would require 'following' teachers for two or three years, observing their classes and asking them to reflect on their own growth in this area. Narrative inquiry would be an excellent tool to use for such reflections. There could be a quantitative element to this study, with researchers assessing pre-identified aspects of PCK regarded as important in terms of a particular curriculum (Golombek & Johnson, 2017).

Translanguaging Classroom Practices

We seem to be thin on classroom observations of translanguaging practices and teacher reflections on their ability to facilitate learning through translanguaging. In this case, audio or video recordings can be used and the context, classroom culture, teacher practice, and subject content could be analyzed qualitatively. Teacher narratives could focus on language negotiations between teacher and the class and amongst learners (see Henderson & Ingram, 2018). To test the extent to which translanguaging can improve understanding and deepen concept knowledge, observations of group discussions or student blogging could be analyzed for such evidence. Madiba (2014) shows how this can be done in the case of group discussions.

Family Language Policies

A study on this topic could investigate teacher awareness of family language policy or family literacy practices in multilingual education contexts. Prospective teachers' own language biographies (in the form of narratives) could be a point of departure for such a study. This very broad topic can be approached from different angles, for example the role of school language dynamics in parental decisions about schooling in a high-status (non-native) language, and teacher awareness of the link between home language literacy and emergent school literacy (see Kajee, 2018). In these examples it would be ideal to record and analyze teacher–parent conferences or, if research participants are wary of allowing an outsider into this space, researchers could interview teachers and parents separately.

English Language Teachers as Gatekeepers

This topic can be linked to language teacher identity in multilingual contexts where a high-status language is used as the language of learning and teaching. Such a topic lends itself particularly well to narrative inquiry. Shohamy (2006, p. 78) refers to teachers as the 'foot soldiers' of repressive language-in-education policies that use access and placement tests to police very specific views of language proficiency. The 'violence' of such educational language policies and the ways in which language teachers may feel complicit in implementing these policies may provide insight into how they see themselves: implementers or subversives? In multilingual contexts where teachers share the learners' minoritized languages, their role as gatekeepers becomes particularly difficult.

Urban and Non-standard Varieties in Education

Language teachers are supposed to 'uphold standards,' specifically the standard form of a language, when they teach and assess. The way in which language variety in the form of 'new languages,' also called urban varieties, street or youth language, are used or suppressed in educational environments is largely dependent on the teachers' attitudes towards them. The usefulness of multilingual teaching practices like co-languaging and the application of a framework like Hornberger's (2007) *continua of biliteracy* in teaching contexts may become problematic when a language variety has no written form. Topics in this area would lend itself particularly well to narrative inquiry when approached from an educational (rather than a linguistic) perspective.

Research Questions

1. What pedagogical content knowledge (PCK) elements regarding linguistic structure can be deduced from a particular curriculum?

This topic would rely on a conceptual analysis of the curriculum and its context to identify the linguistic elements that teachers require for effective teaching of linguistic structures.

2. How do multilingual teachers (by implication second language teachers) develop PCK of the linguistic system of the language that they teach?

The focus in this study should be on beginner teachers and their development over time.

3. How can language teacher education support the development of second language teachers' PCK of linguistic structures?

In contexts where postgraduate students do a teacher qualification (typically a postgraduate teaching diploma) they may not have developed explicit knowledge of language structure. This could be a problem when they start teaching. In such a context pre-service training would need to address their lack of knowledge, and the question in such a case would be both *how* and *what* to teach.

4. In what ways do multilingual language teachers use translanguaging (in the form of code switching, co-languaging, translations) in language teaching, if at all?

There seems to be a strong tradition of language teachers using only the target language in class. If teachers use other languages, why and how do they do this?

5. What are the observed effects of teacher translanguaging practices on learner involvement or detachment at intermediate and advanced levels?

McKay (2002, p. 43) mentions the fact that students are often disappointed when they realize that their teacher is not a home language speaker of the target language. How would they react to the teacher using their home languages?

Student narratives or focus group interviews may provide important data for language teacher education.

6. What are the ways in which pre-service language teachers can be made aware of the home literacy practices of multilingual learners who do not use the school language at home?

There is much evidence to suggest that literacy practices at home support the development of literacy in the school language (Kajee, 2018). Case studies could illuminate ways in which this happens, thereby providing guidelines for teacher educators.

7. How do teachers and parents negotiate family decisions about language choice and use?

A family's decision to school their child in a particular language seems inviolable. Nevertheless, it is important to determine the main drivers of and motivation for parents' decisions. Such a study would probably require careful consideration of teacher and parental consent for the researcher to sit in on and record a discussion.

8. How are English language teacher identities affected in multilingual contexts where they experience pressure to provide access to higher education?

Pressure to increase internationalization in higher education seems to focus on English language proficiency to a large degree. In such cases English becomes the key to further and higher education which often means 'coaching' students for particular access tests.

9. How do language teachers negotiate distinctions between 'correct' language and appropriate language in multi-dialectal contexts?

Varieties of colonial languages may be governed by strong in-group norms but may be stigmatized because they are seen as 'non-standard.' Teacher attitudes will be crucial in determining the extent to which they accommodate language variety.

10. What is the value of a *continuum of biliteracy* in contexts where non-standardized languages form part of the classroom environment?

Although the continuum of biliteracy framework was not developed for teaching contexts specifically, it is widely referenced as relevant in multilingual education. Biliteracy implies the existence of printed matter and an orthography for a particular language. In terms of the continuum of biliteracy it would not be possible to develop biliteracy *per se,* and the framework may only be relevant to a degree in such teaching contexts.

References

Evans, R. (2010). Eeny meeny miney mo! – Choices, and their consequences for graduate students when embarking on educational inquiry. *Per Linguam,* 26(1): 85–98.

Golombek, P.R., & Johnson, K.E. (2017). Re-conceptualizing teachers' narrative inquiry as professional development. *PROFILE,* 19(2), 15–28.

Henderson, K.I, & Ingram, M. (2018). 'Mister, you're writing in Spanglish': Fostering spaces for meaning making and metalinguistic connections through teacher translanguaging shifts in the bilingual classroom. *Bilingual Research Journal,* doi:10.1080/15235882.2018.1481894.

Hornberger, N. (2007). Multilingual language policies and the continua of biliteracy: An ecological approach. In O. García & C. Baker (Eds.), *Bilingual education: An introductory reader* (pp. 177–194). Clevedon: Multilingual Matters.

Kajee, L. (2018). Mapping the literate lives of two Cameroonian families living in Johannesburg: Implications for language and literacy education. *Per Linguam,* 34(1), 1–16.

Madiba, M. (2014). Promoting concept literacy through multilingual glossaries. In L. Hibbert & C. Van der Walt (Eds.), *Multilingual universities in South Africa: Reflecting society in higher education* (pp. 68–86). Bristol: Multilingual Matters.

McKay, S.L. (2002). *Teaching English as an international language: Rethinking goals and approaches.* Oxford, England: Oxford University Press.

Shohamy, E. (2006). *Language policy: Hidden agendas and new approaches.* London: Routledge.

25
SOCIAL REPRESENTATIONS OF MULTILINGUALISM

Alice Chik
MACQUARIE UNIVERSITY, AUSTRALIA

Sílvia Melo-Pfeifer
UNIVERSITY OF HAMBURG, GERMANY

Alice and Sílvia are two multilingual researchers, working abroad, using, among other linguistic resources, the language of the host country in their teaching and research activities. They both live in highly diverse multilingual cities and in binational and bicultural relationships. In common, they also have a passion for multilingual education and visual narratives as a method of collecting data. Alice currently lives and works in Sydney, among another 138,818 Cantonese-speakers. Since moving to Sydney four years ago, she has been fascinated with the cultural and linguistic diversities in urban areas and has worked closely with community language organizations. She is especially interested in the interface between individual and societal representations of multilingualism in Australia. Sílvia is Portuguese and currently works in Hamburg, a city with a large Portuguese community. She is an associate professor in the field of language education. She completed her doctoral degree with a thesis on 'Images of languages in multilingual on-line interaction' at the University of Aveiro (Portugal). Her main research fields are heritage language education and pluralistic approaches in teaching and learning. Multilingual interaction and inter-comprehension across Romance languages are the key themes in her publications.

Multilingualism is a term used to describe the presence of various languages both at an individual and at a societal level. The first level, also called plurilingualism, describes multilingual individual repertoires (e.g., through migration or foreign language education at school), and the second, the presence of different languages in a given space (city, nation, or global). Social representation of multilingualism is a significant topic in language education, including teacher education (Castellotti & Moore, 2002; Kramsch, 2009), and also sociolinguistics, and language policy. It is a significant topic for almost every country given the rapid rise of migration in recent years. Representations of multilingualism are not only limited to multilingual contexts or multilingual individuals. They are anchored in everyday lived experiences and exchanges, and are related to the social contexts in which individuals live.

Strategies for Choosing a Topic

When choosing the research area of 'social representations of multilingualism,' researchers should question whether they wish to research social or individual multilingualism (or the relationship between the two) and if they want to adopt a cognitive or a socio-constructivist stance using qualitative (or quantitative) methods (or a combination of both). Being relatively stable constructs, representations of individual and social multilingualism are also dynamic and can be explored through many qualitative methodologies. These range from more descriptive methodologies, aiming to diagnose the representations at a time–space scale (a more cognitive approach, as in Faneca, et al., 2016), to more interpretative ones, aiming to grasp how representations are co-constructed and circulate in interaction (a more socio-constructivist approach). In the qualitative tradition, social representations of multilingualism can be collected through open questionnaires (language) biographies and narratives, interviews, spontaneous and classroom interactions (both physical and on-line), and visual data, such as linguistic landscapes, linguistic portraits and collages (Barkhuizen, et al., 2014; Chik, 2018). Interviews and interaction have the potential to show how social representations are elicited, emerge and are negotiated in the interaction, and are thus examples of a socio-constructivist approach.

Sílvia, for example, adopted a predominantly socio-constructivist stance to understand how social representations of multilingualism are co-constructed during the interaction between multilingual individuals. She chose to analyze multilingual chat conversations – using conversation and discourse analysis – between speakers of different Romance languages. Her interest in analyzing such a topic came from her regular use of computer-mediated communication tools to communicate in private and professional spheres using different languages and her observation of and reflection about language negotiation and languages change during those multilingual encounters.

Depending on the sociolinguistic environments researchers are immersed in, it may be relevant to choose a topic such as the public understanding and beliefs about languages and their speakers, and the power relations in place. Another way to choose a topic in this field is being attentive to linguistic debates in order to grasp the hidden meaning of arguments put forward, as language debates are about ideologies and representations (Blommaert, 1999). Choosing a topic in this field could involve listening to how people talk, in formal or informal debates, about linguistic policies and practices. Alternatively, one can actively take part in those discussions. If researchers are embedded in educational spaces and they perceive that languages are at the heart of the discussions, it provides an opportunity to analyze the discourses circulating about languages, multilingualism, and multilingual identities. Both Sílvia and Alice used visual data to elicit representations of multilingualism with different research topics in mind, in very different contexts and with different participants. Sílvia, when examining the representations of Portuguese as a heritage language in Germany and working with younger learners, collected hand-drawn language portraits (Melo-Pfeifer, 2015). Using digital multimodal linguistic portraits, Alice investigated how visual imaginary can help university students rethink and express the emotional aspects of language learning. Alice is especially interested in the dissonance between physical and online representation of multilingualism primarily using census data and website analysis. For instance, if the census data show a neighborhood as being inhabited by multilingual speakers, do official and institutional websites reflect those offline diversities? By using a corpus approach to website analysis, it is possible to examine a collective social representation of multilingualism.

Current Research Topics

Representations of Individual Multilingual Repertoires

This topic is about how individuals perceive the organization of multilingual minds and the relationship between languages in their repertoires (Kalaja & Melo-Pfeifer, 2019). This timely topic addresses aspects such as the juxtaposition or the integration of linguistic resources, how languages influence cognition, and how languages are perceived as (un)identifiable and (in)separable semiotic entities. To do so, researchers often use visual methodologies to explore how individuals illustrate the organization of multilingual minds.

Students' Language Representations of their Language Education at School

This research topic is of utmost importance, as it attempts to uncover how social representations positively or negatively influence language choice, language learning, learning motivation and, ultimately, linguistic achievements (Moore, 2006). Furthermore, social representations of multilingualism can also shed light on how students perceive and accept (or not) the use of several languages as cognitive and affective tools in language learning scenarios. So, this topic may help to explain how and why students subscribe (or not) to a monolingual mindset in foreign language education and how they accept monolingualism as the rule in the classroom. Within a qualitative paradigm, researchers dealing with this topic usually use interviews with students, foreign language learning narratives, and the analysis of classroom interaction.

Language Representations in Initial Teacher Training

This topic deals with the role of language representations in the professional development of student teachers. Possible points of interest include how they perceive their future roles as language educators, how akin they are to integrating linguistic diversity as a resource in the classroom, and how willing they are to accept pedagogical proposals that might lead to a rupture of lived and observed monolingual practices in language education (and thus to formative dilemmas and crises). Another focus, one addressing the growing linguistic heterogeneity of student teachers, is whether those having grown up in a bi/multilingual environment are more open to multilingual pedagogies and practices. Such research topics can be studied using interviews with student teachers, and visual and written narratives of language learning and of imagined professional practice.

Heritage Language Education and its Representation

This topic is about perceptions of and bias towards heritage languages. For instance, how do parents and children represent their attitudes towards their heritage language? And what are the social attitudes towards languages other than the dominant language as reflected in the official school curriculum? This will inevitably involve a discussion of curricular spaces for heritage languages. Are schools accommodating the use of heritage languages in mainstream classrooms? Do schools run heritage language classes within school hours, or do heritage language classes operate only during weekends and after school hours?

Refugees' Multilingual Repertoires: Deficit and Divided

Representations of refugees' multilingual repertoires and achievements frequently focus on language deficit in relation to the dominant language. For instance, when many refugees to Germany and Australia are multilingual, there is a focus on perceived lack of proficiency in German and English respectively. Are multilingual refugees considered to be social assets and resources, or are they perceived as deficient in that they do not speak the dominant or national languages fluently *yet*? One question also to consider should be the eventual settlement of refugees. If, for instance, refugees are staying in a refugee camp in Italy as a mid-way transit to another European country, are we discussing their learning of Italian? Or the learning of another language (e.g., English or German or French)? When the wait for an asylum visa and transit could be long, how do we prepare refugees for new lives? And how do we prepare local residents to appreciate refugees' multilingual repertoires?

Research Questions

1. Which social representations of multilingualism circulate in a given society or group, and how do these representations affect language-learning curricula, language choices, and language abandonment?

Researchers could ask if languages with particular positive appeal are offered more often at school, if they are part of an individual's linguistic projects, and what kind of effort is made to achieve competence in those languages. The same kinds of questions could be asked about languages with a negative image. What could be made to reverse such dysphoric social representations?

2. Is there a relationship between representations of the multilingual mind and strategies for foreign language learning and teaching at school?

Imagining a multilingual mind as the sum of multiple monolingual abilities could explain why teachers (and students) are so akin to keeping languages separate in the classroom. This could signal a disconnection between language education in school and languages in the community.

3. How does the value assigned to students' heritage languages impact teaching and learning practices, both of linguistic and so-called non-linguistic subjects at school?

Researchers could ask if a positive representation of some heritage languages would favor their integration in school-settings, and if this means others would be permanently silenced.

4. Are teachers with so-called migrant backgrounds, possibly because of more positive representations of languages, more inclined to accept and integrate multilingual pedagogies and practices in the classroom?

5. Do initial teacher education programs include an additional language requirement?

If teachers do not have experience of learning an additional language, would they still have a favorable attitude towards multilingualism in the classroom?

6. Does language education provision match demographic changes?

Traditionally, language education tends to focus on European languages and English, but migratory trends – at least in our contexts – show that more recent migrants are from Asia, the Middle East and Africa. If language education in school is mostly limited to the former languages, where are the spaces for other languages?

7. Which social representations circulate about refugees (and migrants in general) and about their multilingual repertoires at school and in broader social contexts,

and how do these representations influence language policies aimed at their social, educational and linguistic integration?

It could be anticipated that different perceptions of value and linguistic power lead to different language policies, both at national and school level.

8. In addition, what are the online and offline social representations of multilingualism?

Census surveys around the world are indicating increasing linguistic diversity, but is that diversity also reflected in government and educational websites?

9. Research has shown that urban areas are more likely to attract migrants and thus become more multilingual. Do residents in rural and urban areas hold different representations of multilingualism?

And would these representations impact regional language education provision?

10. In a social representation of multilingualism, is there a contradiction between educational practices and migration policy?

For instance, is there a discourse of dominant-language deficit (e.g., without native-like fluency in German or English), while in schools, students are encouraged to learn a second or additional language?

References

Barkhuizen, G., Benson, P., & Chik, A. (2014). *Narrative inquiry in language teaching and learning research.* New York: Routledge.

Blommaert, J. (1999). *Language ideological debates.* Berlin: Mouton de Gruyter.

Castellotti, V., & Moore, D. (2002). *Social representations of languages and teaching.* Strasbourg: Council of Europe.

Chik, A. (2018). Beliefs and practices of foreign language learning: A visual analysis. *Applied Linguistics Review*, 9(2–3), 307–332.

Faneca, R., Araújo e Sá, M.H., & Melo-Pfeifer, S. (2016). Is there a place for heritage languages in the promotion of an intercultural and multilingual education in Portuguese schools? *Language and Intercultural Communication*, 16(1), 44–68.

Kalaja, P., & Melo-Pfeifer, S. (2019). *Visualising multilingual lives: More than words.* Clevedon: Multilingual Matters.

Kramsch, C. (2009). *The multilingual subject.* Oxford: Oxford University Press.

Melo-Pfeifer, S. (2015). Multilingual awareness and heritage language education: Children's multimodal representations of their multilingualism. *Language Awareness*, 24(3), 197–215.

Moore, D. (2006). *Plurilinguisme et école.* Paris: Didier.

26

LANGUAGE TEACHER EDUCATION IN STUDY ABROAD CONTEXTS

John L. Plews

SAINT MARY'S UNIVERSITY, CANADA

Study abroad (SA) is fundamental to my interest in second languages (L2) and formation as a language teacher. I participated in educational tours and exchanges in France and Germany while attending secondary school in England and twice took part in an undergraduate year abroad, working as an English foreign language assistant in France and Germany. I have since taught English as a foreign language in the public and private education sector in England, France, and Germany, and German studies and teacher education at university in Canada. Having earned doctorates in German Studies (while an international student) and Education, and now working as a Professor of German in Canada and the Director of the Canadian Summer School in Germany, I currently publish on L2 SA in relation to curriculum, teaching, learning, and identity. These interests connect directly to when I taught English as a language assistant in locations abroad where my home university took it for granted I would be *exposed* to and therefore effectively develop my additional languages; there, I became concerned about how it had also been assumed that I could teach English simply because it was my mother tongue. I thus became committed to effective L2 teaching and learning.

L2 SA research has focused on measuring students' gains in grammatical and sociolinguistic domains of communicative competence and exploring their intercultural development; there has been a shift from quantitative to qualitative and mixed methods approaches in order to better understand the consistently evident individual variation and complexity of participants' experiences and learning processes (Isabelli-García, Bown, Plews & Dewey, 2018). Because of their ability to capture the complexity of human behavior and the environment in which humans act, qualitative approaches are especially appropriate for investigating the integrated four skills and whole-language nature of language learning and use in SA and the multi-relational, interconnected, and sometimes contradictory dimensions of the immersion experience. SA scholars have called for research to go beyond the predominant focus on aspects of SA in isolation and often (white, middle-class) US students in France or Spanish-speaking countries by investigating a range of participants by source and destination (Kinginger, 2009; Plews & Jackson, 2017), regarding participants as 'whole persons' (Coleman, 2013), accounting for the social networks (Mitchell, Tracy-Ventura & McManus, 2017) and 'multiple roles' (King & Raghuram, 2013) through which they operate, describing program and pedagogical structures (Plews & Misfeldt, 2018), and integrating the post-sojourn (Plews, 2016). Pre- and in-service language teachers are a distinct population in SA that remains significantly under-researched. Certainly, the aforementioned appeals to SA researchers apply equally to this population albeit with further nuances as the topics below suggest.

Choosing a Research Topic

Scholars write about themselves. They write about phenomena related to who they are: defining aspects of their personal histories, events that affected their lives or the lives of family and friends for good or bad, their pastimes or concerns. Such compassion for the self, once elaborated, is offered to others with similar interests and for social enlightenment. *Writing oneself* applies especially to qualitative research where the researcher engages with complex human experiences and is the primary instrument of investigation. While a junior scholar, still shaped by my experiences of coming out and studying modern languages, I wrote about expressions of queerness in other cultures. Later, once a scholar of language education, I began to explore language students' and teachers' identities in relation to the curriculum or SA; my interest in the meanings underlying cultural phenomena and the stories we tell about ourselves combined in my commitment to analyzing the socially constructed codes that students and teachers draw upon to position themselves and make sense of their SA experiences. I suggest language teacher education (LTE) researchers choose topics that connect foremost with their personal histories. LTE scholars interested in SA are very likely former SA participants or current SA facilitators, instructors, or directors.

When teaching students research methodologies – or helping them find a topic for a paper – I invite them first to answer a series of personal questions: What brought you to this course? What have you enjoyed studying so far? What does the discipline mean to you? What are your concerns, frustrations, passions, and hopes? What are your hobbies, jobs, and plans? What current affairs have you paid attention to this week? What have you read about recently? What do you care about right now? What shocks you? Invariably, the beginnings of a sustainable research topic emerge among the responses. Further useful questions for LTE scholars with SA experience are: What worked for you and do you know how or why exactly? What didn't work or was missing from your experience or observations?

Subsequent strategies – talking with colleagues, reading around the topic, stream-of-consciousness writing, brainstorming what one wants to know about the topic, connecting the topic to a specific place, time, population, event, example, component, or issue – concern generating fundamental, pre-existing ideas about the topic and narrowing them down in order to come to the dilemma that necessitates the basic question that one will explore.

Current Research Topics

LTE Source and Destination

Research on language teachers in SA mainly concerns teachers from English-speaking countries in France, Germany, or Spanish-speaking countries. While these few studies require replication for further insight into the development of individuals from such national populations, attention to teachers from a variety of source countries in a variety of destinations would expand and diversify knowledge, enabling comparison and differentiation of best practices between educational cultures. Ethnographic case studies would capture the rich dimensions and discourses of the source and destination settings, while narrative could reveal teacher-participants' processing of experiential learning. Comparative surveys could investigate the design, implementation, and assessment of programs cross-culturally. Single-source-multiple-site or multiple-source-single-site projects would facilitate comparative data for sending or host cultures, respectively. Bi-partisan projects that include all stakeholders (Isabelli-García, et al., 2018) might increase meaningful cross-cultural cooperation and exchange as a research design effect. They could minimize the risk of repeating neo-colonial power relations in programs where Western participants develop their professional capital in non-Western countries.

The Whole Teacher

Teachers in SA require comprehensive treatment as language teachers, language learners, and teaching learners with complex lifeworlds and personal/professional histories. A broad range of motivations and objectives, therefore, will need to be considered, including language, culture, interculturality, pedagogy, teacher self-identity, professionalization, career mobility, heritage, wanderlust, and so forth. Teachers' personal foci will make them more or less receptive of the systemic goals of a SA program. Research providing a fuller picture of teachers as distinct individuals will reduce the risk of drawing conclusions about single aspects of learning or programming based on oversimplified information. It will avoid categorizing participants as static types rather than regarding the crux of their engagement as a telling moment in the breadth of their ongoing lives. In-depth case studies using (L2) journals, documentary techniques, biographical interviews, and narrative analysis are especially appropriate for generating holistic understandings of participants.

The Social is Professional

Language teachers' L2 SA social networks are always potentially and oftentimes explicitly professional and may positively conflate host, cooperating teacher, friend, and mentor, since teachers uniquely operate on intersecting learner and expert planes. Understanding how teacher-participants interact with host-community teachers and educational professionals and sustain such social relationships (alongside at-home networks) is crucial to encouraging linguistic-intercultural and pedagogical development in SA for LTE. Narrative-informed contact surveys and group think-aloud sessions including participating, cooperating, and administrating members of sending and hosting communities would contribute significantly to understanding the processes involved in fostering reciprocally meaningful social/professional networks.

Specialized Programming

While some language teachers take part in SA programs designed specifically with LTE goals in mind, others participate in SA for L2 per se or for generalist teacher education. Either way, greater description, analysis, and comparison of the design of SA for language teachers is needed to ensure the effective facilitation of desired professional outcomes. Researchers need to determine those structures and tasks best promoting L2 teachers' language development, cultural and intercultural awareness, and pedagogical content knowledge so that learning is not left to mere exposure and chance (Plews, Breckenridge & Cambre, 2010). Research and practice will need to consider the role of teachers' identities, learner agency, and host engagement. Especially important are investigations that elaborate claims (Corder, Roskvist, Harvey & Stacey, 2018; Plews, et al., 2010) that professional homestay, interventions, and mentoring can assist teachers' processing of interactional dilemmas and differing worldviews as learning opportunities, critical engagement, and self-reflection. Narrative-informed surveys and interviews optimally collected across two or more rounds of action research and necessarily involving former participants and administrators (Plews & Misfeldt, 2018) would demonstrate design effectiveness.

Post-sojourn Transfer

The greatest social consequence of LTE SA is the transfer of new linguistic, cultural, intercultural, and pedagogical knowledge to the domestic classroom. It is thus exceptionally important to understand the optimal articulation of teachers' lived experiences of LTE SA with their ongoing work in domestic curricula and their students' learning. Yet this research is the most lacking. Studies that combine pre-, during-, and ongoing post-sojourn classroom observations and longitudinal teacher self-assessment would be effective for tracing structural connections between LTE SA and new or enhanced classroom pedagogy. Such research would focus on teachers' (evolving) actions and their students' (more elaborate) understandings over time. (In this respect, it might be useful to investigate teachers after chaperoning students on SA.)

Research Questions

1. What are the similarities and differences of L2 teachers' experiences on LTE SA programs developed by institutions across one country or in different countries?
2. What is it like, organizationally and academically, to operate a SA program for L2 teachers from one country and with one L1 compared to a program for teachers from various countries and with different L1s?
3. What are the various perspectives of L2 teacher-participants as compared to those of program directors or host teachers, staff, and administrators?

These first three questions take a cross-cultural viewpoint and serve the field by providing overviews while promoting awareness of distinct educational cultures, (inter)cultural sensitivity, and diversity.

4. What is it like for source L2 teacher-participants and host cooperating teacher-participants to work together and how might source teacher-participants' professional learning opportunities also benefit host teacher-participants and their students and schools?

This fourth question takes a transcultural stance and moves away from a neo-colonial research dynamic by focusing on mutual relations and assuming the community accessed to be also a community served.

5. How do L2 teachers go about squaring the professional development goals set for them by education institutions with their personally determined general and professional objectives on SA, or vice versa?
6. What is it like for L2 teachers to develop their personal L2 repertoires and L2 self-identities in specifically professional SA contexts, networks, and homestay?
7. In which ways do L2 teachers' (L1) home lives and networks affect the L2 SA (given the pervasiveness of contemporary communication technology)?

These three questions contribute to a more nuanced picture of teacher-participants by centering on individuals' negotiation of professional, personal, linguistic, cultural, and practical tensions, preferences, and obligations.

8. Which program structures, tasks or interventions, and mentoring strategies most effectively promote L2, intercultural, or pedagogical learning for L2 teachers (and what are the most informative assessment practices in each instance)?

By inquiring after program design, this question enhances program developers' and directors' specialist knowledge. It could be treated wholly or separated by component or desired outcome.

9. What is it like for L2 teachers to implement their SA L2, intercultural, and/or pedagogical learning once working again in domestic schools (i.e., can they maintain and integrate it)?
10. What is it like for domestic students to learn in classes taught by former LTE SA teacher-participants?

These final two questions undergird the very raison-d'être for LTE SA by addressing all-important ongoing effects.

References

Coleman, J.A. (2013). Researching whole people and whole lives. In C. Kinginger (Ed.), *Social and cultural aspects of language learning in study abroad* (pp. 17–44). Philadelphia: John Benjamins.

Corder, D., Roskvist, A., Harvey, S., & Stacey, K. (2018). Language teachers on study abroad programmes: The characteristics and strategies of those most likely to increase their intercultural communicative competence. In J.L. Plews & K. Misfeldt (Eds.), *Second language study abroad programming, pedagogy, and participant engagement* (pp. 257–297). Basingstoke, UK: Palgrave Macmillan.

Isabelli-García, C., Bown, J., Plews, J.L., & Dewey, D.P. (2018). Language learning and study abroad. A state-of-the-art review. *Language Teaching*, 51(4), 439–484.

King, R., & Raghuram, P. (2013). International student migration: Mapping the field and new research agendas. *Population, Space and Place*, 19(2), 127–137.

Kinginger, C. (2009). *Language learning and study abroad. A critical reading of research*. Basingstoke, UK: Palgrave Macmillan.

Mitchell, R., Tracy-Ventura, N., & McManus, K. (2017). *Anglophone students abroad: Identity, social relationships and language learning*. London: Routledge.

Plews, J.L. (2016). The post-sojourn in study abroad research – Another frontier. *Language and culture after study abroad. Comparative and International Education*, 45(2), 1–13.

Plews, J.L., Breckenridge, Y., & Cambre, M.C. (2010). Mexican English teachers' experiences of international professional development in Canada: A narrative analysis. *e-FLT*, 7(1), 5–20.

Plews, J.L., & Jackson, J. (2017). Introduction to the special issue: Study abroad to, from, and within Asia. *Study Abroad Research in Second Language Acquisition and International Education*, 2(2), 137–146.

Plews, J.L., & Misfeldt, K. (2018). Introduction: Shifting attention to second language study abroad programming, pedagogy, and participant engagement. In J.L. Plews & K. Misfeldt (Eds.), *Second language study abroad programming, pedagogy, and participant engagement* (pp. 1–21). Basingstoke, UK: Palgrave Macmillan.

27

STUDY ABROAD FOR LANGUAGE TEACHERS

John Macalister
VICTORIA UNIVERSITY OF WELLINGTON, NEW ZEALAND

I regard myself as something of an accidental academic. It was on a whim that I applied for my first position as an English language teacher and, to be honest, it was the attraction of living and working abroad rather than the teaching itself that triggered the application. I suspect that many of us begin our careers in ELT for such reasons. But for me it has turned out to be a wonderful career, allowing me to live, teach and work with teachers in many parts of the world, including Kiribati, Namibia, Thailand, Cambodia, and, of course, New Zealand, and to develop a deep interest in language teacher education. It has also taken me, through curriculum related work, for shorter periods to countries as diverse as Peru, Vanuatu, and Saudi Arabia. Given this background it is perhaps no surprise that – as a result of indulging another whim, to do a PhD for personal interest – when I ended up working in a university as a fully fledged academic my research interests spanned a broad area. Teachers' work, after all, tends to encompass a breadth of concerns. Thus my research spans language teaching methodology, language teacher education, language curriculum studies, and language policy. Always, however, a central concern has been how to communicate research findings to the classroom. For that reason, I want to focus in this chapter on an area of research I have been working on for several years. It comes by various names including trans-national education, mobility programs, and study abroad, and can vary in many aspects, including the length of the experience, from mere days to years. This is not the place to analyze the terminology, and for convenience I will use *study abroad* and specify that I am thinking of teacher education programs that contain an element of this. I include both pre-service and in-service (i.e., teachers pursuing postgraduate study abroad).

Choosing a Research Topic

So, you now have some idea of why I call myself an accidental academic. And academics do research. However, it should not be academics alone who do research. Research in ELT is not something to be done *to* teachers and *for* teachers; it should also be done *by* teachers. So, when thinking about how to select a research topic, I am primarily thinking of teachers wanting to undertake a project. It is during professional development opportunities that they may start to think about possible topics.

As part of my role as an academic engaged in both teaching and research, I attend conferences. Conferences are a common form of professional development for teachers. Yet occasionally I find myself wondering how different a TESOL conference is from, say, a physics conference. I imagine that in a discipline such as physics researchers start from a shared basis of knowledge, and that their research seeks to test, build on and extend that knowledge. At TESOL conferences, on the other hand, and I apologize in advance if this causes offence, I worry quite often at what I hear. Too often presenters seem unaware of relevant research findings about effective teaching. My worry is that, because they are standing up and presenting as experts, people may believe them. I wonder whether, in fact, they are doing harm. And so I would suggest that a good first step to choosing a research topic is to be a critical listener at conferences. This pre-supposes having some knowledge of the presenter's topic, but teachers are busy people. We need to be realistic and accept that they do not always have time to keep up with the latest research. But even without such knowledge there are simple questions you could ask yourself. Is this personal opinion, or is there evidence supporting it? Would this work in my context? How could I make this work in my context? Would this help my learners meet their needs, or goals? Would this be a better use of time than what I currently do? How will I know?

It is during in-service language teacher education, another form of professional development, that teachers have a chance to develop knowledge about a topic. As I write this, I have just finished teaching a postgraduate course about teaching reading and writing to 30 or so teachers working from early childhood through to tertiary and adult levels. As well as introducing them to current research, one of my goals is to encourage them to be critical readers and critical listeners so that they may, later, go on to be teacher researchers in their own classrooms and contexts. A tool I have adapted to facilitate this is Gary Barkhuizen's QUEST approach (Barkhuizen, 2002). While it is true that not all the questions the teachers on my course have generated are of high quality, some are truly insightful and can be a starting point for a small research project.

These suggestions for choosing a research topic have been fairly general. They refer mainly to the pedagogical knowledge that forms part of language teacher education. In the next section I become more specific and suggest topics for teacher researchers about teachers' engagement in study abroad.

Research Topics

The Rationale for Study Abroad

This is a big question, not least because it can involve a significant financial commitment, whether from the state, an institution, or an individual. It is a question that can be asked in at least two different ways. First, the goal of the study abroad experience needs to be clear. It could be intended to develop language proficiency, or pedagogical knowledge, or inter-cultural awareness. All have been claimed as benefits from study abroad, and it is not that one is inherently superior to another. However, having a clear goal, and the various stakeholders sharing an understanding of that goal, would seem to be a prerequisite for success. In my own work I have found that this is not necessarily the case.

The second way in which the topic can be explored is to question the appropriateness of study abroad models that privilege Western research and researchers. For better or for worse, study abroad in language teacher education remains predominantly centripetal, with teachers and students from the Kachruvian outer and expanding circles being drawn in to the inner circle. This has, of course, been critiqued. A distinction I remain fond of when thinking about this is that proposed by Adrian Holliday (1994); the distinction between the theories and research emanating from Britain, Australasia, and North America and ELT practice in primary, secondary and tertiary contexts throughout the world.

Bringing the Local into the Classroom Abroad

Wherever language teacher education occurs, making it relevant to the local context is generally essential. This is more challenging in a study abroad context, for obvious reasons. Teacher educators in the study abroad setting may not be familiar with, or particularly well-informed, about local contexts. It is difficult to make the general particular, to make it relevant, if you are guessing about the context. Thus, there is a need for teacher educators to find out about, to develop some understanding of, where their students will be teaching in the future, and to ensure such information informs curriculum design.

Creating the Conditions for Change

Lortie's notion of the 'apprenticeship of observation' (Lortie, 1975) is widely known, and the idea that teacher education programs should be change programs is not new. Both link to the field of language teacher cognition research. From this research we know that change is often not the result; beliefs may not be substantially changed, practices may not reflect new understandings of pedagogical effectiveness. Of course, teacher education is not going to stop because of this, but we do need to pay more attention to the features of a program that challenge existing beliefs as a means of promoting change. Some sort of change is, after all, presumably the expectation of those who make the financial investment in study abroad. In order to effect this change, it is essential to have an understanding of what those on study abroad think, know, and believe at the outset of the program.

Dealing with Constraints and Resistance

At the end of the study abroad experience, students generally find themselves back in the home environment, where their new-found knowledge and skills may not be as welcome, or as easy to give effect to, as they might have hoped. Once they are in the classroom, contextual factors may conspire against innovation and change, even when there is an expectation that teachers who have experienced study abroad will become agents of change. Understanding these challenges, and putting in place support to mitigate them, is a topic that has been neglected for too long.

Measuring Impact

A point already made is that those who invest in study abroad expect a return on their investment. My, perhaps overly cynical, impression is that often those who report on the impact of such programs have a vested interest in reporting positively. A more charitable interpretation might be that there is an over-reliance on self-reporting in such evaluations, and that different methodological choices might lead to more convincing results. In a sense this is simply an expansion of the question that teachers should always be asking themselves: How do I know that how and what I am teaching is helping my learners learn?

As my focus here is on the teacher researcher, the teacher educator wanting to be more effective, it should be no surprise that my methodological suggestions rely on understanding the students better. For data creation from large numbers of students, a narrative frame is an excellent tool, as I found in my work with seamen in Kiribati (Macalister, 2012). Working with smaller numbers of students, interviews are a powerful tool for eliciting rich data, as long as they are done well (Mann, 2011). These may result in case studies that illuminate the topic you are investigating. Indeed, as a means of linking research to practice, case studies are hard to beat. They can be brought into the classroom, either as individual narratives representing a particular experience, or as a narrative constructed from multiple individual experiences, and used to promote discussion and reflection (Polkinghorne, 1995).

Research Questions

1. Should study abroad be a part of a teacher education program?

This is a fundamental question that should promote considerations of context appropriateness.

2. How do students view and value the language they will be teaching?

Through narrative research, the relationship between the language, the individual, and her or his immediate and wider society can be explored.

3. How can teacher educators develop understanding of the target educational context?

Teacher educators may lack first-hand experience but they can develop understanding by gathering student stories, either through their pedagogy requiring regular classroom sharing, or through a more structured research approach.

4. How do students on study abroad programs engage with the local society?

The local society is not just beyond the classroom. Direct or indirect observations, interviews and case studies are appropriate here, but the value of interviews will be enhanced if participants maintain some record of interactions they have had.

5. How does target language proficiency affect engagement with the local society?

Having some measure of students' language proficiency has multiple benefits, including the nature of input in the classroom. Such quantitative data allows us to interpret the qualitative with a different lens.

6. What constraints and affordances affect study abroad students' engagement with the local society?

Identifying and understanding these factors though case studies and interviews can lead to improved study abroad programs.

7. What are the optimal features of a study abroad program?

The specific answers may vary from situation to situation, but the application of a principled approach to program design should result in an effective study abroad experience.

8. What formal opportunities for language development exist in a study abroad program?

The general answer seems to be none. This question suggests that's the wrong answer.

9. How can the impact of study abroad be evaluated?

Actual classroom observation and spending time with teachers after they have returned home would be ideal, even if not always financially possible.

10. What forms of support reinforce the study abroad learning when back in the home society?

Case studies of teachers once they have returned to their home context can illuminate challenges teachers may face if they wish to introduce change or to innovate. As potential agents of change they deserve to feel supported, not abandoned.

References

Barkhuizen, G. (2002). The QUEST for an approach to guided critical reading and writing. *Prospect*, 17(3), 19–28.

Holliday, A. (1994). *Appropriate methodology and social context*. Cambridge: Cambridge University Press.

Lortie, D.C. (1975). *Schoolteacher: A sociological study*. Chicago: University of Chicago Press.

Macalister, J. (2012). Narrative frames and needs analysis. *System*, 40(1), 120–128.

Mann, S. (2011). A critical review of qualitative interviews in applied linguistics. *Applied Linguistics*, 32(1), 6–24.

Polkinghorne, D.E. (1995). Narrative configuration in qualitative analysis. *Qualitative Studies in Education*, 8(1), 5–23.

28
GENERATING ACTION RESEARCH TOPICS

Anne Burns

UNIVERSITY OF NEW SOUTH WALES, AUSTRALIA

In the early 1990s I began working at a national research center, funded by the Australian government. Apart from conducting research, this center was responsible for innovative teacher education for teachers working with adult immigrants across Australia. Many were teaching students who were former refugees with limited educational backgrounds and little previous English learning. One challenge was not to be perceived by teachers as 'ivory tower' researchers distant from their classroom concerns.

Besides 'basic' and 'applied' research, we regarded 'practitioner research' (Brindley, 1990) as an important way to reach out to teachers. The close links of action research (AR) with practice makes it accessible to classroom practitioners. Also, although quantitative methodologies can be adopted (Burns, 2010), AR lends itself readily to qualitative and narrative approaches which many teachers find appealing. It falls within an exploratory/interpretive paradigm, seeking evidence that deepens understanding of a research issue, without expecting a definitive outcome. Moreover, incorporating AR would allow us to work in close collaboration with teachers and to feed rich insights from the classroom into the formulation of curriculum policy, research and practice.

For over 15 years I worked with groups of adult immigrant language teachers across the country who investigated particular topics or themes selected from teachers' suggestions. My experiences of facilitating this initiative became a formative learning process that enabled me to acquire deeper understanding of the principles of AR, and also to continue conducting my own research with teachers who did AR.

Strategies for Choosing a Topic

Action researchers I work with have often had a classroom issue in mind for some time that helps determine their research topic. It usually reflects a gap between 'envisioned reality' and the actual reality of their classrooms. Their research aims to bridge that gap. For action researchers uncertain how to pin down a topic, I suggest various strategies:

1. Keep a diary of teaching/learning activities for a convenient time (e.g., a week, a month). What questions or issues emerge about teaching, learning, program management, administration? Do they focus on you, your learners, colleagues, administrators?
2. Spend five minutes listing issues that have puzzled you for some time. Select the most interesting. Place it in the center of a page and circle it. For five minutes write down anywhere on the page any ideas that relate to the central one. Include questions, concerns, hypothetical statements, personal hunches and images. Use colored markers to connect similar concepts. Are there patterns in relation to certain areas?: e.g., topic/problem, age, gender, type of subject, type of educational location, type of interaction, materials, tasks, texts.
3. Select an AR article. List any questions suggested for further research. What questions are not suggested? Which of these questions appeal to you?
4. Brainstorm responses to these 'starter' statements:
   - I don't know enough about how students/colleagues …
   - My students/colleagues don't seem to … What can I learn about this?
   - I'd like to find out more about the way students …
5. Observe a typical work situation: e.g., a classroom, staff room, teacher training session, course you teach, library. If possible observe over a period (e.g., one week) rather than one session. What research questions emerge as a result of your observations? Use suggestion number 2 above to reflect further.
6. Survey your colleagues on what they consider the 'hot issues' or key unanswered questions in their classrooms. Do their perspectives match yours?
7. Look through the recent contents pages/abstracts in journals that publish AR (e.g., *ELT Journal, English Australia Journal, Profile, TESOL Journal*). What are some 'hot' AR topics?
8. Consult some professional association research agendas (e.g., TESOL, 2014). What issues/topics do they identify for practitioner research?

Current Topics

Your own Classroom Issues

Essentially, language classrooms are dedicated to the major skills of listening, speaking, reading, and writing, which provide perennial areas for AR. Several of my doctoral researchers selected topics on dilemmas in teaching these skills. Two useful examples are Siegel (2015) and McPherson (Burns & McPherson, 2017).

Siegel researched listening strategy instruction in a Japanese intermediate class, because of his dissatisfaction with the textbook comprehension-question approach he used and a student's request to know 'how to listen.' Introducing various strategies, his qualitative AR explored his own, a colleague's, and his students' responses through three cycles. He also identified factors contributing to the program's success. Various data-collection methods – questionnaires, group interviews, classroom observations, pre-/post-tests, and research journals – provided rich perspectives feeding into new research cycles.

In Australia, McPherson taught refugee beginners with very low literacy. She treated her students as co-researchers, developing a reading program responding to their learning preferences, their preferred materials, and their identified out-of-class life goals. Eschewing formal interviews or surveys, her own observations and research journal documented her students' daily reactions, body language, and informal interactive comments on her 'trial-and-error' activities. Her AR design was highly exploratory and iterative, as she fine-tuned her practices to students' expressed needs.

Other valuable AR on classroom issues would be investigating materials/technology, teaching approaches (e.g., task-based, genre-based), or assessment (formative, assessment-for-learning).

Teachers Becoming Researchers

One area of continuing interest is teachers' experiences of and responses to becoming researchers. Increasingly, across the world there is growing pressure on English language teachers, particularly at tertiary levels, to conduct research. Many accredited university courses now require an AR component. Teachers may also volunteer to do AR for continuing professional development.

Studies on teachers' experiences adopt a variety of methods. Survey research, where teachers are invited to provide responses to various qualitative statements and/or to offer open-ended responses to questions can capture the views of relatively large numbers at a specific time period. More in-depth insights, however, are obtained through a 'constructivist' case study approach (e.g., Wyatt's 2014 study in Oman) where the researcher develops contextualized and grounded theoretical perspectives by drawing on a combination of tools such as interview, observation, recorded workshop discussions, and reflective journal writing. These studies benefit from longitudinal contact with participants in order to track their emotional responses and skills development over time and identify what transformations are occurring. Although several studies now exist, many are located in first-world or relatively well-resourced locations. More studies in broader international locations would illuminate teachers' actual experiences of conducting AR.

Action Research and Teacher Identity

A few recent studies have investigated how conducting AR reshapes language teacher identities (LTI). These studies are more specifically focused than in the second topic discussed above; they track newly emerging identity constructions, showing the impact becoming researchers has on teachers' sense of themselves. AR can lead to 'disequilibrium' as teachers experience significant personal and professional changes, as well as unpredictable shifts in identity and self-agency.

Here, Trent (2010) is an early study, grounded in theories of LTI as practice (action) and discourse (negotiation of meaning). He taught a pre-service EFL Bachelor course in Hong Kong and, after they conducted AR, interviewed six of the participants through semi-structured interviews. An issue he foregrounds is that he was their tutor; to guard against influencing responses, he assured them that participation was voluntary with no bearing on grades. Interviews occurred after assignments were submitted. More research of this type could illuminate the tensions between teaching perceptions and evidence from teachers' research. Emerging researcher identity may conflict with teacher identity, but also lead to profound professional development and identity changes. More studies, possibly incorporating stimulated recall or reflective journals, could show how teachers navigate boundaries between teacher and researcher communities and the emotional struggles involved.

Support Needs of Teacher Researchers

One area of continuing importance is what kinds of support teachers need to conduct AR successfully. Teachers are not necessarily trained to do research and can face challenges when adopting a researcher role. Two lines of research suggest themselves here. One relates to investigating the perspectives of teachers themselves on their experiences (or not) of receiving support, such as guidance from a mentor, collaboration with colleagues, time allocation, resources/technology, assistance with publishing, or even financial contributions. Xie's (2015) autobiographical narrative of what facilitated and hindered her teacher research in China offers an interesting methodological approach. Case studies, interviews (face-to-face and/or virtually), and video/audio-journals are alternative methods.

The other possibility is studying facilitators' experiences of supporting AR. A recent example is Burns, Westmacott and Hidalgo Ferrer (2016), who mentored a small group of Chilean tertiary teachers. They drew on observational fieldnotes and teachers' evaluations from an introductory workshop, recordings of regular collaborative meetings, and their own reflective responses and discussions as they facilitated the program during its first year. A notable feature of this study was that it traced facilitator experiences from the very first stages and identified what could be learned about initiating and supporting an AR program.

Sustaining Action Research

There is almost no research on how AR is sustained over time and under what circumstances teachers continue to capitalize on it. Clearly individual teacher motivation to continue researching is important, but wider sociocultural factors also play a vital part. Although the literature often mentions that institutional support is crucial, few studies have actually investigated how it interacts with sustaining teacher AR over time.

One recent study by Edwards and Burns (2016) in Australia adopted a socio-constructivist qualitative case study approach, whereby participants create contextually-based meaning. It drew on 18 AR reports published by teachers of international students over three years to design a Likert-scale survey with additional space for qualitative responses. Ten semi-structured interviews were then conducted to identify participating action researchers' micro (their own, colleagues', students') and macro (institutional) responses about how and why they thought impact was sustained (or not) over time. If demands continue to be placed on teachers to develop research skills as part of their professional learning much more research is needed to pinpoint how institutions contribute to sustaining teachers' research efforts. This type of research also needs to investigate relationships between AR and student learning and achievement.

Research Questions

1. What teaching activities/strategies will improve students' speaking, reading, grammar, or vocabulary, etc.?
2. How does using a particular teaching approach, for example, process writing, self-assessment, impact on student learning/achievement?

These are two broad question that enable action researchers to get started. Frequently, AR questions are refined and redirected as the research proceeds.

3. What are teachers' lived experiences of conducting AR?

This question enables the researcher to track teachers' experiences and ideally should be conducted longitudinally.

4. What do teachers learn from participating in AR?

A study based on this question would show what changes occur in teachers' knowledge; e.g., about research, their learners, language learning, themselves as teachers.

5. What factors facilitate or hinder teachers' ability to conduct AR?

This question illuminates what assists or challenges teachers when they conduct AR. Either a longitudinal or a retrospective study could be done.

6. What impact does doing AR have on the identity formation of teachers as researchers?

A study driven by this question would allow researchers to trace the personal struggles, emotions, changes, and achievements experienced by teachers as they move into a new role.

7. What kinds of support do teachers need as they become researchers?

This question helps researchers identify what facilitates successful AR by teachers and what stands in the way of such support.

8. What are teachers' major challenges in doing research and how do they seek to overcome them?

This is a double question with a related focus. The researcher could break the question into two inter-related research goals. The study would focus on what impedes teacher AR and what individual actions teachers take to address their own challenges.

9. What sustainable practices do teachers gain from doing AR?

This question would allow for identifying whether teachers continue to do AR or, if not, how/whether they maintain what they have learned from doing AR in their teaching.

10. What are school leaders' opinions about sustaining AR for their teachers?

This is a question that would enable researchers to identify what place AR has in ongoing institutional development and what role school leaders play (if any) in sustaining it.

References

Brindley, G. (1990). Towards a research agenda for TESOL. *Prospect*, 6(1), 7–26.
Burns, A. (2010). *Doing action research in English language teaching: A guide for practitioners*. New York: Routledge.
Burns, A., & McPherson, P. (2017). Action research as iterative design: Implications for English language education research. In S-A. Mirhosseini (Ed.), *Reflections on qualitative research in language and literacy education* (pp. 105–120). Cham, Switzerland: Springer.

Burns, A., Westmacott, A., & Hidalgo Ferrer, A. (2016). Initiating an action research programme for university EFL teachers: Early experiences and responses. *Iranian Journal of Language Teaching Research*, 4(3), 55–73.

Edwards, E., & Burns, A. (2016). Language teacher action research: Achieving sustainability. *English Language Teaching Journal*, 70(1), 6–15.

Siegel, J. (2015). *Exploring listening strategy instruction through action research*. London: Palgrave Macmillan.

TESOL (2014). *TESOL Research Agenda*. Alexandria, Virginia: TESOL International. Retrieved 26 May 2018 from www.tesol.org/docs/default-source/pdf/2014_tesol-research-agenda.pdf?sfvrsn=2.

Trent, J. (2010). Teacher education as identity construction: Insights from action research. *Journal of Education for Teaching*, 36(2), 153–168.

Wyatt, M. (2014). Action research on a teacher education programme. *ELT Research*, 29, 5–8.

Xie, J. (2015). Learning to do teacher research independently: Challenges and solutions. In S. Borg & H. Santiago Sanchez (Eds.), *International perspectives on teacher research* (pp. 47–56). Basingstoke: Palgrave Macmillan.

29
RESEARCHING TEACHER RESEARCH

Daniel Xerri

UNIVERSITY OF MALTA, MALTA

As an academic working at Malta's main university, I am expected to devote one third of my professional duties to research. One of the reasons why I was expected to hold a PhD when I applied for this position is that this degree is meant to equip people with the knowledge and skills required to do academic research. However, prior to enrolling on a doctoral program I had already worked as an English language teacher in secondary schools. This is where I learnt a lot about research and was encouraged to engage in it.

Despite the fact that research is part of my job description, my interest and willingness to engage in research were nurtured by my experiences in the secondary school classroom. My graduate education prior to becoming a teacher did provide me with an understanding of research principles and methodology, and working on my Master's dissertation enabled me to put into practice the theory I had learnt in my lectures. However, it is only once I started teaching that I realized I had to do classroom research in order to find answers to my questions. These questions varied in nature but mostly revolved around issues concerning my practices as a teacher, my students, and the context in which I taught. Going beyond the research definitions and requirements imposed by graduate education, I found I could experiment with the way I looked for answers. In the ten years I spent in the English language classroom, I engaged in teacher research, which Borg (2013) defines as practitioners' systematic investigation into their own contexts for the purpose of learning more about their practices. Teacher research became one of the main means by which I could develop professionally.

In the process of doing research in my classroom, I became interested in knowing more about other teachers' practices as researchers, especially in terms of how this contributes to their professional development. This led me to become involved in the Research Special Interest Group (ReSIG) within the International

Association of Teachers of English as a Foreign Language (IATEFL). As part of ReSIG, I became aware of how teachers around the world were conducting research in their own classrooms as a means to understand what they and their students do as part of English language teaching and learning. Once I became a university lecturer, I made teacher research one of my areas of interest. I felt that this was a natural choice given my experience of doing teacher research and my professional responsibilities within a graduate program devoted to continuing language teacher education.

Choosing a Research Topic

Researchers interested in investigating teacher research can use a variety of strategies to identify a research topic. Some of these are discussed in methodology textbooks on educational research (e.g., Cohen, Manion & Morrison, 2018); however, in my experience it is helpful to start by considering what one is genuinely curious to know more about. Curiosity leads researchers to ask broad questions about teacher research that can then be narrowed down to topics with a clear focus (O'Leary, 2004). The broad questions are essential since they are driven by something that puzzles researchers and leads them to explore different facets of it. Once researchers have made a note of these questions, they can organize them into different groups according to their main themes, identify any overlapping questions, scrap questions that are impossible to narrow down, and think about which questions lend themselves to being subdivided into narrower foci. Upon selecting a specific focus, researchers can draft more questions related to it, always bearing in mind that the questions asked at this stage need to be answerable. In order to determine whether a question is answerable, researchers have to consider the resources, time, and participants at their disposal. If these conditions are not favorable, then it will be difficult to answer a question about the chosen research topic.

Another strategy that researchers can use to choose research topics related to the field of teacher research is to tap the participants' own curiosity and experiences. Language teachers who do research are not only interested in finding answers to the questions they have about their practices, students, and contexts. On a metacognitive level, they are most probably aware of why they do research and of the benefits that doing research entails. They most likely rationalize what they do and have chosen teacher research in preference over or to complement other modes of professional development. Just as they have questions about their language teaching practices, they also have questions about their research practices. Recording and exploring these questions collaboratively can prove useful to researchers interested in knowing more about teacher research because they can lead them to pinpoint which topics to investigate further. While the method of narrowing the focus of the questions is the same as the one described above, the means by which researchers arrive at a topic are different. Rather than starting from their own puzzles about teacher research, they start from what puzzles those engaged in the activity have. In this way, researchers avoid always having to impose their questions on those at the chalk-face. This seems vital given that teacher-researchers in particular deserve to be respected as professionals who are deeply interested in asking questions.

Current Research Topics

Teacher research as a field has been explored by a number of researchers over the past few decades. My work with teacher educators, teacher association leaders, academics, and teacher-researchers has led me to identify five key topics in this field that merit further research (Xerri & Pioquinto, 2018).

Teachers' Conceptions of Research

The way teachers conceive of research is a fundamental topic because different conceptions of research have implications for their engagement in research. Despite forming the basis of a study published a decade ago (Borg, 2009), the topic remains highly current. As Reynolds (cited in Xerri, 2017, p. 12) says, "the main obstacle is simply the understanding of what research is. It's an understanding that can disempower the teacher; it makes them feel deficient and dependent on the outside expert." Borg (2009) studied teachers' conceptions of research by means of questionnaire responses in addition to follow-up written and interview data. The latter two kinds of qualitative data are especially useful given that they allow researchers to delve deeply into participants' understanding of a topic. Asking participants to produce analogies for research or to provide examples of it might help them concretize an activity that they might consider somewhat abstract. Analyzing written and spoken definitions provides insight into the ways teachers think about research. It can potentially indicate why their conceptions of research might discourage them from pursuing research as a form of professional development.

Research and Teacher Identity

Given the growing importance of the notion of teacher identity in language teaching (Pennington & Richards, 2016), the relationship between research and a teacher's professional identity constitutes another current topic. According to Graves (cited in Xerri, 2018a, p. 38), quite often "Teacher and researcher are not seen as part of the same identity... Teachers may see research as separate from them... Understanding that research is a possible part of your identity as a teacher is important." Researchers interested in this topic may use interviews, reflective writing, and narrative inquiry in order to examine how teachers describe themselves as professionals and what role research plays in their identity. Comparing accounts of teachers who see research as completely alien to their professional identity with accounts of those who position themselves as teacher-researchers would help to throw light on why some teachers distance themselves from research whereas others embrace it.

Supporting Teacher Research

Traditionally, support for teacher researchers was most often described in terms of providing them with the time to do research. However, at present the notion of support is being expanded to include the idea that teachers need to be trusted as professionals who are capable of doing meaningful research (Hanks, 2018). Moreover, support also means that "teachers need to be encouraged to see what they already do as research and shown how they can build on their existing practice to improve and share it" (Smith, cited in Xerri, 2018b, p. 39). In this regard, it would be helpful if researchers were to produce case studies of teacher-researchers who receive support via inside and outside mentors, and who feel empowered to do research because of a school environment that respects them as research-engaged professionals. Inside mentors are usually colleagues who have some research experience while outside mentors are most often professional researchers or academics.

Teachers' Research Literacy

Another notion that is currently being broadened is that of research literacy. While in the past this was sometimes narrowly defined in terms of the knowledge and skills that teachers require in order to do research, nowadays research literacy is understood as encompassing the knowledge, skills, attitudes and beliefs needed to engage *with* and *in* research. Besides the technical competence to ask research questions, design research instruments, and analyze data, teachers also need to know how to critically engage with research, as well as to have appropriate attitudes and beliefs in relation to it. Researchers interested in this topic may choose to observe training sessions focusing on research literacy in order to develop a better understanding of which aspects are given most attention. Interviews with teacher educators and classroom practitioners may also yield insights into how participants describe the training gap.

Benefits and Challenges

While a lot has been written about the benefits of and challenges to teacher research, this topic remains relevant due to the fact that teacher research is a highly contextualized activity. This means that the benefits accrued by a teacher (and learners) from doing classroom research in one specific context might not necessarily be experienced by another teacher (and learners) in another context. The same applies to the challenges experienced by teachers in different contexts. The literature discusses some generic benefits and challenges; however, in order to fully understand what these entail for a teacher-researcher it is crucial to use qualitative tools that enable one to probe what each participant's experience of doing research translates into. In-depth interviews and ethnographic research might serve a useful purpose in this respect.

Research Questions

After having considered the currency and value of five key topics within the field of teacher research, it is now worth looking at some questions that researchers may pose in order to explore each topic further.

1. What are teachers' conceptions of research?
2. What do teachers compare research to?

Researchers interested in learning more about how teachers think of research may consider examining participants' conceptions of research, as well as the activities or objects they compare it to. Such comparisons can help them to concretize something they might otherwise consider abstract.

3. How do teacher-researchers describe themselves?
4. What role does research play in teachers' professional lives?

These two questions enable researchers to interrogate the notion of teacher identity with respect to research by looking at how teachers describe themselves and the role research plays in their lives.

5. What kind of support do teacher researchers receive?
6. What are the attitudes of school managers towards teacher research?

These two questions are suitable for researchers wishing to investigate the support that teacher-researchers are provided with, whether of a material or emotional nature, by their colleagues, institutions or beyond.

7. Which aspects of research literacy does language teacher education focus on?
8. How is teachers' research literacy developed by means of language teacher education?

Researchers examining the role of language teacher education in developing teachers' research literacy may seek to identify the aspects that are focused on, as well as the techniques employed to do so.

9. What are the benefits of teacher research for the participants?
10. What are the challenges of teacher research for the participants?

These two questions enable researchers to study the benefits and challenges that participants in a specific context experience with respect to teacher research.

References

Borg, S. (2009). English language teachers' conceptions of research. *Applied Linguistics*, 30(3), 358–388.

Borg, S. (2013). *Teacher research in language teaching: A critical analysis*. Cambridge: Cambridge University Press.

Cohen, L., Manion, L., & Morrison, K. (2018). *Research methods in education (8th edition)*. London and New York: Routledge.

Hanks, J. (2018). Supporting language teachers as they engage in research. *ETAS Journal*, 35(3), 48–50.

O'Leary, Z. (2004). *The essential guide to doing research*. London: Sage.

Pennington, M. C., & Richards, J. (2016). Teacher identity in language teaching: Integrating personal, contextual, and professional factors. *RELC Journal*, 47(1), 5–23.

Xerri, D. (2017). 'Teachers want to know answers to questions': Dudley Reynolds on teacher research. *ETAS Journal*, 34(3), 12–13.

Xerri, D. (2018a). 'Generating knowledge for themselves': Kathleen Graves on teacher research. *ETAS Journal*, 35(3), 38–39.

Xerri, D. (2018b). 'Research by teachers for teachers': Richard Smith on teacher research. *ETAS Journal*, 35(2), 38–39.

Xerri, D., & Pioquinto, C. (Eds.). (2018). *Becoming research literate: Supporting teacher research in English language teaching*. Sursee: ETAS Journal Publications.

30

TEACHER RESEARCHERS

Kenan Dikilitaş

BAHÇEŞEHIR UNIVERSITY, TURKEY

I have been an English language teacher for almost 25 years and a teacher educator for about 15 of these, with my whole career in Turkey, where I was born and grew up. Despite very limited overseas travel opportunities, I have been able to establish an international network for projects and research, mainly using online facilities. My main area of interest is language teacher education, particularly in-service teacher development though action/teacher research. For the past ten years, I have dedicated a great deal of time to mentoring teacher researchers across Turkey, and organized conferences in my role as the main contact for IATEFL ReSIG (Research Special Interest Group). In collaboration with various co-editors, I have also edited and published teacher researchers' accounts, hoping that these would lead to the further development of the genre of teacher research. I have always believed in the key role of teacher-led inquiry in sustainable development and learning, and particularly in promoting motivation and autonomy, as well as in improving teaching practices. All these experiences have helped me to develop research perspectives on teachers' practical knowledge development, and to theorize teacher learning through multiple lenses, taking an emic approach, with which I have a strong affinity.

Topic Selection in Teacher Research

Topic selection for qualitative research in language teacher education is a challenging process and involves several issues that deserve consideration. The process has traditionally consisted of identifying a gap that has previously been insufficiently explored, if at all, and addressing it through innovative research methods (Nassaji, 2018). However, it does not necessarily mean abandoning the topic if it has already been investigated, but rather, finding novel approaches with different robust and innovative methods to generate data and evidence.

I suggest the following initial questions to consider: (1) Have you observed teachers while engaging in research? (2) Have you yourself engaged in either doing teacher research or in mentoring others in the process? This is key to bringing an emic perspective into the research process. (3) Do you know any teacher researchers? Have you held informal discussions or interviewed them before? These experiences are important for those intending to conduct research into teacher research, since they can increase awareness of the practical dimensions that theoretical aspects of teacher learning must support. In other words, the complex interplay between theory and practice is key to creating a close connection to local practices (Kumaravadivelu, 2001).

From my own contextualized, local experience of teacher research as an academic, I have found myself doing the following. First, I have observed teacher researchers and identified what they do and why. However, observing is not enough. It is also necessary to write reflective notes on what was observed. I take thick notes, identifying the specific procedures they follow, in the form of a teacher educator/teacher log. Meanwhile, with sensitivity to teachers' preferences for openness, I continue to discuss how they feel about doing research and what specific strategies they follow. Such background work will give access to the research site and also build rapport, which will be useful for any future collaboration with these participants.

Second, I regularly read publicly available research accounts written by teachers themselves, which are increasingly available, particularly online (see ReSIG website, http://resig.weebly.com/). In this process, I thematize topics that have been investigated, challenges that have been experienced, and benefits reaped, as well as issues repeatedly mentioned, which could help suggest recurring themes. Such a list can help both in understanding the concerns of teachers and in identifying an overarching topic for future research.

Finally, I read published research about teacher research and, visualize this, for example, by creating a mind map of all the topics covered. In this way, I can see which specific areas are covered, to what extent, and more importantly, which are missing, and therefore may be worth investigating.

Teacher Research Topics

Impact on Student Learning and Teacher Practices

Although there are a number of studies that explore teachers' practical development through research engagement, there is an area that has not been addressed so far: whether learners in researched classrooms learn relatively more than those in non-researched classrooms. This topic can be addressed by observing teacher researchers' classrooms for instructional and interactional changes in their practices. More specifically, pre-teacher research observation can help understand teachers' current practices, whereas while- and post-teacher research observations help identify developing or changing teaching practices. Learner and teacher journals can be collected in order to understand how teacher research-driven research activities influence their learning processes.

Autonomy Development in Doing Research and Teaching

By doing research into their classroom practices, teachers often develop their autonomous learning skills since teacher research allows them to make pedagogical and methodological decisions during their research engagement. However, there is still a need for understanding how autonomy is promoted by the different aspects of research engagement. This process is important for assessing the value of teacher research in teachers' autonomy building. To investigate autonomy development through research engagement, a design including technology-integration into research (e.g., Burns & Kurtoğlu-Hooton, 2016) could be established where teachers are invited to participate in a telecollaboration program involving teachers from international contexts to develop teacher research plans. This approach has been insufficiently investigated, despite its potential to create an environment where teachers can utilize their autonomous skills to access and create innovative ways of engaging in research and sustaining collaboration with other teachers.

To address this topic, teachers' synchronous and asynchronous conversations in telecollaboration could provide rich insights into the process of autonomy development, as they discuss challenges and learning opportunities. Researchers could also monitor how teacher researchers establish networks to access knowledge, how they interact and collaborate, what kind of decisions they make as a result of their research experiences, and what pedagogical changes they implement as part of the research-based evidence they generate.

Identity Reconstruction and Development

It is argued that research is transformative learning, which influences teachers' identity (who they are, how they are seen by others, and how they interact with others and discover self). Studies consider how teachers' identity is influenced by research engagement (e.g., Dikilitaş & Yaylı, 2018); however, the range of studies needs to be increased to include diverse contexts. Teacher research encourages critical reflection over issues of interest to them, offering a wide range of opportunities to discover their own beliefs about teaching practices, and to become more reflexive and self-critical, thus giving new insights into the knowledge system. Think-aloud protocols and stimulated recall are two qualitative methods that can be used to investigate cognitive changes. The think-aloud protocols – during or after the research process – might give insights into how teachers problematize the research issue based on their local experiences and explicate or justify the instructional decisions. These two methods also help capture teachers' thought processes, giving insights into their own practical knowledge development and that of their learners.

Self-efficacy Building and Motivation in Research and Teaching

There is little research on how research engagement develops self-efficacy beliefs and increases motivation. One such study is Wyatt and Dikilitaş (2016), a multi-case study of Turkish English teachers' self-efficacy beliefs over time. Self-efficacy and motivation were examined with introspective data collection methods involving teachers' reflection on their own practices through self-observation. It was concluded that self-observation and self-reflection form a strong basis for understanding classroom practice. Further case studies from diverse international contexts could help explore the complex process of self-efficacy development through teacher research engagement, based on written and verbal expression of feelings, emotions, perceptions, expectations and underlying personal understandings of lived experiences.

Research questions in this area could shed light on the intricacies of self-efficacy-building capacity and motivational development that research engagement might lead to. One of the methods for investigating this research focus is interviews; however, to ensure reliable data, these should be in the form of democratic discussion, where the interviewee is allowed to confront the questions posed by the researchers, rather than only answer them. Such open and honest exchanges might generate greater insights into changes or development in teacher researchers. Teacher or action research emerged as a reaction to prescriptive and inflexible academic research, emancipating and liberating teacher researchers from external expert input. This underlying principle should be sustained, even in the data collection process, particularly in interviews with teacher researchers. Thus, teachers are deemed to be an active participant of building knowledge through interaction, and not simply sources of information. Interviews in the form of critical discussion enable teachers to feel that they are self-regulating their thoughts without any potential researcher manipulation or leading questions.

Teachers' Research Writing Experiences: Narratives of Teachers as Researchers

Teachers, when engaged in doing research to improve their teaching practices, may also engage in writing up these research experiences for publication. There is as yet no study that investigates the actual process of this writing. As a research topic, teachers' written research could be approached as a specific genre, increasing understanding of how this process influences their written language development, and revealing how they position themselves within the research experience. In addition, discourse analysis can enlighten the process of becoming a reflective and critical teacher through research, providing tangible evidence for how they conceptualize their learning process. The reflective/reflexive writing can also offer researchers understanding of the practical challenges that teachers face. Therefore, a careful analysis of their research narratives has the potential to yield authentic and contextualized experiences, which further research could meaningfully interpret.

Teachers could also themselves produce narratives about their teaching experiences and challenges, classroom interactions, and relations with students as well as other teachers. These could constitute data for investigating identity embedded in their teacher stories. Methods for data collection could include voice recorded oral as well as written data. Some teachers may feel more comfortable telling their stories orally, while others may prefer writing. If it is possible, students can also be asked for narratives about their teachers, which would allow for delving into students' perspectives of their teachers' identity (see Varghese, et al., 2005, for example, regarding learners' 'image texts' of teachers.)

Research Questions

1. What instructional and interactional changes are adopted during the implementation of the teacher research?
2. How does teacher research support student and teacher learning?
3. How does research engagement influence teacher researchers' autonomy development in research and teaching?
4. How does that influence contribute to teacher professional development?
5. How do teachers construct their understanding of themselves as 'teacher' through research engagement?
6. How does research engagement help teachers develop their professional identity?
7. What role does teacher research play in the development of teachers' self-efficacy and professional motivation?
8. How does teacher research change teachers' self-efficacy beliefs and motivation to teach and do research?
9. How reflective are teacher researchers in their written accounts?
10. What specific writing strategies do teachers employ to express reflectivity?

References

Burns, A., & Kurtoğlu-Hooton, N. (2016). *Using action research to explore technology in language teaching: International perspectives (ELT Research Papers 16.06)*. London: British Council.

Dikilitaş, K., & Yaylı, D. (2018).Teachers' professional identity development through action research. *ELT Journal*, 72(4), 415–424.

Kumaravadivelu, B. (2001). Toward a postmethod pedagogy. *TESOL Quarterly*, 35(4), 537–560.

Nassaji, H. (2018). How to add to knowledge. *Language Teaching Research*, 22(2), 143–147.

Varghese, M., Morgan, B., Johnston, B., & Johnson, K.A. (2005). Theorizing language teacher identity: Three perspectives and beyond. *Journal of Language, Identity and Education*, 4, 21–44.

Wyatt, M., & Dikilitaş, K. (2016). English language teachers becoming more efficacious through research engagement at their Turkish university. *Educational Action Research*, 24(4), 550–570.

31

EXPLORING ISSUES IN LANGUAGE AND CONTENT INSTRUCTION

Sandra Zappa-Hollman and Patricia A. Duff
UNIVERSITY OF BRITISH COLUMBIA, CANADA

We (Sandra and Patsy) both work in the area of TESOL and applied linguistics at the University of British Columbia, Canada. Our research examines how best to describe, interpret, and support multilingual language learners' academic English discourse socialization, especially in higher education. Some of that research takes place in programs that integrate language and content instruction, which is the focus of this chapter. Sandra has, in addition, been doing research on collaborations between language and disciplinary university instructors and on the use of genre theory and Systemic Functional Linguistics in English for academic purposes. Patsy has been doing research involving the teaching and learning of Chinese as well as English, and has a longstanding interest in qualitative research methods.

Many potential challenges face pre-service or in-service teachers aiming to integrate a focus on both language and disciplinary content in diverse educational settings, particularly given the growing global phenomenon of English medium instruction (EMI). Curriculum, instruction, and teacher development need to be informed by research on how teachers (and teacher educators) learn to integrate language and content (L&C) in effective ways. In this chapter, we propose topics and methods for studies exploring L&C instruction. Our interest in this topic arises from our own experiences – and those of our colleagues and graduate students – of fostering professional socialization within new discourse communities and undertaking research examining the processes and outcomes involved, and considering ways of improving educational practice.

Strategies for Choosing a Topic

Choosing a research topic can be facilitated by attending and presenting at conferences, participating in online forums, receiving updates from relevant journal publications, engaging in informal conversations with colleagues or by working alongside (other) teachers. In addition, suggestions may come in the form of published research agendas (see Snow & Brinton, 2017).

Researching both familiar and unfamiliar settings typically entails spending time with teachers; negotiating permissions and access (research ethics); discussing pedagogy and instruction; and listening to teachers' stories, particularly what concerns, excites, or frustrates them, and what their various needs are. Researchers may wish to conduct reflective inquiry into their own experiences (both positive and negative) as teachers or teacher educators (Farrell, 2016).

Research Topics

Developing Effective, Sustainable, Interdisciplinary Collaborations

This topic involves examining the nature of partnerships between instructors whose expertise is in teaching additional languages (e.g., ESL) and those who teach a disciplinary subject (e.g., physics, sociology). Such collaborations are known to require significant resources (time, money, goodwill) as well as strong support from administrators (Pawan & Greene, 2017) in order to be successful and sustainable. While there is general agreement about the value of interdisciplinary collaborations, there is also an acknowledgement that teachers face major issues as they establish such partnerships. Several internal and external factors impact the effectiveness and sustainability of collaborations (Zappa-Hollman, 2018).

Given the proliferation of EAP programs that draw on integrated L&C approaches, there is a need to expand our understanding of how cross-disciplinary collaborations are best supported. In particular, there is an underrepresentation of the instructors' (emic) perspectives on the topic, particularly of 'content' teachers (Goldstein, 2017). Narrative inquiry is one promising research approach through which teachers share their experiences of collaboration. Research in this vein requires systematic data collection, often using structured journaling by teachers (to capture their accounts as well as personal reactions/emotions), interview-based accounts, detailed notes on meetings, and other exchanges between collaborators, and an analysis of materials produced jointly to assess their effectiveness and suggest improvements.

Developing Curriculum that Integrates Language and Content Instruction

Investigating collaborative instructional relationships and/or the integration of L&C instruction delivered by one instructor primarily might also entail examining curriculum and materials, curricular innovations, and assessment practices. Such research might elicit the perspectives of participants and the analysis of documents by researchers: policies, guidelines, syllabi, and other curriculum documents and resources. In addition, the research might involve observing the enactment and use of these curricula and materials in classrooms. Classroom observation is included in many types of (qualitative) educational research (see Zappa-Hollman & Duff, 2017). The observational research component (like narrative inquiry by teachers discussed earlier) may be relatively short in duration (e.g., over several hours, days, or weeks) or longitudinal, conducted over an extended period of time (e.g., a semester or a year), particularly when new curricular approaches are being implemented. Although observations might involve field-note-taking by researchers, they are usually audio- or video-recorded as well. The researcher then must choose to focus on particular types of interactions, activities, or linguistic practices, as guided by the research questions, and then transcribe and code the relevant data accordingly (typically looking for recurring themes or patterns in the data).

Research on this broad second topic might involve visiting and recording classes, attending planning meetings, interacting with instructors, interviewing program/course participants and (other) stakeholders, and noting issues that arise. The research questions explored should (ideally) dovetail with other current published research as well, as ascertained from reviews of relevant literature on the same topic, to ensure that the theoretical framing and findings will be of interest to scholars and teachers outside of the immediate educational context as well as those within.

Using Technology to Optimize Learning, Communication, and Assessment

Increasingly, technology is a key component of course delivery and instruction, using a variety of new course learning management systems and tools, such as multimodal online forums and other collaborative tools, various feedback/assessment tools, and more recently, augmented or virtual reality software. Yet, insufficient research has documented how instructors and students learn to engage with these tools and with others in their courses in the online environment, and to what effect, particularly in the context of L&C integration. In addition, technology can facilitate assessment, through online portfolios (e-portfolios), peer feedback, rubrics, and automated feedback systems, for example. Some of the issues involved in L&C assessment, and research possibilities, are explored by Andrade and Green (2017), including the artificial separation between language and content. As Huang (2018) points out, based on her research with EAP practitioners at various Canadian institutions, knowledge about current testing/assessment approaches is often lacking among (language) teachers and therefore constitutes a critical area for both research and professional development.

This third set of topics can be researched using structured (digital) logs, or blogs, where teachers (and students) keep detailed notes on their own engagements with instructional technologies, analyses of the discourse and interaction found in online learning forums, and an examination of assessment tools, both formative and summative, in terms of their effectiveness, practicality, validity, and so on.

Deepening Connections between Research, Theory, and Practice

In the spirit of narrative inquiry described earlier, research for this topic might have teachers reflect deeply on how their beliefs, identities, and backgrounds inform and mediate their current practices, and how and why their practices, understandings (or theories), and identities have changed over time (Farrell, 2016). Zappa-Hollman and Duff (2017) discuss the value of research investigating how teachers who have been socialized within one cultural and instructional setting move into another and develop the expertise needed within the new context. For example, English as a foreign language (EFL) teachers who move to an ESL, English lingua franca, or EAP setting and must now emphasize L&C integration across particular genres with a very different population of learners must adapt to their new context. This adaptation may require in-service professional socialization mediated by mentors, peers, curriculum documents, observation of others, feedback, and other forms of experience. Having teachers make explicit tacit understandings of their beliefs and practices and then analyze them is valuable for practitioners as well as other newcomers to the profession and the institutions in which they work.

Developing Expertise in (New) Linguistic Orientations and Pedagogical Approaches

As professionals, language teachers need a strong foundation in the language(s) they teach, as well as the linguistic theories, pedagogical approaches, and learning theories that inform their practice. Yet, as noted above, at different points in their careers (including when they first enter the field, and possibly years later), teachers may find themselves in situations in which they require further training or development. For example, in an integrated L&C setting, an EAP teacher may be tasked with designing and teaching an adjunct course linked to a chemistry class – a science discipline in which he/she lacks sufficient background. This would require the EAP teacher to become familiar with the disciplinary genres, language features, and ideally at least an ability to grasp key concepts and ideas of the content of that discipline, as well as with materials and assessments used in that course (which in turn, as mentioned in the first topic above, would likely involve cross-disciplinary collaborations). Or they may be expected to draw from a particular language orientation (such as genre theory, or Systemic Functional Linguistics) that may be unfamiliar to them. What these scenarios have in common is the potentially unsettling feelings of insecurity and frustration teachers may face before (hopefully) regaining their confidence as they develop new kinds and levels of expertise. Learning about the challenges teachers encounter as they go through such transformations, and finding out what advice they would provide to others based on research would yield insights for program developers as well as scholars of professional socialization. Self-study by teachers, through a careful review of videos or other artefacts based on their own teaching or through lesson study, for example, is another productive approach to professional development and, thus, another topic for potential research (Farrell, 2016).

Research Questions

Qualitative research methods in language teacher education offer many possibilities for studies on the five topics above, whether by means of case studies of teachers and/or learners within particular programs, ethnographies, narrative inquiry accounts, discourse analyses of classroom instruction, online discussion, or instructional planning sessions, or textual and semiotic analysis of materials teachers and students must read and produce, to name just a few possibilities. Furthermore, these methods – and others – can also be combined in creative and complementary ways to explore important issues in integrated L&C instruction.

1. What are teachers' experiences with cross-disciplinary professional collaborations in programs combining a focus on language (e.g., ESL/EAP) and disciplinary content (e.g., geography)?
2. What factors, according to L&C teachers and (other) researchers, contribute to highly successful, sustainable collaborations?
3. What processes are involved in curricular reform and enactment, from teachers' perspectives, particularly in programs with an emphasis on language and content integration?
4. How and why might the L&C curriculum-as-planned and the curriculum-as-enacted be different?
5. How do L&C teachers engage with new learning and assessment technologies?
6. How do teachers make informed decisions about assessment design (type, focus, content), and how do they evaluate their effectiveness in measuring students' ability to meet language and content objectives?
7. What beliefs, assumptions, and theories of teaching and learning, according to teachers, underpin their teaching of integrated language and content?
8. What internal and external factors affect the decisions teachers make about what to teach, when, and how? How much agency do teachers feel they have?
9. What can be learned from a comparison of novice and expert teachers' reflections on their professional transformations as they learn to use new instructional approaches for language and content integration?

10. How can L&C teachers be best supported in their professional development by their peers, academic leaders, administrators, and the institutions in which they work?

References

Andrade, M.S., & Green, B.A. (2017). Fundamental principles in content-based assessment. In M.A. Snow & D.M. Brinton (Eds.), *The content-based classroom: New perspectives on integrating language and content* (2nd edition) (pp. 297–308). Ann Arbor, MI: University of Michigan Press.

Farrell, T.S.C. (2016). The practices of encouraging TESOL teachers to engage in reflective practice: An appraisal of recent research contributions. *Language Teaching Research*, 20(2), 223–247.

Goldstein, L. (2017). Looking back and looking forward at the adjunct model: Are we still smiling through the turbulence? In M.A. Snow & D.M. Brinton (Eds.), *The content-based classroom: New perspectives on integrating language and content* (2nd edition) (pp. 337–351). Ann Arbor, MI: University of Michigan Press.

Huang, L-S. (2018). A call for critical dialogue: EAP assessment from the practitioner's perspective in Canada. *Journal of English for Academic Purposes*, 35, 70–84.

Pawan, F., & Greene, M.C.S. (2017). In trust, we collaborate: ESL and content-area teachers working together in content-based instruction. In M.A. Snow & D.M. Brinton (Eds.), *The content-based classroom: New perspectives on integrating language and content* (2nd edition) (pp. 323–337). Ann Arbor, MI: University of Michigan Press.

Snow, M.A., & Brinton, D.M. (Eds.). (2017). *The content-based classroom: New perspectives on integrating language and content* (2nd edition). Ann Arbor, MI: University of Michigan Press.

Zappa-Hollman, S. (2018). Collaborations between language and content university instructors: Factors and indicators of positive partnerships. *International Journal of Bilingual Education and Bilingualism*, 21(5), 591–606.

Zappa-Hollman, S., & Duff, P. (2017). Conducting research on content-based language instruction. In M.A. Snow & D.M. Brinton (Eds.), *The content-based classroom: New perspectives on integrating language and content* (2nd edition) (pp. 309–321). Ann Arbor, MI: University of Michigan Press.

32

LTE IN PRIMARY AND SECONDARY SCHOOLS

Takaaki Hiratsuka

TOHOKU UNIVERSITY, JAPAN

I was born and grew up in a tiny Japanese village surrounded by glorious rice paddies, mighty rivers, and spectacular mountains. None of my family members spoke a word of English, nor had they ever been to English-speaking countries. It was not until age 18 that I met and spoke to a non-Japanese person. It happened in a relatively large city in Japan where I had just started to live as a university student. The person asked me in English for directions to his hotel (or so I presumed), to which I just replied "No." I felt mortified because that was all I could say after six years of public English education! This incident made me think for the first time about my English language education in a critical way. It dawned on me that, for many people in English as a foreign language (EFL) contexts like Japan, the English lessons offered in primary and secondary schools are the first and possibly only chance to learn English, and therefore they are absolutely crucial for the development of confident and capable users of English. A few years later, to everybody's (and my own) surprise, I became an English language teacher at a secondary school in my hometown. After I worked in that capacity for a decade, I resigned to gain a deeper understanding of English education by studying for and completing a PhD in the field. Since then, I have devoted my career to working with pre-service and in-service teachers in primary and secondary schools in Japan. My research interest thus lies in elucidating the complicated experiences of language teachers, improving the quality of language teaching and learning, and evaluating the educational assumptions held and policies implemented in these contexts.

In this chapter, I first outline some strategies for the selection of LTE-related research topics. I then address some current and germane areas of interest within LTE that relate to primary and secondary school English education in an EFL context. I conclude with specific research questions that I believe can greatly enrich LTE.

Choosing a Research Topic

There are three strategies I address in this section. The first strategy is to understand the essential characteristics of a potential topic. To do this, I ask myself the following set of questions: (a) Am I passionate about this topic and can I sustain my interest in it throughout my research? (b) Is it relevant, meaningful, and useful for me, my participants, my colleagues, and most importantly my students? (c) Is it timely, valuable, and therefore beneficial for the field? (d) Is it clear, specific and carefully defined for the research to be feasibly carried out? If the answers are positive, I then consider researching the topic by using methods that are the best fit for my research purposes. I then choose a variety of participants who work and live in under-researched contexts so that my study has originality in its focus, methodology, and context.

The second strategy is related to replication studies. I do not mean that we should repeat a previous study on the same topic by employing precisely the same methods to determine the generalizability of the results within different contexts. Rather, I mean that we should conduct additional research on the same or similar topics to explore the issues further and potentially create new knowledge that can support, add to, or challenge the findings of the previous studies. This is particularly warranted when these studies have added tremendous value to the field.

The third strategy involves attending to two or more (sub-)fields and finding a gap in the combined field. For instance, I did a great deal of reading and became familiar with the literature in the areas of non-native/native English speaking teachers, team teaching, and teacher research within the broader field of LTE. As a result, I realized that there was no previous study that had integrated these three areas holistically to make explicit how individual language teachers' team-teaching experiences affected their professional development. This strategy promotes inter-disciplinary research that can lead to new theory building.

Current Topics

Early English Language Education

One assumption that is commonly held around the world is "the earlier you start learning a second language, the better." An example of a recent policy that reflects this belief is that the Japanese government has decided to extend its primary school English program by making English an official school subject for grades 5 and 6 (it has been an unofficial subject only since 2011) and to introduce English lessons in grades 3 and 4 from 2020. This decision was reached despite the relatively limited information available on how young learners learn English as well as mounting criticisms of its presumptions (Butler, 2015). What makes the matter particularly unprecedented is the fact that, until very recently, primary school teachers in Japan have not been trained to become English language teachers and, in general, their knowledge of English language teaching and their English language competence is quite limited. There is an urgent need, therefore, for researchers to explore primary school teachers' English classroom practices by, for example, focusing on their teaching methodologies (e.g., audio-lingual methodology, task-based language teaching) and their use of the first language (L1) and second language (L2). These kinds of studies could be examined effectively through qualitative studies that include classroom observations and interviews.

Teaching English through English

English as the medium of instruction (EMI) has become widespread around the globe. However, several concerns about this shift are evident: (a) there is no agreement on the level of teachers' linguistic competence for successful EMI classes, (b) there is little information on adequate EMI instruction, and (c) there is little or no pre-service/in-service teacher education involving EMI (Dearden, 2014). Although heated debates surrounding the topic continue, the Japanese government has decided that all English lessons at secondary schools will, in principle, be carried out exclusively in English from 2021. Against this backdrop, one focus of LTE research could be on the relationship between the teachers' (self-perceived) English proficiency and their pedagogical performance in EMI language lessons at Japanese secondary schools (see Richards, 2017). Researchers could adopt classroom observations, interviews, diary studies, and a review of school documents to probe into this issue. Another research agenda could be to challenge the privileging of monolingualism and champion the emerging notion of multicompetence (Cook, 2016). That is, researchers could look into how successfully local teachers (and foreign teachers), particularly in secondary schools, can demonstrate multilingualism by teaching English through both English and the students' L1 rather than teaching English only through English. Qualitative discourse analysis of classroom talk and interaction is best suited to this kind of research.

Reflective Teaching

There is growing recognition within the field of LTE that teachers who become reflective practitioners, via constant examination of their teaching beliefs and classroom practices, obtain insight into their current teaching and make informed decisions for their future classes (Farrell, 2018). Despite this, the practice of reflective teaching in Japanese primary or secondary education remains scarce (however, see Hiratsuka, 2017). In order to broaden our knowledge about the complexity of language teachers' development in primary and secondary schools, future researchers could incorporate in their methodology a reflective practice component (e.g., stimulated recall, journal writing) and examine how it changes (or doesn't) the teachers' perceptions and practices. In doing so, they can track the transformation of the teachers' professional lives over time by means of ethnographies, in-depth interviews, and a discourse analysis of teacher journals.

Teacher Research

Teacher research is teacher-initiated systematic inquiry into their professional practices in their own contexts. An embedded notion of teacher research is that teachers can develop as professionals via a spiral of research actions (i.e., formulating a research plan, collecting and analyzing data, reflecting on the results, and sharing them with others). One kind of teacher research called Exploratory Practice (EP) is the research *of, for,* and *by* teachers and learners conducted at the grassroots level (Hanks, 2017). EP attempts to conduct research *with* teachers and students, not *on* them, and to gain understanding of their classroom lives by exploring 'puzzles' that are based on their personal experiences within their particular contexts. Promoting teacher research, including EP, in primary and secondary schools is currently of key importance, not only because it has recently attracted more practical attention as a professional development opportunity within LTE in general but also because successful examples are now available in those contexts (e.g., Hiratsuka, 2016). One possible research topic is how participation in teacher research (EP) affects the professional experiences of language teachers in primary and secondary schools. Another is the ways in which researchers effectively engage in collaborative teacher research (EP) with teachers and students in these settings in pursuit of answers to their own puzzles. Teacher research might be best accomplished through a case study approach that utilizes, for example, classroom observations, focus group discussions, and student feedback sheets.

Team Teaching

Team teaching partnerships between native English speaking teachers and non-native English speaking teachers in EFL classrooms have been widely adopted in Japan. Local Japanese teachers of English (JTEs) and foreign assistant language teachers (ALTs), hired through the government-sponsored Japan Exchange and Teaching (JET) program, have been collaboratively teaching to enhance foreign language education for many years. The number of ALTs has increased from 848 in 1987 to 5,163 in 2017. The government aims to accelerate this trend with plans to hire 50,000 ALTs by 2023 so that there is at least one ALT for every primary and secondary school in the country. Much research on the team-teaching arrangement has focused on team teachers' general perceptions of their experiences, primarily through surveys.

However, some qualitative studies have begun to appear (e.g., Hiratsuka & Barkhuizen, 2015). One specific direction for future investigation is to scrutinize the team teachers' assigned roles, talk, and movements in the classroom through classroom observations and discourse analysis. The focus of such studies could be to examine the effects of the teachers' practices on their students' motivation and learning. Another research direction is to qualitatively document and analyze veteran JTEs' team-teaching experiences with different ALTs over the years, as well as ALTs' experiences prior to, during, and after the JET program. The results would generate useful implications for constructing effective pre-service, in-service, and post-service education programs for team teachers in Japan and in other similar contexts.

Research Questions

1. What are the instructional approaches primary school teachers in Japan, as novice teachers of English, employ in their English lessons and what are the types and amount of L1 and L2 they use in their lessons?
2. What impact does the English proficiency of language teachers in secondary schools have on their pedagogical performance in EMI language lessons?
3. How does employing a multicompetence perspective in classrooms affect the professional experiences (e.g., teacher self-efficacy) of language teachers in secondary schools?
4. How do reflective teaching practices (e.g., stimulated recall, journal writing) help language teachers in primary and secondary schools recognize, interpret, and challenge their educational philosophies, principles, and theories?
5. What are some obstacles to adopting reflective teaching practices for teacher development in primary and secondary school contexts and what are some solutions for overcoming them?
6. What effects does participation in teacher research (EP) have on language teachers' professional experiences over time?
7. How can researchers effectively carry out teacher research (EP) in collaboration with teachers and students in primary and secondary schools and find answers to the puzzles that emerge from their local contexts?
8. How do team teachers' classroom practices (e.g., their assigned roles, talk, movements) affect their students' motivation and learning?
9. What team-teaching experiences have veteran JTEs had with different ALTs over the years and what are some viable recommendations for pre-service and in-service JTEs for their team teaching with ALTs?
10. What professional and personal experiences do ALTs have before, during, and after the JET program and what are some viable recommendations for the hiring processes of JET participants, professional development opportunities for in-service ALTs, and post-program initiatives for JET alumni?

References

Butler, Y.G. (2015). English language education among young learners in East Asia: A review of current research (2004–2014). *Language Teaching*, 48, 303–342.

Cook, V. (2016). Where is the native speaker now? *TESOL Quarterly*, 50, 186–189.

Dearden, J. (2014). *English as a medium of instruction – a growing global phenomenon: Phase 1*. London: British Council.

Farrell, T.S.C. (2018). Reflective practice for language teachers. In J.I. Liontas (Ed.), *TESOL encyclopedia of English language teaching*. New York: Wiley.

Hanks, J. (2017). *Exploratory practice in language teaching*. Basingstoke: Palgrave Macmillan.

Hiratsuka, T. (2016). Actualizing Exploratory Practice (EP) principles with team teachers in Japan. *System*, 57, 109–119.

Hiratsuka, T. (2017). Pair discussions for reflecting on action: Stimulated recall. In R. Barnard & J. Ryan (Eds.), *Reflective practice: Options for English language teachers and researchers* (pp. 89–97). New York: Routledge.

Hiratsuka, T., & Barkhuizen, G. (2015). Effects of Exploratory Practice (EP) on team teachers' perceptions in Japanese high schools. *JALT Journal*, 37, 5–27.

Richards, J.C. (2017). Teaching English through English: Proficiency, pedagogy, and performance. *RELC Journal*, 48, 7–30.

33

RESEARCHING TASK-BASED TEACHING AND ASSESSMENT

Martin East

UNIVERSITY OF AUCKLAND, NEW ZEALAND

For ten years, between 2008 and 2017, the primary focus of my work as a language teacher educator was with beginning (pre-service) teachers, those who would go on to become the next generation of teachers of languages other than English, principally in the New Zealand secondary school sector. The New Zealand school system underwent radical transformation during this period, due to the introduction of a revised national curriculum for schools and subsequent alignment with revised curriculum expectations of New Zealand's high-stakes assessment system – the National Certificate of Educational Achievement (NCEA). For languages, these revisions led to the promotion of task-based language teaching (TBLT). TBLT is based on the learner-centered experiential premise that learners "learn to communicate by communicating" (Nunan, 2004, p. 8), drawing on collaborative tasks to enhance second language acquisition. Attendant assessment renewal resulted in a new way of assessing learners' speaking skills which in several respects reflected a task-based language assessment (TBLA) approach (Norris, 2016). A traditional teacher-student end-of-year summative interview test was replaced by an on-going assessment model (called 'interact'). Evidence of students' spoken proficiency was collected via a series of peer-to-peer paired or group interactions, taking place (and recorded) in the context of teaching and learning programs. This new TBLT/TBLA focus led to considerable challenges for teachers. My research agenda, which has followed predominantly qualitative approaches, has principally addressed how TBLT/TBLA were being understood and operationalized by teachers who were being required to navigate substantial curricular and assessment changes.

Strategies for Choosing a Research Topic

TBLT is increasingly widely investigated in applied linguistics research, where often the focus is on exploring task efficacy through experimental studies.

Nevertheless, despite considerable empirical support and a relatively long history (TBLT has been developing since the early 1980s), TBLT is still seen as innovative, and therefore unfamiliar, threatening, and suspect. Contexts where TBLT is being encouraged or mandated therefore provide rich sources for researchers who are thinking about choosing an LTE-related research topic within a qualitative/narrative research paradigm.

When choosing a research topic, it is important initially to situate that topic within a suitable theoretical framework. Working with my own students, I very quickly became aware of several tensions as we engaged together with theory and practice around TBLT throughout the year. For the beginning teachers, the program integrated time on the university campus with time spent teaching in schools. Tensions appeared to arise from two intersecting spheres: first, the beliefs and understandings that these beginning teachers brought with them into the program right at the start, based on their own prior experiences with learning a language; and second, the beliefs and understandings of more senior colleagues with whom they were working in schools, who often saw things differently to the theory we were exploring on campus, and who, it seemed, often 'guided' their mentees towards more traditional practices (and away from principles of TBLT). This created a challenging environment in which to promote and advocate for TBLT.

In essence, two underpinning theoretical frameworks informed not only how I worked with my students but also how I conceptualized researching their experiences: teacher cognition (e.g., Borg, 2015) and reflective practice (e.g., Brandenberg, Glasswell, Jones & Ryan, 2017). With these two intersecting theoretical frameworks in mind, I allowed research questions to emerge that would enable me to explore teachers' reception of TBLT as innovation, alongside the success of their engagement with innovation and the barriers to its implementation. I undertook a series of studies, all qualitative in nature. These studies not only tracked teachers' progress and development over several years but also compared beginning teachers' cognitions and practices with those of more experienced teachers. The student voice was also included. Below I articulate what this range of studies, which included both teaching and assessment, means for choosing a research topic.

Research Topics

Pre-service Teachers' Emerging Beliefs about TBLT

One immediate topic is how beginning teachers (that is, those with minimal experience in classrooms) cope with TBLT as innovation in the context of an LTE program. Bearing in mind the experiences and beliefs that novice teachers might bring into such a program, one important way of investigating teachers' engagement with theory and practice is to look at how their thinking and actions change and develop in the course of being introduced to the innovation. Novice teachers' thinking can be collected via, for example, questionnaires and/or interviews towards the start of the program, and collected again in the same way towards the end (that is, asking much the same questions, but in ways that link two different points in the program: What do you think about TBLT at the start of the course? What do you think about TBLT at the end of the course?). Themes emerging from the data can then be compared to determine whether, and to what extent, a process over time (in this case what happens in an LTE program) can be successful in challenging and changing beliefs and understandings. A positivist research paradigm would describe this as a pre- and post-intervention (before-and-after) design. Qualitative researchers can also utilize this kind of design quite successfully. This is the approach I used for one of my own studies (East, 2014a), but in that study I drew on aspects of participants' coursework as data sources.

In-service Teachers' Developing Beliefs about TBLT

It is one thing to investigate changes by virtue of a dedicated LTE program (and perhaps to demonstrate that beliefs and practices can change). Another important question is the extent to which these changes are sustainable once beginning teachers take up positions in real contexts and become immersed in the day-to-day practicalities of teaching. Another important topic is therefore the extent to which beginning teachers are able to sustain TBLT as innovation after several years in the real world. A useful design here is what might be referred to in a positivist paradigm as a within-subjects comparative design, a research project that draws on the same participants, but collects data at two different measurement points. Again, from a qualitative perspective teachers' thinking and practices can be collected via questionnaires and interviews (and perhaps observations), both at the end of an LTE program and, for example, after a period of time teaching in classrooms (see East, 2016b, for an example). Again, themes emerging from the data can be compared to determine whether, and to what extent, TBLT principles can be successfully maintained, and the barriers to maintaining them.

Comparing Pre-service and In-service Teachers' Beliefs about TBLT

Another form of comparative study is comparison between novice teachers and more experienced colleagues. In the positivist paradigm this might be labelled a between-subjects comparative design, where different groups of teacher participants are compared. Once more, this design can be used quite successfully by qualitative researchers. An example of a study I undertook (East, 2014b) compared the pre-service teachers who were part of the one-year initial teacher education program with more experienced teachers who were taking part in a one-year professional development program. Both sets of participants were exposed to similar input during the program. Following East (2014a), I adopted a before-and-after design, comparing teachers' reflections towards the beginning of the year-long courses with their reflections towards the end, based on coursework assignments. This provided the opportunity not only to consider changes in beliefs and practices at these two points in time, but also to consider whether changes differed between pre-service and in-service teachers.

Comparing Teacher and Student Beliefs about TBLA (Survey)

LTE studies that involve students on the receiving end of the teaching and learning experience may also prove to be rich sources of qualitative data. These studies are important in eliciting broadly based stakeholder feedback that can influence directions for subsequent LTE. Two comparative studies I have undertaken investigated teacher and student reception of an assessment informed by task-based principles in the context of New Zealand's curriculum and assessment reforms. One larger-scale project (East, 2016a) drew on surveys and interviews to collect data on teachers' and students' reception of the new assessment. My interest here was mainly in the new assessment as compared to the traditional interview test that it had replaced, with student data used to triangulate with teacher data. The surveys, widely distributed, contained both closed-ended and open-ended questions, worded somewhat differently depending on the audience (teachers or students), but still designed to elicit comparative data. The data were analyzed thematically and I was able to draw conclusions that demonstrated the similarities and differences in perception between teachers and students. This kind of study allows for collection of stakeholder feedback that can inform subsequent LTE by highlighting similarities and differences in perception and experience between two groups of stakeholders across a range of contexts.

Comparing Teacher and Student Beliefs about TBLA (Interviews/Focus Groups)

A contrasting highly focused follow-up project investigated one teacher in one school. It involved an interview with the teacher and a focus group with a small class of seven of his students (East, in press). Again, I was interested in the comparative angle on what was and was not working well with the new assessment. This time the comparison specifically focused on the new assessment, and was between a teacher and his own students. This kind of study is important in eliciting stakeholder feedback that can inform subsequent LTE by highlighting similarities and differences in perception and experience between two groups of stakeholders working in the same context.

Research Questions

1. Does critical reflection lead to changes in practitioners' beliefs about TBLT/TBLA?

This overarching research question provides a bridge between the two theoretical frameworks (teacher cognition and teacher reflection).

2. What do beginning/experienced language teachers/language learners believe about TBLT?
3. How do beginning/experienced language teachers/language learners enact/engage in TBLT in classrooms?
4. What impact does reflection on practice have on beginning/experienced language teachers'/language learners' enactment of/engagement with TBLT?

The above three research questions take account of the intersecting nature of the two theoretical frameworks but enable these to be addressed in a somewhat discrete way (beliefs – practices – reflection).

5. What understandings about TBLT do beginning teachers have as they begin an initial teacher education program?
6. Do understandings about TBLT change and develop as beginning teachers complete the program?
7. What possibilities and challenges for the implementation of TBLT are highlighted by the data?

These three research questions are based on East (2014a). They might be appropriate when researching beginning (pre-service) teachers, but they can also be applied in other teacher education/professional development contexts.

8. To what extent do practicing teachers understand and enact TBLT in their classrooms?
9. What do practicing teachers perceive as the barriers to successful implementation of TBLT?
10. What responses do teachers make to the perceived barriers?

The last three research questions are based on East (2016b). These might be appropriate when researching experienced teachers' engagement with TBLT in the context of real classrooms.

References

Borg, S. (2015). *Teacher cognition and language education: Research and practice.* London: Bloomsbury Academic.

Brandenberg, R., Glasswell, K., Jones, M., & Ryan, J. (Eds.), (2017). *Reflective theory and practice in teacher education*. Singapore: Springer.

East, M. (2014a). Encouraging innovation in a modern foreign language initial teacher education programme: What do beginning teachers make of task-based language teaching? *The Language Learning Journal*, 42(3), 261–274.

East, M. (2014b). Mediating pedagogical innovation via reflective practice: A comparison of pre-service and in-service teachers' experiences. *Reflective Practice: International and Multidisciplinary Perspectives*, 15(5), 686–699.

East, M. (2016a). *Assessing foreign language students' spoken proficiency: Stakeholder perspectives on assessment innovation*. Singapore: Springer.

East, M. (2016b). Sustaining innovation in school modern foreign languages programmes: Teachers' reflections on task-based language teaching three years after initial teacher education. *The Language Learning Journal*. doi:10.1080/09571736.2016.1221440.

East, M. (in press). Addressing the possibilities and limitations of implementing a new classroom-based assessment of oral proficiency. In M. Poehner & O. Inbar-Lourie (Eds.), *Toward a reconceptualization of L2 classroom assessment: Praxis and researcher-teacher partnership*. Berlin: Springer.

Norris, J. (2016). Current uses for task-based language assessment. *Annual Review of Applied Linguistics*, 36, 230–244.

Nunan, D. (2004). *Task-based language teaching*. Cambridge, UK: Cambridge University Press.

34

LANGUAGE TEACHING APPROACHES

Jessie S. Barrot

NATIONAL UNIVERSITY, PHILIPPINES

With my almost two decades of experience in teaching, I have gathered a wealth of insights into the ways language teachers teach English to students of varied linguistic backgrounds and learning styles. Several years after my first teaching engagement, I became interested in research because of our university's 'publish or perish' culture. I attended numerous research seminars and training workshops. I read a lot of top-tier journals in language teaching and was mentored by experienced researchers in my field. At that point, it was clear to me that I wanted to concentrate on language teaching approaches and, by extension, on language teacher education (LTE). Specifically, I focused on how a principles-based language teaching approach can be translated into learning materials and actual classroom practices.

English language teaching has shifted from a focus on methods to a postmethod condition, which is a "state of affairs that compels us to refigure the relationship between the theorizers and the practitioners of method" (Kumaravadivelu, 1994, p. 27). In short, it allows the power to reside among the practitioners to develop classroom-oriented theories of practice instead of compelling the practitioners to apply knowledge-oriented pedagogical theories constructed by theorizers. Despite this paradigm shift, qualitative studies on language teaching approaches continue to be of current interest among language teaching scholars and practitioners (Demir & Koçyiğit, 2018). I therefore continue to embark on qualitative research projects within this field of study and have published my work in reputable education and linguistics journals.

Choosing a Research Topic

One of the struggles that I experienced when I was just starting as a qualitative researcher was selecting relevant topics that would advance knowledge in this field. The same might be true for other novice researchers. Hence, this chapter offers a research agenda in the field of LTE, particularly in teaching approaches. Many research methodology books recommend that research topics conform to several criteria (Barrot, 2018). First, the topic should be relevant. Does it address the needs of the target audience and their pressing practical issues? Second, it should be interesting for both the researcher and the readers. Third, the topic should be within the abilities of the researcher and given time constraints. If you want to embark on an ethnographic study, do you have technical expertise in this kind of research? Do you have sufficient time to complete the study over a period of a few months? Finally, the topic should match the available financial resources, human resources, and relevant bibliographic materials. Is your research funded? Do you have enough human resources to implement it? And by human resource, I mean both quantity and quality. Do you also have access to reputable journals and major research databases?

One personal strategy I use when choosing qualitative research topics within the field of English language teaching is surveying recent articles (i.e., published within the last five years) from top-tier journals, such as *TESOL Quarterly*, *System*, *Language Teaching*, *Language Teaching Research*, *The Modern Language Journal*, and *ELT Journal*. As I read the articles, I focus specifically on the conclusion section, which presents the limitations of the study and recommendations for future studies. This section becomes my source of possible research topics. In some cases, purely quantitative research in language teaching suggests that follow-up studies use qualitative design to obtain a clearer picture and deeper understanding of the phenomenon being investigated.

Research Topics

Isolated and Integrated Form-Focused Instruction (FFI)

Spada and Lightbown (2008) introduced two forms of FFI in terms of the pedagogical timing of attention to form: *integrated* and *isolated* FFI. While much has been studied in this area, research examining teachers' understanding of what these two mean and their implementation in lessons remains very limited. This study could provide insights into how teachers respond to instructional innovations and reveal the potential gap between the intention of the approach and its implementation. Aside from showing how teachers implement the approach, these accounts could also indicate the contextual and cognitive factors that influence their decisions in teaching linguistic forms. As such, possible interventions for proper implementation could be proposed. A qualitative approach using observation and semi-structured interviews could be used to elicit the needed data. Observational data may be collected from the teachers' regular classes with the researcher as a non-participant observer. Thereafter, teachers may be interviewed as to the hows and whys of their implementation. Participants may come from different teaching contexts that adopt FFI. However, these contexts should be clearly described, which may include the curriculum they use, the students they are teaching, and the school and its resources.

Technical-practical Knowledge among Teachers

Another issue that haunts scholars is the difficulty experienced by teachers in accommodating technical knowledge, especially when they are confronted with classroom challenges; instead, they embrace practical knowledge (Borg & Burns, 2008). Why do teachers struggle to embrace technical knowledge? Why is it difficult for some experienced teachers to change their way of teaching despite training and retooling? Why do they revert to their original teaching practices after attempting to integrate innovative teaching practices? Is the force behind this phenomenon their embedded teaching framework? Thus, future studies may zero in on surfacing this invisible force and how it shapes their instructional delivery and decision-making in the classroom. This study might involve two groups of participants: experienced and inexperienced teachers. Researchers could attempt to uncover and compare the embedded teaching framework of these two groups of teachers using a grounded theory approach. Since the study will employ grounded theory, it requires an interplay of data collection and data analysis, consequently allowing the framework to emerge from the data (Glaser, 1992). Hence, appropriate data collection techniques for this study are interviews and observation.

Constructive Alignment

With the teacher training I have conducted, I have come to realize during workshops that language teachers struggle with applying constructive alignment to their teaching practices. Constructive alignment refers to the use of teaching–learning activities and assessment to support the achievement of learning outcomes (Biggs, 1996). It involves four major steps: (a) defining the intended learning outcomes (ILOs), which are statements about what students are expected to do; (b) selecting teaching–learning activities that are likely to lead to the achievement of ILOs; (c) assessing students' performance to see how well they match the ILOs; and (d) transforming assessment into a final grade. To address this issue head on, future qualitative studies may investigate the potential causes of this problem and the factors that contributed to it through a descriptive qualitative research design. Specifically, lessons produced by teachers can be analyzed as to how the teaching–learning activities and assessment help achieve the learning outcomes and how the lesson components are linked with one another. To further understand the causes of the identified problems, document analysis may be supplemented with in-depth interviews.

Task-based Language Teaching

Studies on teaching methods reigned supreme until the end of the twentieth century. It started with the instructional effects of traditional approaches in the 1970s and learners' cognitive processes in the 1980s. In the 1990s, the focus shifted to task-related studies as manifested by a great amount of research on task-based language teaching (TBLT). Until now, TBLT continues to be a prevailing approach in language classrooms across the globe. Although numerous studies have already evaluated the effectiveness and appropriateness of TBLT in various learning contexts, very few studies have explored how the social nature of teaching interplays with the implementation of TBLT. Thus, future studies may examine the interaction between teacher cognition and TBLT implementation in the classroom. An ethnographic approach could be carried out for this purpose, which might use interviews and participant observation field notes as the primary source of data to be collected over a period of several months (e.g., four to six months). Researchers may also use a teacher's log to supplement observation.

Technology-enhanced Language Teaching

My reflection so far on qualitative research has focused on traditional language teaching approaches. However, a future research agenda in this area would need to consider technology integration in the language classrooms. Undoubtedly, advancement in technology has revolutionized language pedagogy and its impact on learners (Chen Hsieh, Wu & Marek, 2017). Of particular significance are the affordances of social networking sites (e.g., Facebook) that change how teachers teach and how learners learn. It may be timely to initiate narrative studies on how teachers integrate these affordances into their teaching practice, the challenges they encountered, and how they address these challenges. Narrative studies refers to the accounts teachers tell about their professional practices and experience (Barkhuizen, 2014). Since school leaders are also vital to the successful implementation of technology-enhanced pedagogy, their beliefs and experiences may be explored as well. This requires an interview or a focus group discussion. The implications of technology integration for classroom teaching and learning provide a rich area for future research and should be at the core of any research agenda on English language pedagogy.

Research Questions

1. What beliefs about integrated and isolated FFI do English teachers hold?

This question explores teacher's understanding of isolated and integrated FFI. It also allows the researcher to discover if there is a gap between what they know and what these two forms of FFI really are.

2. What is the extent of teachers' implementation of integrated and isolated FFI and the factors that influence the implementation?

This question will reveal how faithful the teachers are in implementing isolated and integrated FFI. The answers to this question will provide relevant information on the causes of misapplication or weak implementation of the approach.

3. How do teachers' background, beliefs, and classroom practices interact?

This question will reveal how teachers' experience, attitudes, and knowledge influence the way they teach, and possibly vice versa.

4. What 'theory of practice' can be developed from teachers' classroom experience?

The main goal of this question is to identify the theory of practice used by experienced and inexperienced teachers. Theory of practice refers to the teaching framework generated from the teachers' own personal teaching practices in their respective learning contexts. It is an "ongoing, living, working theory" that results from constant reflection and action (Chambers, 1992, p. 13).

5. How much does alignment of teaching–learning activities and assessment help in achieving learning outcomes?

This question will reveal whether teachers faithfully practice constructive alignment in their lessons and whether there is coherence in the way they teach.

6. How do contextual factors influence teachers' adherence to constructive alignment?

This question will reveal the factors that contribute to misalignment in teachers' classroom practices. By identifying these factors, proper interventions can be done.

7. How does teacher cognition influence teachers' decision making and practices in TBLT classrooms?

This question aims to reveal teachers' awareness of TBLT and how this understanding shapes their decision making and classroom practices.

8. How does teachers' identity shape their implementation of TBLT?

This question will reveal how specific TBLT classroom practices are influenced by the teachers' identity and how they use these practices to project the identity that they hold.

9. In what ways do teachers integrate technology into their teaching approaches?

This question will reveal the specific ways teachers employ technology-enhanced teaching approaches in their respective classrooms.

10. What challenges do teachers face in integrating technology into their teaching practice?

With this question, problems that teachers encounter during technology integration will surface. Their strategies for overcoming these challenges will also be probed.

References

Barkhuizen, G. (2014). Narrative research in language teaching and learning. *Language Teaching*, 47(4), 450–466.

Barrot, J. (2018). *Practical research 1: A guide to effective qualitative research*. Quezon City: C&E Publishing.

Biggs, J. (1996). Enhancing teaching through constructive alignment. *Higher Education*, 32(3), 347–364.

Borg, S., & Burns, A. (2008). Integrating grammar in adult TESOL classrooms. *Applied Linguistics*, 29(3), 456–482.

Chambers, J. (1992). *Empiricist research on teaching*. Dordrecht, Netherlands: Kluwer Academic.

Chen Hsieh, J.S., Wu, W.C.V., & Marek, M.W. (2017). Using the flipped classroom to enhance EFL learning. *Computer Assisted Language Learning*, 30(1–2), 1–21.

Demir, Y., & Koçyiğit, M. (2018). A systematic review of research on English language teacher education published in three flagship journals (1997–2016). *JETPR Journal*, 4(1) 128–138.

Glaser, B. (1992). *Emergence vs. forcing: Basics of grounded theory analysis*. Mill Valley, CA: Sociology Press.

Kumaravadivelu, B. (1994). The postmethod condition: (E)merging strategies for second/foreign language teaching. *TESOL Quarterly*, 28, 27–47.

Spada, N., & Lightbown, P. (2008). Form-focused instruction: Isolated or integrated? *TESOL Quarterly*, 42(2), 181–207.

35

STRATEGY INSTRUCTION

Carol Griffiths

AUCKLAND INSTITUTE OF STUDIES, NEW ZEALAND; UNIVERSITY OF LEEDS, UK

Language learning strategies (LLS) have been my main area of research interest since I chose them as the topic for my own PhD many years ago. Personally, I believe in the power of strategies for anything we want to achieve in life, a conviction that stems from an experience trying to learn English grammar for a test, which I describe in my most recent book (Griffiths, 2018). Over the years, I have thought long and hard about issues surrounding the strategy concept, which have been the subject of much controversy: How can they be defined? What is the underpinning theory? How can they be classified? What is the appropriate research methodology? There is no space to go into all of these issues here (for further discussion, see Griffiths, 2018). Suffice it here to say that in my book I give a very concise definition of language learning strategies as "actions chosen by learners for the purpose of learning language" (p. 19). This definition includes the elements about which there is general consensus: they are active, chosen by learners (rather than being imposed by others), goal-oriented, and for learning language. In addition to these broadly agreed characteristics, however, there may also be dimensions of variation (Gu, 2012), such as whether they are conscious, deliberate, or automatic (e.g., Cohen, 2011; Oxford, 2017), or whether they are mental or also physical (e.g., Macaro, 2006; Oxford, 2017).

Choosing a Topic

As with all research, in order to choose a topic within this area, it is necessary first of all to review the literature. An area of strategy research that remains under-developed is that of strategy instruction, which is the area I focus on in this chapter. There has been some skepticism about the effectiveness of strategy instruction (SI), such as Rees-Miller (1993), who points out some of the unsuccessful attempts at instruction reported in the literature and suggests that it would be more useful to use the time to teach the subject matter, at least until the question of the effectiveness of strategy instruction has been clarified by further research. A more recent systematic review by Hassan, Macaro, Mason, Nye, Smith and Vanderplank (2005) concludes that "there is sufficient research evidence to support claims that training language learners to use strategies is effective" (p. 2). Several years later, a meta-analysis by Plonsky (2011) also concluded that there was a "small to medium overall effect of SI" (p. 993). There are also ongoing publications promoting the value of strategy instruction, such as the book by Tang and Griffiths (2014), who describe a study that found that students given strategy instruction achieved higher test scores than those who did not receive such instruction, and another by Chamot and Harris (forthcoming). Of course, when choosing a topic, you are looking for the gap, something which has not been researched to date, or about which there are conflicting views. In fact, as stated previously, strategy instruction is an under-researched area, so there are many gaps.

Research Topics

The Relationship between Language Learning Strategies and Successful Learning

The first question that has long eluded a clearly positive empirical result is that of the relationship of language learning strategies to successful learning. The question that follows logically from this, is: are LLS worth teaching? Intuitively, LLS have strong appeal. However, consistent empirical proof of their effectiveness has proven elusive. Certainly, some studies have shown a correlation between LLS and successful learning, but there are others that have failed to show a relationship (for more details, see Griffiths, 2018). This is, therefore, an absolutely fundamental question awaiting further research. If we accept that language learning strategies do contribute to effective learning, and we accept that they are, therefore, worth teaching, the question then becomes: what is the best way to teach them? As Rees-Miller (1993) pointed out, by no means all attempts to teach LLS have been successful, and even the studies that have been done since (e.g., Hassan et al., 2005; Plonsky, 2011) are fairly guarded in their positivity. Over the years, a number of strategy instruction programs have been promoted (again, see Griffiths, 2018, for a summary), one of the most recent being the *Keys to Effective Learning* by Tang and Griffiths (2014), which suggests a five-step procedure (consisting of raising awareness, explicit instruction, practice, implicit instruction, and evaluation), but this procedure is waiting further research to determine its effectiveness or to suggest modifications. An issue that is related to this is that of materials development. It is well recognized that most published materials currently pay scant attention to strategy development. It would be very helpful for teachers to be able to refer to effective and well-structured strategy instruction programs in the materials they are required to use.

The Relationship between Context and Language Learning Strategy Use

The issue of context has received much attention in recent years. In relation to our current topic, the issue is that strategies that may be effective in one context may or may not be effective in another. Given that language is currently taught in a vast number of different contexts all over the world, this opens up a huge pool of potential research topics. A study done in an African environment, for instance, may or may not produce the same results as one done in Asia, Europe or South America. Differences between foreign-language contexts (EFL – that is, where the target language is not spoken in the local environment, such as English taught in China or Turkey, or French taught in Australia) and target-language contexts (e.g., Chinese students who go to study in the UK or USA) also present opportunities to research what the differences may be and how successful students manage these differences. Another contextual issue that is beginning to be more and more popular is that of the use of English as a medium of instruction (EMI), as well as content and language integrated learning (CLIL), and content-based learning (CBI). Although there are some differences among these three approaches, they all have in common the fact that the target language is used to teach content; the potential problems with this approach are only just beginning to be recognized, which presents yet another fertile area for potential research.

The Relationship between Individual Differences and Language Learning Strategy Use

Individual differences are another area that has attracted a great deal of research interest. In relation to strategies, we cannot assume that all strategies work equally well for all individuals. A multitude of individual differences (such as age, gender, personality, style, aptitude, affect, and motivation) have the potential to influence the effectiveness of a given strategy for any particular learner. For instance, a social strategy that works well for a student with an extroverted personality may not be useful for a more introverted personality; what works for younger students may or may not be as effective for more mature learners, and so on. Given how many individual differences have been identified, there is much scope for research initiatives in this area.

The Relationship between Learning Target and Language Learning Strategy Use

Yet another under-researched area is the relationship between learning target and language learning strategies. It would seem merely common sense to suggest that the strategies a student uses to learn General English will need to be adapted if, for instance, s/he decides to sit a major exam. But there is very little existing research into goal-specific strategy use by students, or how strategy instruction needs to change to best support students according to their learning target.

The Relationship between Complex/Dynamic Systems Theory and Language Learning Strategies

And the final research suggestion that will be made here relates to the current interest in complex/dynamic systems theory. Contemporary theory recognizes that learning is not a simple or a linear process; it is, in fact, highly complex, and this relates no less to strategy development than to any other factors. Strategy development inter-relates with all other individual variables, to the context, and to the learning target, and all of these need to be considered when attempting to research the strategy phenomenon and to come to meaningful conclusions regarding how they are best instructed. Furthermore, not only are strategies complex, they are also dynamic, that is they are constantly changing, and we must consider that, just because we get a particular result at one point in time, it does not necessarily mean we will get the same result at a later point in time.

Research Questions

1. Are language learning strategies related to successful learning?

If so, what is the relationship (e.g., is it a matter of how often, or how many, or are there other factors that contribute to LLS effectiveness)? How does this relate to what is required of the teacher in terms of strategy instruction? Teacher interviews, either as individuals or in focus groups, might be a way of approaching this question.

2. How can language learning strategies be effectively taught?

This question might be approached by identifying an interested teacher or teachers, constructing a strategy instruction program, and getting them to conduct the program. The results would then be analyzed, perhaps by means of interviewing some of the students who had participated in the program and recording their perceptions.

3. What would be useful for teachers in the way of strategy instruction programs embedded in the teaching materials they are required to use?

A way of approaching this question might be to arrange focus groups of teachers to meet and examine a range of available materials, to identify gaps, and to suggest improvements.

4. How does geographical context (e.g., Africa, Asia, etc.) relate to effective strategy use, and how do teachers need to adapt their instructional practices?

This question could either take an in-depth look at a currently under-researched context or it could compare two different contexts. Teacher journals, interviews and/or observation might be useful research techniques for this question.

5. Does a foreign or target language environment require different strategies?

If so, what are the differences? How can teachers respond to the need to help students adapt? As with Question 4, teacher journals, interviews and/or observation might be useful research techniques for this question.

6. What strategies are required for successful learning in an EMI, CLIL or CBI context?

How can teachers support and provide useful instruction for these strategy requirements? Again, teacher journals, interviews and/or observation might be useful research techniques for this question.

7. How are individual difference factors related to effective strategy use?

Although this question has the potential to provide interesting insights, a possible difficulty may be measuring the individual differences in order to be able to compare them with strategy use. Biographical differences (such as gender or age) are, of course, relatively easy to identify, but psychological differences (such as personality or beliefs) are more complicated and may require appropriate instruments to operationalize them before they can be compared with strategy use.

8. What are the strategies students need for a variety of learning targets (e.g., General English, English for academic purposes, etc.), and how does strategy instruction need to change to facilitate student success according to these differing goals?

A useful way of approaching this question might be to obtain student journals or using think-aloud protocols with students at the point of change and then eliciting feedback from teachers regarding how best to deal with issues raised.

9. How can strategy instruction accommodate the complexity of learner strategy development?

Actually, this is a difficult question, and difficult to operationalize, since there are so many possible variables to include that it tends to become unmanageable.

Nevertheless, this is the reality, so finding ways to research complex systems (such as strategy development) is, in itself, a worthwhile and much needed research goal.

10. How can strategy instruction accommodate the dynamics of strategy development?

This question calls for a longitudinal design, perhaps interviewing students and/or teachers at one point in time (e.g., the beginning of a semester) and then again at a later point in time (e.g., at the end of the semester, after a key test).

References

Chamot, A., & Harris, V. (Eds.) (forthcoming). *Learning strategy instruction in the language classroom: Issues and implementation*. Bristol: Multilingual Matters.

Cohen, A. (2011). *Strategies in learning and using a second language* (2nd edition). London: Longman.

Griffiths, C. (2018). *The strategy factor in successful language learning: The tornado effect* (2nd edition). Bristol, UK: Multilingual Matters.

Gu, Y. (2012). Learning strategies: Prototypical core and dimensions of variation. *Studies in Self-Access Learning Journal*, 3(4), 330–356.

Hassan, X., Macaro, E., Mason, D., Nye, G., Smith, P., & Vanderplank, R. (2005). *Strategy training in language learning: A systematic review of available research*. London: EPPI-Centre, Social Science Research Unit, Institute of Education, University of London.

Macaro, E. (2006). Strategies for language learning and for language use: Revising the theoretical framework. *The Modern Language Journal*, 90(3), 320–337.

Oxford, R. (2017). *Teaching and researching language learning strategies: Self-regulation in context* (2nd edition). New York: Routledge.

Plonsky, L. (2011). The effectiveness of second language strategy instruction: A meta-analysis. *Language Learning*, 61(4), 993–1038.

Rees-Miller, J. (1993). A critical appraisal of learner training: Theoretical bases and teaching implications. *TESOL Quarterly*, 27(4), 679–687.

Tang, Y., & Griffiths, C. (2014). *The keys to highly effective English learning*. Shenzhen: Jiangxi Education Publishing House.

INDEX

academic freedom 116
academic literacy experience 18
academic reading 16–7, 18
action research 132, 133, 167–72, 183; classroom issues 168–9; support needs 170; sustaining 171; teacher identity 170; teachers becoming researchers 169
adaptability 64
African American Vernacular English 37
agency 58, 65; contexts 94–5
Andrade, M.S. 188
anxiety 56, 59, 64–5; effects 65
apartheid 33–4
apprenticeship of observation 163
Arizona State University 63
Asia 21
assessment 107, 188, 206; and language ideologies 36; task-based language 198, 201–2
assimilation failure 18, 19
assistant language teachers, foreign 195–6
attentional deployment 66
attrition 53
audiovisual resources 123
Australia 149, 152, 167, 169, 171
autonomy 65, 182
Azerbaijan 45

Barahona, M. 29
Baratz-Snowden, J. 129
Barkhuizen, G. 162

beliefs 28, 46–7, 52, 199; and emotions 72, 73; formation of new 93–4; and identity 72; learners 122; and race 122–3; and task-based language assessment 199–201, 201–2; and teacher education 73; teachers 46–7, 52, 123
Benesch, S. 57, 58
between-subjects comparative design 200–1
big data 79
bilingual classrooms 35
bilingual researchers 25
biliteracy, continua of 146, 147–8
blogs 83, 188–9
book knowledge 20
Borg, S. 174, 176
boundaries, topic 64
Bourdieu, P. 78
brainstorming 168
Brazil 72
bridging programs 111, 112
Bucholtz, M. 122
burnout 53
Burns, A. 170, 171

Canada 79
Canadian Summer School 155
capital 78
career span, identity development across 84
caring, teaching as 59
Casanave, C. 1, 15, 112
case studies 123, 157, 169, 171
challenges 96

Chamot, A. 211
change: and study abroad 163–4; sustainable 200
Cheung, Y.L. 78
Chile 29, 170
China 39–43, 170
circumstances, adapting to changing 32
citation practices 99
classroom interaction: and gender 128–9; and race 123
classroom practices 29–30, 32; action research 168–9; and identity 83; and language and content instruction 189; and language ideologies 36–7; and multilingualism 138–9, 139, 140, 141, 145; and teacher research and researchers 181–3; translanguaging 145
cognition 28; socially mediated 94; Vygotskian sociocultural theoretical approach 89
cognition research 163
cognitive change 66, 182
cognitive positions 29
co-languaging 146
collaborations, interdisciplinary 187
Colombia 126
colonial languages 147
combinational thinking 22
commitment 95
communication, language and content instruction 186–91
communicative experience 121
community engagement 4
comparative studies 100
comparative surveys 157
complex/dynamic systems theory 212–3
computer assisted language learning 79
computer-mediated communication tools 150
conferences 162
constructive alignment 206
contact surveys 158
content-based learning 212
content knowledge 28, 30–1
contexts 67: agency 94–5; commitment 95; diverse 24, 25; EAP 118; and language learning experiences 25; and language learning strategies 212; learning 94; local 163, 165, 212; multicultural 53; multilingual 35, 77, 143–8; new beliefs and practices formation 93–4; perezhivanie 95; in sociocultural theory 92–6; study abroad 155–60; teaching 94; topics 92–3

contextual factors 96
contextually-based meaning 171
continua of biliteracy 146, 147–8
conversation analysis 67, 90, 128
counter-storytelling 123
courses, taking 71
creativity 21, 22, 23–4
critical discourse analysis 128
critical incidents 59–60
critical literacy 34
critical pedagogy 34
critical perspective 115–9, 120–4
critical reflection 53
critical thinking 106–7
critiquing 41–2
cross-cultural cooperation 157
cross-fertilization 57, 138
cultural historical activity theory 29
curiosity 4, 16, 70, 175
curriculum: Global Englishes 132–3; integrating language and content instruction 187–8; and language ideologies 36

Dagenais, D. 79
Darling-Hammond, L. 129
Darvin, R. 79
decision-making 28
Denzin, N.K. 2–3
description, need to go beyond 16
Dewey, J. 87
dialogue 50–1
diaries 168
digital interaction 79
digital multimodal linguistic portraits 151
digital research tools 79
digital world, identity in 78–9
Dikilitas, K. 183
disciplinary differences, academic writing 99
disciplinary knowledge 28
discipline faculty, and academic writing 112–3
discipline-specific tuition 99
discourse analytic techniques 90
discursive psychology 67
discussion groups 83
disequilibrium 170
diverse contexts 24; and language learning experiences 25
doctoral advising 16
doctoral dissertation writers, working with 15–20

dominant-language deficit 154
Doran, M. 72
Duff, P. 189
duoethnographies 133
Dyson, A. 37

East, M. 202
ecological approach 24
ecology 22
educational policies 29, 31; and race 123–4
educational psychology 22
Edwards, E. 171
EfECT project 46
emotional challenges 41–2, 60
emotional labor 65–6
emotional regulation strategies 54
emotional responses 58
emotional rewards 60
emotion labor 57–8
emotion management 65–6
emotions 56–61, 63–9, 70–4; and agency 58; anxiety 56, 59, 64–5; and beliefs 72, 73; and caring 59; and critical incidents 59–60; definition 63; discourse 67; function 67; identifying 71; and identity 58–9, 72; management 65–6; negative 65, 82; positive 24, 65; regulation 59, 66–7; role 71; rollercoaster 54; and teacher actions 71–2; and teacher development/learning 72; and teacher education 72–3; teachers 54; and teaching 71; Vygotskian sociocultural theoretical approach 89
emotion work 65–6
English as a medium of instruction 134, 194, 212
English, as an international language 131–6; curriculum 132–3; implementation policies 134; learners attitudes 133; and multilingualism 134; teaching 133; variation in 133
English for Academic Purposes 110, 115–9; contexts 118; management 117–8; pedagogy 117; teacher identity 117
English language education, primary and secondary school 192–6; early 193–4; English as the medium of instruction 194; reflective teaching 194–5; teacher research 195; team teaching 195–6
English language proficiency 45–6
epistemological violence 128
ethics 60, 118, 121
ethnography 21, 24, 123, 157, 207

Europe 138
evaluator feedback 17
experiences, unexpected 22–3
experimental studies 198–9
Exploratory Practice 195

factor analytic theory 52
family language policy 145
feedback 17, 107, 188, 189, 201
Feminist Poststructuralist Discourse Analysis 128
Feryok, A. 89, 94
field research 133
Finland 139
first-hand experience 20
focus groups 213
foreign language anxiety 65, 137
form-focused instruction 205–6
France 155, 156, 157
frustration 189–90
funding 121

gender 126–30; absences 127; and classroom interaction 128–9; discourses 127–8; identities 127; invisibility 127; and learning materials 128; non-normative sexualities 126; own assumptions 127; representations 128; social representations 126; and teacher education 129
generalizability 193
genre theory 186, 189
geo-political location 33
Germany 152, 155, 157
Global Englishes 131, 132; curriculum 132–3; learners attitudes 133; and multilingualism 134; teaching 133; variation in 133
globalization 78, 105
goal-specific strategy 212–3
Golombek, P. 72
Greece 59
Green, B.A. 188
Griffiths, C. 211
grounded theory 206

habitus 78
Hamburg 149
Harris, V. 211
Hassan, X. 211
heritage language education, perceptions of 152, 153
Hidalgo Ferrer, A. 170
high-status language 145

historicity 29
Holliday, A. 163
home language 27
home language literacy 145, 147
Hong Kong 170
Hornberger, N. 146
Huang, L-S. 188
Hyland, K. 107

ideas: cross-fertilization 57; emergence of 21
identity: across the career span 84; and beliefs 72; categories 121–2; development process 81, 82, 83–4; development support 84; in a digital world 78–9; disequilibrium 170; and emotions 58–9, 72; formation 59; gender 127; and language 82–3; methodological issues 79; postcoloniality and 77; and practices 83; processes of change 81; racial 78, 123; social 96; and social class 78; in teacher education 76–80, 83–4; and teacher research and researchers 176–7, 182; teachers 117, 170, 176–7; understanding 81–5
identity changes: literacy-related 17; research questions 19
identity work 56, 65
idiographic research 29
implicit beliefs 52
India 79
individual differences, and language learning strategies 212, 214
influence, relationship of 88, 89
inner lives, of teachers 89–90
inner worlds 29
innovation, and learning outcomes 133
insecurity 189–90
inspiration 63; sources of 50–1, 127, 138, 168, 186–7
Institutional Research Board 116
instructional practices, professional development 45
integrated form-focused instruction 205–6
interdisciplinary collaborations 187
International Association of Teachers of English as a Foreign Language, Research Special Interest Group 174–5, 180
internationalization 147
international language, English as 131–6
international students 116–7
intertextuality 100
inter-university communities, professional learning 42

interventions 96
intervention studies 100
interviews 16–7, 18, 45, 52, 83, 84, 205–6; semi-structured 171; text-based 100
isolated form-focused instruction 205–6

Japan 120, 192–6
Japan Exchange and Teaching (JET) program 195–6
Johnson, K. 93
Johnston, B. 28
Journal of Language, Identity, and Education 78
Journal of Multilingual and Multicultural Development 77
journals and journal writing 17, 42, 169, 182

Kanno, Y. 78
Kaufer, D. 106–7
Keys to Effective Learning 211
knowledge: book 20; content 28, 30–1; development 180; disciplinary 28; linguistic 144; pedagogical content 28, 31, 144; practical 28; propositional 46; teacher 28, 28–9, 46; technical 206
knowledge-for-teaching 28–9
Kubanyiova, M. 89
Kumaravadivelu, B. 204

language: conceptualizations of 82–3; and identity 82–3; teacher's conceptualizations of 140, 141
language and content instruction 186–91; and classroom practices 189; curriculum development 187–8; and interdisciplinary collaborations 187; and professional development 189–90; and technology use 188–9
language anxiety 53
language attitudes 133
language choice 121
language concept 96
language hierarchies 36
language ideologies 33–7; and assessment 36; and curriculum 36; definition 34; and language policy 35–6; and learning opportunities 35; and pedagogy 36–7; students 35; teachers 35
language-in-education policies 35–6, 77, 145
language integrated learning 212
language learning strategies 210–5; and complex/dynamic systems theory 213; and context 212; definition 210;

goal-specific 212–3; and individual differences 212, 214; and learning target 212–3; strategy development 211, 213; and successful learning 211
language policy 33, 77, 145, 149; and language ideologies 35–6
language proficiency, teachers 45–6
language representations 151
language teacher education 3
language teacher identity 76–80; postcoloniality and 77; understanding 81–5
Language Teaching 76
language teaching approaches 204–9; constructive alignment 206; form-focused instruction 205–6; task-based 207; and teachers technical knowledge 206; technology-enhanced 207; theory of practice 208
language use 35
learner achievement 52
learners: anxiety 56, 57, 59; attitudes 133; beliefs 122; cultural and linguistic backgrounds 139, 140; lived experiences 139; and teacher research and researchers 181. See also students
learning: contexts 94; successful 211; and sustainable development 180
learning materials: and gender 128; and multilingualism 139, 141; and race 123
learning opportunities, and language ideologies 35
learning outcomes 206; and innovation 133
learning strategies. See language learning strategies
learning target, and language learning strategies 212–3
life-histories 81, 84
life skills 53
Lightbown, P. 205
Lincoln, Y.S. 2–3
linguicism 28
linguistic anthropology 34
linguistic diversity 36–7, 154
linguistic knowledge, teachers 144
linguistic orientations, developing expertise in 189–90
linguistic resources, integration of 151
listening strategy instruction 169
literacy activities 16, 17, 18–9
literacy practices 16
literature 4; absences 127; engagement with 50, 57, 132, 205

lived experiences 81, 116–7, 139
longitudinal perspective 83–4
longitudinal research 88, 100, 144
Lortie, D.C. 163
love 73

Macaro, E. 211
McKay, S.L. 146
McKinley, J. 134
McPherson, P. 168–9
Malta 174
marginalization 78, 118, 120, 121, 123
Mason, D. 211
matched guise technique 133
media 138
mediational means 88
mentoring 180
metadiscourse 101
metalanguage 104, 107
metaphors 28
methodological issues 79
methodologies, qualitative research 3
Mettler, S. 29
Mexico 79
mindsets 52
misogyny 128
mode 67
Modern Language Journal, The 76
monolingualism, privileging of 194
most significant change stories 45
Motha, S. 123
motivation 52, 63, 65, 175, 183
multicompetence 194
multicultural contexts 53
multilingual contexts 35, 77
multilingualism 134, 137–42; and classroom practices 139, 140, 141, 145; conceptualizations of 140, 141; contexts 35, 77, 143–8; definition 149; family language policy 145; in foreign language classrooms 138–9; and learning materials 139, 141; and policy documents 140; refugees 152; repercussions 138; social representations of 149–54; teachers 194; terminology 137; translanguaging 145
multilingual mind, the 153
multilingual repertoires, representations of 151
multi-voicedness 29

narrative 64, 68, 88, 133, 183–4
narrative inquiry 123, 144, 187, 189
narrative studies 207
native-like proficiency 143

native-speakerism 28, 78
negative emotions 65, 82
new emerging themes 23
new languages 145–6
New Zealand 110, 111–2, 198, 201
non-native speaking language teacher, legitimacy 78
non-normative sexualities 126
non-standard Englishes 133
non-standard language 145–6, 147
Norway 47
novice teachers, professional learning 41
Nye, G. 211

observational research 188
online ethnography 79
online portfolios 188
ontological violence 128
opportunities 96
opposite, the, doing 23
Oranje, J. 94
outside the box thinking 21–6

Palmer, D. 35
Park, G. 123
Park, K. 78
participants 176; appropriate 4; categories 41; reflection 24; study abroad 156
participation format 67
passions 4
patchwriting 100
patriarchalism 128
pedagogical approaches, developing expertise in 189–90
pedagogical content knowledge 28, 31, 144
pedagogy 29–30: descriptive studies 16; EAP 117; and language ideologies 36–7; teacher education 87–8; technology-enhanced 207; Vygotskian sociocultural theoretical approach 87–8
Pennycook 122
perezhivanie 87, 93, 95
peripheral English language teaching contexts 21
personal quest 21
phenomenological approaches 89, 117
plagiarism 100
Plonsky, L. 211
policies 29, 31, 96; and race 123–4
policy documents, and multilingualism 140
policyscapes 29
Positive Education 53
positive emotions 65

Positive Language Teacher Education 53–4
positive psychology 65
Positive Psychology Interventions 53
post-colonial contexts, language policy 33
postcoloniality, identity and 77
post-modern paladins 28
post-structuralist approach 94
power, and gender 128–9
power hierarchy 121
power relations 34
practical knowledge 28
practitioner research 167
pragmatics 106–7
primary and secondary schools, English language education 192–6
Prior, M. 4
professional development 30, 32, 162, 174, 195; confidence 47–8; English language proficiency 45–6; impact 44–8; instructional practices 45; and language and content instruction 189, 189–90; most significant change stories 45; teacher knowledge 46; teachers' beliefs 46–7
professional learning 29; aspects of 41; China 39–43; emotional challenges 41–2; inter-university communities 42; novice teachers 41
professional outcomes, study abroad 158
proficiency 31
propositional knowledge 46
proximal development, zone of 93, 94
psychology research 50–5; teacher–learner relationship 51–2
publish or perish culture 204

Q methodology 52
qualitative methods, and topics 16–8
qualitative research: definition 2–3; features of 3; methodologies 3; processes 1; topics 1–14
QUEST approach 162
questionnaires 116, 176
questions: critical 115–9; what, who, and where 124

race: and classroom interaction 123; critical perspective 120–4; and educational policies 123–4; and identity 78, 123; and learner beliefs or subjectivities 122; and learning materials 123; negative connotation 122; and teacher beliefs or subjectivities 123

222 Index

racial identity 123
racism 34
rapport, building 52
reader-responsibility 101
reading 16–7, 18, 57, 71, 132, 168, 181, 193, 205
Rees-Miller, J. 210, 211
reflection 183; critical 53, 182; participants 24
reflective practice 58, 199
reflective/reflexive writing 183–4
reflective teaching 194–5
refugees 86, 152, 169
relationship of influence 88, 89
relationships 51–2
replication studies 193
representations, gendered 128
research: teachers' conceptions of 176; utilitarian 22
research engagement 181, 182, 183
research literacy 177
research narratives 183–4
research perspective 40
research questions 1, 15–6, 105, 175 105
research skills 4
Research Special Interest Group, International Association of Teachers of English as a Foreign Language 174–5, 180
research strategies, critical perspective 116
response modulation 66
Richards, K. 3
Rondón, F. 129

Said, S.B. 78
School of International Training 27
school policies, and language ideologies 35–6
Schulze, E. 79
second language acquisition 57
self-efficacy building 183
self-formation 56
self-inquiry 88
self-observation 183
self-reflection 183
self-reflective journals 42
sense-making, emergent 89–90
Siegel, J. 168–9
situation modification 66
situation selection 66
Skyrme, G. 112
Smitherman, G. 37
Smith, P. 211
social class, and identity 78
social constructivism 104, 106

social identity 96
social networking sites 207
social networks 156, 158
social turn, Vygotskian sociocultural theoretical approach 88–9
socio-constructivism 150
sociocultural positions 29
sociocultural theorists 42
sociocultural theory, contexts in 92–6
socio-emotional competences 52
sociolinguistic environments 150
sociolinguistics 149
sources: integrating 100; using 100
South Africa 33, 77, 110
Spada, N. 205
specialized programming, study abroad 158
stakeholders 50, 53, 201
standards 145–6
status 53
stimulated recall 83, 182
strategy instruction 210–5; program structure 211
stress 58
students: interest 24; international 116–7; language ideologies 35; language learning experiences 25; language representations 151; and learning 71–2; lived experiences 116–7; postgraduate 112; teacher–learner relationship 51–2; working with sources 100. *See also* learners
study abroad 155–60, 161–6; and change 163–4; destination countries 157; goals 163; impact 164; local context 163, 165; participants 156; post-sojourn transfer 158–9, 164; professional outcomes 158; rationale 163; social networks 158; source countries 157; specialized programming 158; teachers 157
studying across 121
studying down 121
studying up 121
Sunderland, J. 128
support needs, action research 170
surveys 169, 201
sustainable development, and learning 180
Sydney 149
Systemic Functional Linguistics 186, 189

Talmy, S. 123
Tang, Y. 211
task-based language assessment 198; and beliefs 199–201, 201–2

task-based language teaching 198–201, 202, 207
Taylor-Mendes, C. 123
teacher actions, and emotions 71–2
teacher cognition 199
teacher education 27–32; and beliefs 73; design theory 27; and emotions 72; focus 53; and gender 129; and identity development 82; identity in 76–80; in-service 162; language representations 151–2; pedagogy 87–8; Vygotskian sociocultural theoretical approach 87–8; and wellbeing 53–4
teacher knowledge 28, 28–9, 46
teacher–learner relationship 51–2
teacher learning 27–32; China 39–43; and emotions 72; Vygotskian sociocultural theoretical approach 88
teacher–parent conferences 145
teacher research and researchers 1, 169, 174–9, 180–4; autonomy development 182; benefits 177; challenges 177–8; conceptions of research 176; English language education, primary and secondary school 195; Exploratory Practice 195; and identity 182; impact on classroom practices 181–3; impact on student learning 181; mentoring 180; motivation 175, 183; promoting 195; and research literacy 177; self-efficacy building 183; support needs 177; and teacher identity 176–7; writing experiences 183–4
teachers: academic writing 113; becoming researchers 169; beliefs 46–7, 52, 123; conceptions of research 176; conceptualizations of language 140, 141; confidence 47–8; emotions 54; engagement with 4; English language proficiency 45–6; as gatekeepers 145; identity 117, 170, 176–7; inner lives 89–90; knowledge development 180; language ideologies 35; legitimacy 78; linguistic knowledge 144; lived experiences 139; misunderstandings 37; multilingualism 194; novice 41; research literacy 177; study abroad 157; technical knowledge 206
teacher talk, quality of 24
teacher thinking 28
teaching: aim 94; as caring 59; contexts 94; and emotions 71; English, as an international language 133

Teaching Knowledge Test 46
teaching/learning environments, interest and 24
team teaching 195–6
team work 138
technical knowledge, teachers 206
technology: integration 207; and language and content instruction 188–9
technology-enhanced language teaching 207
telecollaboration 182
terminology, multilingualism 137
TESOL Quarterly 76
text-based interviews 100
textbooks 123, 128
thematic content analysis 3
theoretical frameworks 199
theoretical perspective 40
theory of practice 208
think-aloud protocols 83, 182
think-aloud sessions 158
thinking 106–7; combinational 22; critical 106–7; higher order 24; outside the box 21–6
Toohey, K. 79
topic development 15, 98–9
topics 98–9; action research 167–72; big 28; boundaries 64; building 28; construction 4, 63–4; contexts 92–3; criteria 205; decision-making 144; development 15, 98–9; emergence of 86–7, 127; essential characteristics 193; feasibility 111; finding new 21–6; flexibility 111; generalizability 193; grounding 28; implications 28; inspiration 99; passion for 110; and qualitative methods 16–8; selection 1, 3–6, 15–6, 104–5; selection drivers 27–8; selection strategies 22–3, 39–40, 50–1, 56–7, 70–1, 77, 81–2, 92–3, 110–1, 120–1, 131–2, 137–8, 143–4, 150–1, 156–7, 162, 167–8, 175–6, 180–1, 186–7, 193, 198–9, 204–5, 210–1; sources of inspiration 50–1, 127, 138, 168, 186–7; strengths 111; thinking outside the box 21–6; Vygotskian sociocultural theoretical approach 86–7
transformation, spaces of 87
translanguaging 145
Trent, J. 170
trust 18
Tse, P. 107
Turkey 180
Turner, J. 112–3, 113

Uganda 77
underprivileged contexts 24
unexpected, the 4, 22–3
University of Auckland 92
University of Aveiro 149
University of British Columbia 186
University of Otago 92
University of Wisconsin 76
urban language 145–6

Vanderplank, R. 211
Vandrick, S. 78
verbal guise technique 133
virtual observation 100
visual imaginary 151
Vygotskian sociocultural theoretical approach 86–91
Vygotsky, L.S. 87, 88–9

washback effect 107
wellbeing 52–4, 66
Westmacott, A. 170
workplace exploration 4
writer-responsibility 101
writing, academic 16–7, 18, 19–20, 98–103, 110–4; bridging programs 111, 112; challenges 111; disciplinary differences 99; discipline faculty and 112–3; engagement 101; genre-based instruction 101; integrating multiple sources 100; L2 student cohorts 111–2; L2 (thesis) writers 112; metadiscourse 101; models 101; stance 101; standards and norms 106; summarizing 100; teachers 113; using sources 100
writing, English L2 104–9, 121; assessment 107; critical thinking 106–7; fluency 106; metalanguage 107; pragmatics 106–7; social constructivist lens 106; standards and norms 106
writing oneself 156
writing skills courses 99
Wyatt, M. 183

Xerri, D. 176, 177
Xie, J. 170

Yamada, M. 123

Zappa-Hollman, S. 189
Zembylas, M. 71
Zhao, H. 106–7